All Things Considered

AN AUTOBIOGRAPHY BY

Richard Carr-Gomm

1922-2004

Born in 1922 at Mancetter Lodge near Atherstone in Warwickshire, Richard Carr-Gomm was educated at Stowe school in Buckinghamshire before joining the Coldstream Guards in 1941. He resigned his army commission in 1955 in order to work with the lonely in Bermondsey, London. He started the Abbeyfield Society in 1956 and founded the Carr-Gomm Society in 1965 and the Morpeth Society in 1972. Other societies affiliated to Carr-Gomm include St Matthew Housing, Byker Housing Association, the Solo, Richard and Solon Societies. The author – father of five and grandfather of eight – lives with his wife, Susan, in the village of Batheaston, Somerset.

DEDICATION

To Susan

To Anna, who typed the first manuscript, called 'Push on the Door' and to Harriet, who, also with speed and without fault, did the same for this full and, probably, final one.

To these three and to Elizabeth, Adam and David ... this book is dedicated.

Copyright © by Richard Carr-Gomm 2004

Published 2005 by Trafford Publishing (UK)

All rights reserved. No part of this publication may be reproduced, stored in a retrieval system, or transmitted, in any form or by any means, electronic, mechanical, photocopying, recording or otherwise, without the prior permission of the Copyright owner.

CONTENTS

INTRODUCTION 6
PREAMBLE 7

PART I 10
Family history, childhood, schooldays, a soldier in war and peace, marriage, children, family life, African adventures, retirement

1 IN THE BEGINNING ... TWIGS FROM THE FAMILY TREE 10
2 CHILDHOOD 1922-1933 14
3 SCHOOLDAYS 20
   Stowe School, Buckinghamshire 1934-1940
4 IN THE FOOTSTEPS OF FIELD-MARSHALL GOMM 25
   Coldstream Guards: training in England 1941-1944
5 FIGHTING IN EUROPE 1944-1945 30
   Active Service in France and Germany 1944-1945
6 "WAKEN ... THE BLUE MEDITERRANEAN" 40
   Palestine 1945-1948; travels while on leave 1945-1950
7 EGYPT TO ENGLAND 51
   Egypt, the Canal Zone 1952-1954; escort duty for Imperial Defence College; tour of Middle East, 1953; travels home to England 1952-1954
8 DOUBT AND DOUBTING 59
   Reflections on career & non-aggression; army & social life in England 1948-1955
9 PUBLIC DUTIES WITH THE COLDSTREAM 66
   Ceremonial duties on state occasions and at official functions; entertaining on guard 1943-1955
10 1955: A YEAR OF TRANSITION 75
    Final decision to resign army commission, leave Chelsea Barracks Sept 1955
11 TWO MONTHS IN BUGANDA 83
    A kind of 'ADC' to the 35th Kabaka of Buganda 1956
12 WEDDING BELLS AND FAMILY LIFE 89
    Marriage to Susan Gibbs; 'This is your Life'; family homes 1957-1962
13 IN THE WAKE OF ABBEYFIELD 94
    Restorative holiday in Uganda and family holiday in Corfu; return to England and work; the family grows; Morley College; retreat to Somerset 1964-1967
14 THE KABAKA: LIFE AND DEATH IN ENGLAND 105
    The Kabaka's escape from Uganda; his life and death in England; his state funeral in Uganda 1966-1971
15 HESITANT COUNTRY-DWELLERS 113
    Illness and convalescence; financial decline; move to Mells; life at Mells 1974-1982
16 OLD FAMILY FACES 125
    A crowded life at the Batch, Batheaston; children and grandchildren; holidays with Susan 1982-1991
17 RETIREMENT 1992 135
    Public engagements; Abbeyfield 40th anniversary; home-life and hobbies at Batheaston; Ruby Wedding anniversary; poverty and need in the 90s 1992-1999
18 UGANDA REVISITED 140
    Ssabataka's (Ronnie Mutebi) Coronation 1993; Carr-Gomm family holiday 1998; Ronnie Mutebi's wedding 1999
19 HOME AND DRY ... 149
    Back at the Batch 1998-2004

CONTENTS

PART II 152
First house for the lonely in Bermondsey; the societies: Abbeyfield, Carr-Gomm, Morpeth, St Matthew Housing, Byker Bridge Housing, Richard, Solo, Solon

20 WORK BEGINS IN BERMONDSEY 1955 152
Begin new life in Bermondsey; work as home help; open first house (50 Eugenia Road) for the lonely and first residents move in 1955-1956

21 FOUNDING THE ABBEYFIELD SOCIETY 168
Buy 36 Gomm Road; founds Abbeyfield 19th November 1956; house prayers; residents' stories 1956-1958

22 THE EARLY YEARS 181
Open-door policy; fundraising; Abbeyfield in Macclesfield and Brighton; the society's aim and principles; Abbeyfield in Canvey Island and Oxford 1957-1959

23 ONWARDS AND OUTWARDS 190
New administrative approach brings period of rapid growth and development; financing expansion; a visionary team; the lonely rich; extra care and specialist houses; Abbeyfield in the early Sixties 1959-1962

24 DIVISION, DISMISSAL, RECONCILIATION 200
Internal divisions; dismissal from Abbeyfield (1963); Abbeyfield International (1988-2001); reconciliation and return to work with Abbeyfield (1996); reflections 1962-2004

25 A FRESH START, A NEW SOCIETY 210
Reshaping life in the aftermath of Abbeyfield; work as a librarian (1964-1967); advent of the Carr-Gomm Society (1965); Carr-Gomm houses in Major Road and Storks Road (1965); return to full-time social work with Carr-Gomm Society (1967); Bermondsey Abbeyfield split/Bermondsey amalgamates with Carr-Gomm (1967) 1964-1967

26 ALONG THE ROAD 220
Establishing the Carr-Gomm Society to house a mix of young and old; funding through charity shops 'What Next', Greenwich (1968), Kensington High Street and Knightsbridge (1971/2), Eccleston Street, Victoria (1974); funding from state and residents' contributions; St Matthew Housing, Lambeth tie-in (1967); Carr-Gomm in Thamesmead (1970-1976) including first houses at Lensbury Road and Wolvercote Road 1965-1976

27 NEITHER POOR NOR RICH 235
The Morpeth Company begins with Morpeth Mansions (1972); memorable residents and distinguished visitors at Morpeth Mansions; Morpeth Society formalises administration (1975); London flats at Oakwood Court, Holland Park (1973), Wyndham House, Chelsea (1975) and Richmond Mansions (1984), plus Bath (1981) 1972-2004

28 ALL THINGS CONSIDERED ... 244
Carr-Gomm Society growth and development in the UK since 1972 (includes Plumstead and Ealing in London, Sydney Grove in Newcastle-upon-Tyne, Norfolk, Bath, Suffolk, East Grinstead, Hove, Launceston, Hereford, Cambridgeshire and Frome); own 'pet projects'; office ditty (1989); centralisation and national constitution for national Carr-Gomm Society (1993) and Abbeyfield (2003); allied societies – St Matthew Housing; Byker Bridge Housing Association; Solo Society; Richard Society; Solon Society 1972-2004

ENVOI 259
INDEX 260

CONTENTS

ILLUSTRATIONS

1. Mancetter Lodge in Warwickshire 14
2. RC-G with his parents and brothers 15
3. 4th Battalion in Munster, April 1945 32
4. Belsen 33
5. RC-G cartoon, Schonboken, May 1945 35
6. RC-G, 1948 40
7. House of Commons 1950 67
8. Uganda 84
9. Kabaka Mutesa of Buganda with Sarah, sons and daughter 85
10. Susan and Richard – an engagement photograph 89
11. Ceremonial procession, The Order of St. John, 1985 115
12. The Corps of Drums playing in Ulundi Road, Greenwich 118
13. Christmas card 1978 119
14. Family group at Mells 1981 123
15. 9 The Batch, Batheaston 126
16. Modelling with granddaughter Matilda Kime 130
17. Family group at Batheaston Sept 1996 132
18. Laying foundation stone for Abbeyfield Community Centre, Bukalango, 24 July 1998 146
19. 50 Eugenia Road, Bermondsey, the first Abbeyfield House 160
20. RC-G and housekeeper 162
21. Abbeyfield Road, Bermondsey 169
22. Abbeyfield committee group, Wokingham 1959 190
24. Abbeyfield House, Masterton, New Zealand 205
23. Abbeyfield International, Canada 2003 209
25. Contrast in the Society's places 233
26. Churchill cutting, Morpeth Mansions 236
27. Morpeth: an evening meeting in the Morpeth Society 237
28. Abbeyfield House, in the centre of Malmesbury 243
29. Carr-Gomm Society house, Frome 246
30. Carr-Gomm Society reflection conference, Mells 1982 248
31. Family group, Templeton Award 1984 253

INTRODUCTION

I wrote most of the preamble, which follows, in 1970 while we lived in Greenwich. Fortunately for me, others – some named here – now bear the brunt and do the work I once did for the societies. Each year this work seems to grow larger and become more varied and complicated, yet those who carry it out cope ever better. I am only grateful that I was in at the beginning, when everything seemed more simple, easier and more straight-forward.

Many people have cooperated during the writing of this book and I am very grateful to them all. For the first edition "Push on the Door" Mark Amory was wonderfully helpful in guiding and correcting with patience and much-needed tact. His advice was invaluable and his knowledge of the literary world guided me in decisions over its printing and publishing.

This book, however, breaks totally new fields for me in that its existence is entirely due to technology on the Internet. Allan Snowie of Abbeyfield International pointed the way, Mark nodded and Piers Newton, our son-in-law, became a mentor and more in the intricacies of how one goes about such a thing.

For the societies involved I hope that this is just a beginning book. Others could tell the stories as they unfold. Here, I do not offer a definitive account of all that each society does: the legal, professional, financial and technical aspects as well as the experimental and research ones will, I hope, one day be written up comprehensively.

It is, though, really to all the societies' committees and staff through the decades that the greatest thanks should go. Their faith and leadership has and does, always, inspire others and gives shape, strength and momentum to all that has been, and is being, achieved. Sometimes, for the sake of anonymity, I have needed to change the names of people and places, but the heroes and heroines are here, and should be, in bold to emphasise them and their stories.

This, therefore, is a personal story in which the societies with which I have been and am still involved play a very large part. It comprises a collection of memories with fragments added about our family and its background – there is much more in family storybooks, unprinted. Photographs help and, anyhow, I'll probably never reach the end with words alone.

Richard Carr-Gomm
April 2005

9 The Batch, Batheaston
Bath, Somerset, BA1 7DR

PREAMBLE

When St Luke first became an author (about 65 AD), he introduced his work to Theophilus, a Roman official, who later became Bishop of Antioch with these words:
> No-one has undertaken to draw up an account of the events, which have happened among us. So I, as one who has gone over the whole course of events in detail, have decided to write a connected narrative.

Here, these words are a high-flying introduction to a small family story and some social history, with the history part put within an autobiographical context. Nevertheless, if I'm forgiven for vanity this St Luke's statement sums up roughly how I have come to tell this individual story.

When I wrote "Push on the Door" (my earlier attempt at an autobiography) Susan, my wife, told me: "One thing is certain, you mustn't write the book. You waffle and use too many adjectives."

As we were dropping off to sleep the telephone rang; it was one of our societies' housekeepers: "I'm frightened. Donald's got a knife, Jimmy's run off and I don't know what's going to happen." "I'll be over." By 2.00 am, having brought the housekeeper home with me, I was back in bed and Donald (without his knife) lost on the streets of Bermondsey. I had warned the police.

Next day was Saturday so I thought I'd catch up on some sleep. During my afternoon snooze the telephone rang; a woman, very drunk, and with a lot of money said: "A man's on his way to borrow off me. I know I won't be able to refuse." I told her I'd be there to meet him. He didn't turn up but I had missed my nap.

Over the weekend I thought about being an author. I had no time and Susan was probably right in what she had about not writing the book; but the work was beginning to grow and who else was there to tell the story? Susan hadn't volunteered.

The Carr-Gomm Society was small (1978) but could be bigger; we were trying to help lonely people of all ages and, through this, we were engaged in situations such as those I have just described. We had (and have) small houses or flats in which the residents lived and around them, we hoped, they had the care and concern of neighbours. With that they could live their lives constructively or, where necessary, make a fresh start.

To the office at Gomm Road two men, straight from an all-night soup-run, came wanting to hear about our work. A blind boy came in to sell some tools, successfully, and an African dropped in with a message. An Irishman, fresh from riots in Londonderry, asked for a room – he said he was lonely in London but preferred it to returning home.

As I was trying to deal with the mail a probation officer came in with a young man who had formerly sung in a well-known pop group. For three years he'd lived beside the King's Road in Chelsea, in rooms well stocked with liquor; slowly he'd begun to drink too much, soon no longer remembering nor keeping appointments at recording sessions and shows. After a car crash in which a member of his group was killed, he drank more and more until he lost his job with the group. He attempted suicide and ended up in a psychiatric hospital. After a long period there, he was out and prepared to take any job, labouring or factory. Would we help? Did we have space? A Welsh girl from a voluntary youth organisation offered to help but, unlike many, took one look and thought it would be too much for her. The afternoon soon came to an end.

In the evening, I was at prayers in one of the houses and went to another for its monthly meeting. It has often been said that only the old are interested in sing-songs, poetry reading and such things, and that we'd never get the young to join in; however that evening nine out of the 12 present were younger than me and I was (then) 49.

It was not until the next day that I was able to get down to letters and correspondence. I had asked the well-known author Godfrey Winn to join our Christmas party. He replied:

> I find Christmas hell and yours will probably be my only party. Twelve million people know me through my books and yet I have almost to beg to get a scrap of company. Twenty years ago I had 15 callers every Thursday [his regular "at home"]. Yes, week after week, and so happy. Now if I get one a month I'm grateful but it is the everyday that rots me. Silence all day, silence all day and not a word spoken.

I had asked him to give a short talk during the party:

> Oh, yes, I can give a merry talk, I can make people laugh, I have done so for 29 years. I go tonight to Norbury to make 160 men laugh. I know I won't make a single friend and not a soul will help me there. I shall be an odd novelty. Laugh, clown, laugh. Please God, I need some laughter now.

A young resident dying in hospital wrote:

Oddly enough, I have never had a moment's real pain, in fact the damnable thing about cancer is that you don't know you've got it but the discomfort that comes with it can drive you potty at times.' A new correspondent wrote, 'I wonder if you would be able to help me. I am an unmarried mother and my daughter is thirteen months old. The situation at the moment is so terrible; it has made me so that I just cannot go on living here. I hope you will be able to help.

Such letters as these are interspersed with all the bills, rent demands and official correspondence with statutory bodies and voluntary organisations with whom we are in contact. A proper secretary, to deal with the typing, filing and documentation would obviously make all such basic office work easier and more efficient. At the moment we tend to rely too much on voluntary helpers who appear and disappear. Perhaps one would volunteer to write the book – but so far no one has.

Meanwhile the telephone rang. "Get us some bric-a-brac for the shop," said one of our helpers. "We've got far too many clothes. It's beginning to look like a jumble sale." But we made £700 in the first four months, I replied. "I know," she said, "But the Oxfam shop over the hill made £8,000 in 18 months and that's far better." I didn't do the arithmetic; but that afternoon I received a copy of *The Times* of 1805 with a report about a naval engagement off Cape Trafalgar – perhaps this would give our worker something important to sell? Sadly, though genuine, it was only worth £1.

A long distance call from Inverness: they'd put a man with a scarred face on the train for London and would I find him somewhere to stay when he arrived? "Why not a hotel?" I said. They told me he was so badly disfigured he didn't want to be seen in any public place; could I find him somewhere else?

A young boy or girl in care needing somewhere to live. A lonely person, who wants some help, an ex-Ambassador, whose foreign wife had left him and who has no real friends in England – so it goes on. Perhaps I'd better get on with it and write the book myself. So I thought and so I did – first with "Push on the Door" which ended in 1979, and now with this in 2004

PART I
Family history, childhood, schooldays, a soldier in war and peace, marriage, children, family life, African adventures, retirement

1

IN THE BEGINNING ... TWIGS FROM THE FAMILY TREE

Both my parents' family trees were long but none could be longer than my mother's which went back to Adam and Eve. I have a large piece of parchment which shows a direct line from Adam and Eve (reputedly about 4000 BC) through Noah, Boaz who married Ruth and produced David, followed by his son, Solomon and other biblical characters, to us. Doubtless there are plenty of similar such trees about. Our particular line included George, Duke of Clarence, who died in a butt of malmsey wine, King Alfred, who burnt cakes, and Sancho the Great, first King of Spain.

My mother's name was Amicia Dorothy Heming and her father maintained that their family was originally Danish and that the original Duke Heming was the leading Viking chief who led their successful invasion of the north of England around 800 AD. Whether he was or not, into his line (11th century) came Lady Godiva. She was the wife of Leofric, Earl of Mercia (around Warwickshire), who founded a monastery at Coventry. By taking her clothes off in public she forced her husband to withdraw a heavy tax he had imposed on the poor and they, in gratitude, helped her modesty by remaining in doors while she did her naked ride (except Peeping Tom).

On my father's side there were two main branches to the tree. The Carr branch, joined in marriage to the Lothian Kerrs (and Kers), was a Northumberland family coming from Eshott and Hexham. The Gomm branch shows that in 1768 William Gomm was Lord of the Manor of Nethercote in Oxfordshire. While he and his forebears were thoroughly English, two of his great-grandchildren were married to Prussians: Marie to the strategist General von Clausewitz and Frederick William to the Countess Hedwig Gneisenau.

The third great-grandchild was my great uncle, Field-Marshal Sir William Gomm who, as an honour to his father for fighting and being killed in Guadeloupe in 1794, was given a commission at the age of ten. He died on the active service list (as did all Field-Marshals; the rank was abolished in 1998) in 1875 at the age of 91, thus holding a commission for 81 years; a record in the British Army.

William Gomm's first wife was Sophia Penn, granddaughter of William Penn of Pennsylvania. Having been given the land (in the now USA) by Charles 2nd in order to discharge a debt owed to his father by the King, Penn immediately established the State in 1681 so that it could be used as a refuge for the Quakers who were being persecuted in England; Penn having helped start the Sect about 20 years earlier.

My various, and varied, forebears include Leonard Childers, who around 1700 bred Flying Childers, "the fleetest horse that ever ran at Newmarket". Then, later, came Michael Childers who devised the Childers's Fly – still used for fishing on the River Tweed – and who sold the command of his regiment, the 11th Hussars, to the 7th Earl of Cardigan – later to achieve Balaclava fame.

There was Sampson Gideon, who died in 1762 and was the Government financial adviser; he personally supervised the finances for the resistance to Bonnie Prince Charlie in 1745 and raised all the loans necessary for the Seven Years War. Gideon's father was a travelling Jew from Portugal but, as Horace Walpole wrote, Sampson "breeds his children Christian". Sampson's third daughter married Sir Culling Smith, and that is how my second Christian name of Culling first came into the family.

Another forebear, William Gomm, lived in Russia and in 1752 married a Russian/French lady from the Barraud family in Normandy. He is reputed to have constructed the port of Onega on the White (Barents, off the Arctic Circle) Sea, between Archangel and Stalingrad.

In middle age Field-Marshal Sir William Gomm succeeded to the family property in London at Rotherhithe and Bermondsey. This had come to the family in 1816 through his spinster aunt Jane Gomm, the friend of a Miss Goldsworthy who was by inheritance the Lady of the Manor there. These two ladies were governesses to the younger children of King George III and Queen Charlotte (six daughters and nine sons), and they stayed on at Court after the children had grown up. They had then for many years been retained in waiting upon the three princesses who had remained spinsters. (There is an unconfirmed report of a relationship between Jane Gomm and the King, which produced a Colonel Godwin).

When Miss Goldsworthy died she left everything to her "dear friend Jane Gomm". This, though no doubt infuriating to the

Goldsworthys, was both kind and lucky for Miss Gomm who had undertaken to bring up the three children orphaned when her brother William was killed at Guadeloupe in 1794 and his wife died two years later; it was one of these children who would later become Field-Marshal Sir William Gomm.

The Field-Marshal and his wife were childless and thus, after their deaths, the property descended to their niece, Emily Blanche Carr. When in 1876 Emily wanted to marry Francis Culling Carr – a widower and her first cousin – it was provisional on her inheritance that she should add her aunt's surname, Gomm, to theirs; this the couple did by royal license on 9th March, 1878. The double name Carr-Gomm has not, therefore, been going very long.

Emily and Francis were my paternal grandparents, whom I never knew. They lived in a large country house at Farnham Royal in Buckinghamshire called The Chase. It was a happy place, and family memories evoke cricket weeks, croquet, large house parties, military bands and music.

And The Chase had a ghost. My grandfather's first wife, Jeannie Elizabeth Franklyn (born 1837) had died, aged 29, after her exertions in producing and looking after their four children. She then, however, remained around the house as a kind, friendly, family ghost and had, by the time of writing in 2004, appeared on nine occasions to members of our family, wearing white and helping them in times of trouble.

From The Chase my grandfather played the part of country squire, incorporating all the best of Victorian charity. He was also colonel of the local Volunteers, a Justice of the Peace and chairman of the London Hospital.

Sanctuary and friendship for Joseph Merrick

As chairman of the London Hospital Francis Carr-Gomm made a mark by befriending Joseph Merrick, who became known as the Elephant Man – played by John Hurt in David Lynch's 1980 film "The Elephant Man" and whose story was written by Frederick Treeves. Born in 1862, Merrick was an intelligent man but with a head so large and a body so deformed that to avoid unwelcome attention when he went out he shrouded his body in a cloak and wore a veil over his face. Merrick had been exhibited in this country and abroad by fun-fair proprietors – made to sit in a cage, half-naked, being laughed at all day long.

My grandfather, through lobbying friends and by writing a letter to

The Times, helped stir up public interest and concern for Merrick's plight and, thanks to his efforts, the Elephant Man was given the unprecedented gift of a home, two rooms and a bath – the bath much needed as his skin was reportedly "very smelly" – in the London Hospital. Here, he lived out his last few years; happy, in comfort, cared for by the hospital nurses, and visited by many eminent people including members of the Royal Family. Merrick died, quite young, in 1890 when his head slipped off the pillow one night and broke his neck with its weight.

He had made a cardboard model of Southwark Cathedral, which he could see from his window, and given to my grandparents. They stood it on the drawing-room mantelpiece, where it stayed for many years. A housemaid later knocked it off by mistake as she dusted and, being smashed, it was thrown away. Family memory recalls Merrick visiting The Chase and records how my grandfather once came across him murmuring quietly to himself the words of the Lord's Prayer; his mother was a Baptist. For my part, I knew nothing about Merrick or of his existence until I had long been involved in social work.

Carr-Gomm family estate

My brothers – Antony (Tony), Roderick and Eardley – and I rarely talked about family history or inheritance until almost middle age, and it was not until after the war that I began to want to learn more.

When, in 1816, the family inherited the property at Rotherhithe it was mainly meadows and vegetable gardens. My forebears had then let most of it go on a 99 year lease to people who subsequently built rows of houses to last that number of years. Much of the remainder was sold to the Port of London Authority to add to Surrey Commercial Docks and 60 acres was given, I believe, for the formation of Southwark Park.

All the family money was in the estate, and my father did not inherit until 1937. He told us, his sons, little about it and we took no interest until he formed a property investment company, the Gomm Estates, in 1948; with us four boys as directors he was chairman until his death in 1963, after which it was divided equally amongst us. When the buildings returned to our family in the 1950s and 1960s most were, due to the wartime bombing and the fact that the houses had reached the end of their natural life, in a poor condition. The whole Estate was sold and finally wound-up by 1994.

2

CHILDHOOD

Before I was born I was a twin. I never knew the other because my mother miscarried early in her pregnancy and he or she, my twin, was never born. When my time came, I believe I appeared the wrong way around and I'm certain I was late. My mother was hoping for a New Year baby but, instead, I was born at 2 am on the morning of the 2nd January 1922. I have always found it easier to work late at night but whether or not this relates to my arrival in the early hours I don't know. Some think it does.

I was born at Mancetter Lodge near Atherstone in Warwickshire; a country house belonging to my mother's parents Mancetter had a large garden, sloping lawns and a paddock. The house is on the Roman Watling Street and I romanticise, and some historians believe, that it was in our garden that Boudicea died after pursuing the Romans from St Albans in 62 AD.

1. Mancetter Lodge in Warwickshire

My maternal grandfather was a stern product of the Indian civil service (Commissioner of Police in Madras), he suffered from occasional bouts of melancholia and I don't remember him ever smiling. I do remember sitting on his knee while he read me the Ugly Duckling; the story was near the knuckle because it was how I felt I looked.

But my childhood was happy and conventional, although I recall being very bored lying in my pram aged around two. I was the third of four boys – Antony, Roderick, myself and Eardley – who arrived at two-year intervals and we had a nanny (Nanny Rice) and a nursemaid. We were bought down, usually for tea and sometimes for breakfast, but for the rest of the time we took over the top floor with our nursery overlooking the drive, gardens and river.

In matters of taste, my dislike of things such as "country clubs" with fake old furniture and cocktail bars in private sitting-rooms came, I think, from an unconscious remembrance of the lovely things in my grandparents' house. Mancetter Lodge was Georgian and full of nice things and it is not, perhaps, a coincidence that my wife Susan and I have now chosen to live in a similarly attractive Georgian house (she having grown-up in like houses in Gloucestershire and Hertfordshire).

My parents, my brothers, and me ...

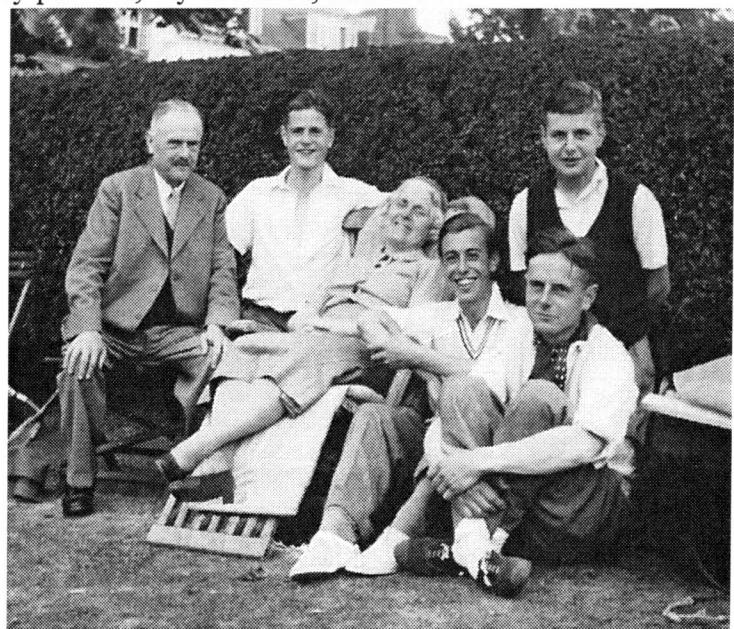

2. RC-G with his parents and brothers. Left to right: Eardley, RC-G, Roderick, Antony

When I was eight, my grandparents died and we moved to a London flat and a closer family life. My father had little money and my mother less. We could not run a car but, still, we had a governess. However, living cheek by jowl, we began to get to know our parents. They were a devoted couple, growing in later life to look like Tweedledee and Tweedledum and though they quarrelled it was never very serious.

Although my mother was the stronger character (she had a theory that it was the stronger partner of a marriage who produced the opposite sex children), my father quietly held his own. During a first-war job as ADC to the Commander of the forces liberating the Cameroons in West Africa from the Germans, he fell into a concrete gun emplacement and hurt his head; this, according to my mother (and, not in my hearing, denied by him) led to his slowness and an unemotional reaction to things. Both my parents, however, played an equal part in guiding our lives.

I wasn't very bright. My mother fell down the stairs at Mancetter just before I was born, and whether this had any effect on me I don't know. A doctor said that a cell in my brain was slow developing, so I was considered delicate as a child and my brothers were not supposed to knock me down. I was usually left to push the wheelbarrow while they careered about on bicycles. I was allowed to arrange the toy farm and animals, whilst the others organised busier things such as model railways, boats and soldiers.

My brothers must have been driven mad by my slowness, but a patient governess, Miss Jones (Mippy) got me into Mowden, a prep school in Hove. I was happy there and remember best a cricket match, in which I took a hard catch, on one knee, close to the batsman. It won the match and I returned a hero, promptly promoted to the first eleven.

In London (1930-1939) our family lived in a two-floored flat in Courtfield Gardens, South Kensington. We laughed a lot and enjoyed conventional outings to museums, Madame Tussauds, London Zoo and other edifying places. We walked to and along the Embankment on Sunday afternoons and along the Broadwalk and the flower walk in Kensington Gardens on other days. We watched the Silver Jubilee of King George V and Queen Mary from a jeweller's shop in Regent Street and father for this and other royal occasions was a Gold Staff Officer and appeared at Westminster Abbey in court dress, which he had to hire.

He inherited the job from his deceased brother Hubert (one time Liberal MP for Bermondsey and Private Secretary to Winston Churchill, before the latter changed to the Conservatives), who got it through a Court contact at King George V's Coronation in 1910. My father passed it on to my brother Roddy because Tony didn't want it at the 1953 Coronation of Queen Elizabeth II, after her Accession in 1952.

We were kept largely on our own as a family and did not get to know other children of our age; of cousins we had few. Although we used to have children's parties, the ones I remember were the grown ups' tennis parties at Mancetter. The grass court was usually damp causing the balls to skid off below flailing rackets; thus we became useful ball boys to our elders.

Family holidays were at such places as St Leonards, Rhyl, Ventnor or Angmering. Again, we spent them on our own as a family, but not knowing any different we never minded and had great fun. The first holiday abroad was when Antony, Roderick and Eardley went with my parents to Belgium. Then aged seven I was miserable at being left behind but, apparently, considered still too delicate for the dangers of continental cooking.

Two years later we went to Berneval in France; some cousins came with us and I have awful memories of them tying me up and leaving me locked in a dark cellar. I was recovered weeping and miserable by Mippy. While she was untying me, father came along and was, uncharacteristically, very angry with the cousins – which cheered me a little.

My immediate family was very self-contained, perhaps because we were four boys we didn't need others for companionship or to play games. But as a result, we had no great crosscurrents of ideas and arguments to make us think. Nor did I have great friends with whom I could pool ideas; in old age I have no friends who have been with me since childhood and school. I do, though, see my brothers often and we usually get together over Christmas and family affairs including our responsibilities in Bermondsey *(Ch. 1)*.

I was in my late teens before I began to meet girls. In retrospect I realise how little sex of any sort came into my life as a young man. Life seemed full enough without it. Certainly, being told about sex had been left out of my upbringing and only the exploratory interests at school or semi-drunken experiences on the social side of army life involved me in any sort of encounter.

Spending the night, sharing a home or my life with a woman never seemed to come into it for me or, as far as I could see, for any of my friends. Marriage, a wife and family, all lay quietly in the future. This, too, was because of our family's closely-knit, all-male set-up and, perhaps, single-sex schooling. I never minded at the time.

My mother never noticed this lack of female company until, after 25 years of completely masculine family life, she began to acquire daughters-in-law competing for attention. It wasn't easy for her.

Eardley was the first to marry, then Roderick and Antony. Thus the female element in the family rose sharply with daughters-in-law, and later granddaughters; my mother's matriarchal control was, consequently, weakened.

After spending the war in a little house in Colwall, on the west side of the Malvern Hills, my parents bought a house near Hassocks in Sussex which became our home for the rest of their lives. Not a pretty house, it was nevertheless modern, practical and geographically convenient for me and my brothers. The house had been used as a fire brigade headquarters during the war and the lawn had been a car park with the rest of the garden full of Nissan huts.

Slowly and not without the difficulty of post-war shortages, improvements were made. A couple – Russell and his cat-loving wife came to look after the garden and moved into one of the Nissan huts. Russell was principally in charge of the small Dexter cow which kept the grass short and provided everyone with milk. Mother was particularly good at homemaking and getting life to rotate around the family and when I was in the army I used to make weekend visits home to Hassocks.

Little Christian Soldiers

From our earliest years church going was a regular part of Sunday mornings. At Mancetter the old church dominated the village green and into the first pew we would go, as regular as clockwork. Nanny remembered how beautifully we sang the hymns and how "serious our dear little faces looked" as we tried to pronounce each word properly. We remembered the long sermons and splendid decorations – mostly put there by us – on harvest festivals and holy days.

Mother always impressed us with her awareness of God. Once, at Mancetter, she described heaven so pleasantly to Roderick that he asked if he might go there that afternoon. She had great faith and was always conscious that: "underneath are the everlasting arms", and speaking these words would throw her arms wide open. This complete confidence and faith remained with my mother throughout her life.

She also had great enthusiasm for music and built up a family band with herself at the piano, Roderick on flute and Eardley on clarinet (they being the most competent members), while Antony played the xylophone and I became proficient on the drums. Father accompanied us singing, almost in tune, songs such as Alphonso, the Toreador.

From her father, who under the name of Col Bowlong (drawing 'a long-bow') wrote extravagant, short stories about life in India, mother had inherited a flair for writing. In 1938 she enjoyed West End success with "Adventure", a children's play which ran for the Christmas season at London's Victoria Palace and, with my father, co-wrote short, contemporary works which were sometimes staged by amateur dramatic societies. Among these collaborations was "The Light", a longer, religious play combining my parents' spiritual creed with their shared sense of the dramatic. And here, while writing about the writers in our family I should mention the finest and most distinguished – albeit a distant cousin by marriage – Erskine Childers author of "Riddle of the Sands".

3

SCHOOLDAYS

After prep school at Mowden I went to Stowe School in Buckinghamshire where I achieved little. Nevertheless I enjoyed it and again got my best fun playing cricket and trying – and nearly succeeding – to get to the top in the Officers Training Corps, or army cadets as they are now.

In an article in the *Sunday Telegraph* in 1988 Anthony Quinton – himself an old Stoic – wrote about the history of public schools in general and Stowe in particular:

> The English public school as we know it is less than a century and a half old. The mid-Victorian foundations, often set up on the remains of old charitable grammar schools for the able children of the poor, answered a clear and social need. A trading and industrial empire could not fill its more practical jobs simply by the patronage and influence method of the 18th century. A wholesome patriotic manliness fostered and protected by compulsory games and religious services were the great benefits these schools aimed to confer. Herd-mindedness, preoccupation with correct form, lack of imagination, disdain for learning and the arts, the English disease of 'undeveloped heart' were of course also prevalent.

A group of Protestant high Anglicans in 1922 were provoked into action and ... having bought and converted Stowe, they elected John Ferguson Roxburgh as the Headmaster, and he became one of the great headmasters of the century.

When I went there in 1934 I had no idea Stowe was so new; no one told me this sort of information.

We were a mixed lot. Prince Rainier of Monaco was in my house. Once a week we lined up for our pocket money and beside each name on the list was entered our weekly allowance – 2s 6d, 3s, 5s ... – as approved by our parents. Beside Rainier's name was always a question mark so that he could have asked for a fiver, or more, if he'd liked. I don't think he ever did but I suppose that, if he had, he could have taken us to the tuck shop with it. He didn't do that either but we all liked him.

Thinking of old boys, I also remember Christopher Robin Milne, who wanted to sink through his chapel seat when the preacher quoted from his father's book "Winnie the Pooh": "Christopher Robin went down with Alice ..." Then others come to mind: John Langley, a brilliant golfer; Leonard Cheshire, who was awarded the VC and the OM and started the Cheshire homes for handicapped people; several millionaires and Ian Moncrieffe who, pompous to the extreme, maintained his dignity even when falling down the lectern steps after reading the Lesson in chapel.

In 1957 (aged 35) I attended an old boys dinner in the House of Commons. As a distraction from the excessively dull speeches I fell to observing my fellow diners: their bald heads, moustaches, large features and bloated bodies – hard to believe they ever been schoolboys.

At Stowe, we all pulled together happily because we had a fine and fair housemaster, David Brown, and a superb headmaster, JF Roxburgh. Brown was an ex-rugger international but memory gives him neither false heartiness nor toughness. He taught me to enjoy rugby while at the same time, keeping my love of cricket. The games master discovered me bowling leg-breaks in the nets on the South front, and put me into the third eleven; thereafter, I tended to live on, rather than fulfil my promised brilliance – I had five minutes of that later when, in an inter-village match at home, I achieved a hat-trick and had the ball mounted and hung on the wall.

A pioneer headmaster

JF Roxburgh (known by all as JF), had come from Lancing to be headmaster at Stowe when the school was founded in 1922. He presided with easy familiarity over 500 of us and, somehow, knew each of us by name. I was "Ricardus", even though he only spoke to me about once a year. Whenever he wrote in our prize books, however small the distinction it represented, his handwriting was cherished. He died soon after leaving the school, aged 65, and it was a great pity that he was never honoured publicly.

His influence and the atmosphere of the school should have rubbed off on me. But I was more concerned over my perceived ugliness – keeping my head bowed in the Creed thinking those behind were looking at me, walking around head down to hide my face. I had also cultivated a habit of turning up my overcoat collar to hide the lower half of my face, though this more in imitation of the sinister, semi-criminal look popularised by anti-heroes such as Humphrey Bogart. So, it was vanity which influenced me.

The two ideals which "JF" especially wanted to imprint on his pupils were admiration of beauty and the liberation of minds so that thought or belief would not be moulded into rigid, narrow channels. Noel Annan in an article in the *Daily Telegraph*, again in 1988, wrote about JF Roxburgh:

> He came from being a housemaster at Lancing and he accepted the public school system – houses, prefects, fagging and the rest; but he wanted to make the school less regimented, less dominated by the worship of games and, above all, less philistine. He wanted the athlete and the intellectual to respect each other and both to be better mannered, less insular and prejudiced. He wanted schools to stop neglecting literature and the visual arts, and his religion seemed to be based on his regularly repeated sermons covering the topics of Fellowship and Service.
>
> He preached a social creed, which was not a harsh one. Much emphasis was laid on good manners and understanding; that example needed also a mild and persuasive consideration of others. Individuality and originality were also virtues, and he realised they could not flourish until the boys had leisure.
>
> While the old guard filled every minute of the day to prevent boys getting into trouble, Roxburgh thought that boys could learn responsibility only if they had leisure; leisure to learn something other than set books. There were no absurd boy-made rules about dress or who could walk where. Indeed there were as few rules as possible and the ones that were had to be kept by seniors as well as juniors.

According to a contemporary, Roxburgh taught the actor David Niven: "the grace and elegance, which were the kind of behaviour, which became the Niven manner on screen and off".

Perhaps JF's ideals of individuality and behaviour did rub off on me and did, subconsciously, liberate my mind. The beauty of the architecture and landscape around me, of language, music and art, of the natures (mainly kindly ones) and abilities of people around me, led me later to react against the ugliness of poverty – its expression in squalid housing, dirty surroundings, unhappy faces and unfulfilled talents. Also, too, the ugliness of cheap lino and cracked plasterboard walls, of chipped mugs and rusting corrugated tin roofs, of crude words and provocative gestures. An American boy once told me that I was "a typical English schoolboy". I don't really know what he meant but it made me feel proud and did my ego a lot of good.

The opening of outlook which JF so strongly preached helped me, I'm certain, to look over horizons, to be un-noticing of the conventional and keen to break new ground if it seemed the better thing to do. This is sometimes called eccentricity, but has, I think and hope, no element of madness in it for me. Stowe was a pioneer school and JF a pioneer headmaster – perhaps that rubbed off on me, too.

Many stories are told of his courtliness, his good manners, his sartorial elegance and his tact. My wife, Susan, often reminds me that I've missed out on all these but, perhaps, those earlier, subtler, elements in understanding and behaviour did get home to me. I needed, however, to read the words of those wise writers, Anthony Quinton and Noel Annan, quoted earlier, many years later, in order even to think that it might have been so.

Was it these influences also, which made me later so at ease when taking part in and hearing the beauty and truth of the traditional speeches in Freemasonry, and in the dignity of the ritual ceremonies carried out in the chivalric Order of St John and in the Brigade of Guards? Perhaps it was so, but I know that my parents, without the benefit of this knowledge and these experiences would have felt, instinctively, much the same as I did and their enormous influence on and example to me, must not be left out of the equation.

Schooling in its broadest sense must cover all the influences which come to play upon our lives. I find such influences on my life hard to remember and am unsure how much importance I ought to attach to them. I can, however, bring a few to the surface: Nanny Rice's gentleness, for example, and her kindness to animals, and the "not giving up" which Mippy imparted.

All my parents had taught me centred, certainly, on religion. From my mother this was the surety of everlasting life and, from my father, the wry resignation to the inevitable. Independence and do-your-own-thing from my brothers, and fair play in sport and losing cheerfully from Edward Snell, headmaster of Mowden. These were a few of the earliest influences which somehow got into my make-up.

But what part, particularly, did Stowe (which, with Mowden and a pre-prep school in Collingham Gardens, London, comprised my school education) play in my life, my thinking or in the development of my subsequent career? How do I know and what can I assume?

Stowe has the most beautiful buildings in England, a noble 18th-century mansion set in a park landscaped by Capability Brown and Kent and spangled with temples and follies. Its grandeur and history should have meant something to me, yet I neither knew nor cared about them. Built by Vanburgh, this former home of the Dukes of Buckingham had been brilliantly adapted to become a public school. Many new rooms had been added but my house, Cobham, was in the old block and had more character than the modern additions – that I had noticed and I was glad of it.

But I always regret that throughout my time at Stowe I neither properly noticed nor fully appreciated the school's architecture, its grounds or its headmaster or, for that matter, the ethos and history of the school and its originators.

4
IN THE FOOTSTEPS OF FIELD-MARSHALL GOMM

War was declared during my last year at Stowe (1939-40). Aged 17, I joined the school Local Defence Volunteers (LDV), probably under compulsion however disguised, in order to defend that remote spot in Buckingham should the need arise.

While still at Stowe I went to Oriel College, Oxford, where Antony and Roderick already were, to see if I could pass their entrance exam, called "Responsions". I did pass, despite the fact that my swotting time the evening before the exam was taken up in retreating after an air-raid warning to a shelter with the Provost and his family, but although the War meant little to me, it enthused me enough to decline the opening I was offered at the University and to volunteer instead, with a school friend, to join the army.

My family connections were with the Coldstream Guards through my great uncle, the Field-Marshal, who had been its Colonel from 1863 to 1875. I never thought of joining any other regiment. On leaving school, however, I was too young (17½) to join the Coldstream Guards and thus, in 1940, I enlisted in the Young Soldiers Battalion of the Royal Berkshire Regiment.

When I joined, the Regiment was under canvas in a meadow at Oxford but we soon moved to Thame and occupied the Masonic Lodge – an admirably suitable platoon barrack room. I was made a lance-corporal and later a full corporal.

Thame holds pleasant memories for me. I had a great walkout with the local greengrocer's daughter, and while our affair never got beyond late-night hot chocolate in the sitting room, it was a happy time.

And it was at Thame that the war first, and quite suddenly, became real and serious to me. My parents had come to visit – they were staying at the famous Spread Eagle Hotel – and we were bombed. I helped organise the cordoning of the area and recovery of salvage. It was a night of great excitement.

New recruit
In the spring of 1941 I joined the Coldstream and went first to the Guards Depot at Caterham as a recruit. Fortunately, the normal

peacetime medical standards did not apply and my colour blindness, which would now prevent me from joining the army, was no bar, nor, as it turned out, did it ever pose me any problem.

The Coldstream unit in which I was trained as a recruit Guardsman was called a brigade squad and comprised some two dozen cadets, potential officers for all the different regiments of foot guards. My brigade squad was marched swiftly and frequently up and down the square but the training was generally straightforward and not too hard.

One of the odd military manoeuvres we learned was marching backwards in slow time wearing gas masks. It taught us balance and showed whether we had kept our gas masks properly de-misted; if we had not, the lenses soon fogged up and we had no idea which way we were turning or moving and so usually fell down.

From Caterham I wrote to my parents:

> The Colonel commanding the Regiment came down and interviewed me the other day. The first question he asked was how often had I played rugger for the Depot and, when I told him twice, he seemed very pleased. Then he asked my company commander how I had got on so far and was told all right so he told me definitely that I should go to Sandhurst. I shall need for it a bicycle, sheets, cricket outfit and bag, squash and tennis racquets and a swimming suit; also a dark suit and all that goes with it ... I forgot to add golf clubs, old trousers and white trousers.
>
> All this to be taught how to fight a war.

I also wrote of a cookhouse fatigue (not a punishment) during which I scrubbed dishes, peeled potatoes and cleaned out drains, and of my first "short back and sides" which left me hairless to the crown. I remarked on the introduction of the new Bren automatic machine gun: "bit heavy but pretty good", and that I had begun to wax my moustache. The King, we were told, thought the soldiers guarding the Palace looked too young so we were encouraged (ordered) not to shave. There was a prize for moustache growing but I did not win it. I began smoking – even a pipe – but the keenness of others for my cigarette coupons helped me to stop; I, anyhow, preferred the chocolate coupons they offered in exchange.

Sandhurst

From Caterham I went to Sandhurst in the summer of 1941, and was later commissioned. Sandhurst, like Stowe, is a historic building of architectural note but, again, I failed to notice it. I remember more the hot sausages eaten with beer, endless brass polishing and quick uniform changing.

My first appointment as an officer, later that year, was to our holding battalion at Regent's Park Barracks in London where I was made weapons officer. I thoroughly enjoyed trying out all sorts of weapons, and sticking armour onto armoured cars. Unfortunately a lot of weapons disappeared during this time but my commanding officer, Jimmy Coates, the Cresta runner, wrote off more than £100 – the amount of my annual income above my army pay – to clear it up. Coates was known as an extremely generous man, but I think this kindness was partly prompted by the recognition that I couldn't yet be expected to have control over all departments of my job.

It was from Regent's Park Barracks with our holding battalion that I did my first guard on Buckingham Palace. We marched there through Regent Street and round Piccadilly Circus in battledress and steel helmets. Later, I drove past Marble arch, down Park Lane and around Hyde Park Corner in a tank. Both these experiences seemed, somehow, unreal.

Training for war: 1942-1944

From the holding battalion, I was posted, in 1942, to the 4th service Battalion, and stayed with it until the end of the war, almost four years. My first reaction to its officers was that they were a very unfriendly lot. For the first six months there, nobody called me by my Christian name and I was such a miserable, and therefore bad, soldier that I was given an adverse report by the commanding officer. This gave me only a short time in which to improve before being thrown out of the battalion, but I managed to stay and began to enjoy myself.

We soon became part of a completely separate brigade, the 6th Guards Tank Brigade. We were put into tanks because it had been decided that six-foot guardsmen were too tall to fit into Halifax troop-carrying aeroplanes; otherwise we would have become parachutists, which I would not have voted for.

With the heaviest possible tanks, Churchills, we were sent to train in many different parts of the country: Salisbury Plain, the Derbyshire Dales, a Lancashire firing range, Sherwood Forest and, finally, around villages in Kent. A good way of training tank crews was to drive across the plains chasing rabbits. The gunner would train his unarmed gun on the animal while the commander practised giving directions and the driver honed his speed and handling skills. Often, the rabbits just gave themselves up and sat waiting, dejected; then we would let them go.

We worked hard but also enjoyed a full social life and made good friends. We took every possible weekend off and hurried to London to stay in the smartest hotels – Claridges, the Ritz, the Savoy and the Berkeley. There we gave breakfast parties, drank champagne and, although at that time I belonged to a total of 40 clubs, we spent most of our nights in the "400" nightclub in Leicester Square. Breakfasting in Lyons Corner House and dancing, in battledress, in the most sophisticated places completed our picture of wartime gaiety.

I had number 8 Troop in number 2 Squadron. This was my first real command and I held it for more than three years before being promoted to second-in-command of the squadron in 1944. Each troop's tanks were named after first letters of different animals; ours was "E" (elephant, eland, elk) and my tank was called Elephant.

Elephant was adopted by the town of Brighton after a Salute the Soldier fund-raising week in 1944. I used to keep the local MP in touch with its movements, although these were not particularly significant until it was knocked out by the Germans – just a few days after I had been wounded and had left it – in Normandy in 1944. However, being adopted gave my tank an added interest and I looked on Elephant with affection and served with her, or various improved models of her, for nearly three years. My friends even used to send me Christmas cards with elephants on them.

After being knocked out, Elephant was replaced for the Rhine crossing. With an even bigger gun, the "new" Elephant weighed about 70 tons and needed nine gallons of petrol for every mile covered – what a supply task! It churned up concrete roads when it turned because the two tracks revolved in opposite directions.

Driving across country at 15 mph (which feels like 60 mph) in the heaviest tank in the allied army, as mine once was, is a wonderful feeling. It's not just the power and the noise; it's the feeling of control and the sense of responsibility which is exhilarating.

During training on the Yorkshire Wolds, around Leyburn and along Swaledale, we used to have small exercises on which we were allowed to take our tanks wherever we liked – provided we avoided trespass or wanton damage. The Government was very reasonable about compensation and the value to our training was immense compared to any loss to the farmers; to have been always road-bound would have been stultifying to the tank crews and have taken away all initiative from us junior leaders.

In 1943, while stationed at Rufford Abbey in Nottinghamshire, we used to practice night drives in our tanks. Once the move was over and everyone had arrived in the middle of some piece of waste land, each five-man crew would dig a large hole in the ground and run their tank over it; the crew then crawled into the hole between the tank tracks and went to sleep – thankful for the dry and warmth, we slept incredibly well.

To make our tanks waterproof for going into the sea we extended the exhaust pipes (like periscopes) so the fumes were expelled above the height of the waves. We practiced this by crossing rivers and driving along their beds, but we did it for real during a beach landing when we were forced to evacuate a landing craft earlier than planned. We had to submerge our tank before running it up the shelving beach, and seeing water pushing against the windows provoked a very strange feeling.

5
FIGHTING IN EUROPE 1944-1945

After three years' training in England we took our Churchill tanks and landed on Juno Beach, near Caen in Normandy, on 20th July 1944. D Day was earlier, 6th June 1944, but we were not needed. Our tanks were so heavy that they needed a firm beach, better if specially prepared to land. The crossing had been rough, wet and miserable; one man took a look at me in our tank landing craft and immediately left his potato-peeling to go below and be sick. When we finally disembarked on the sands at 2 am, I called out the tanks in the wrong order.

We moved to various concentration areas in turn and as we waited it continued to rain. We kept cheerful with the help of some local Calvados. Leaflets dropped by the Germans said we were "foxes caught in a trap" and showed a girl telephoning with the caption "you'll never hear her sweat (German spelling) voice again"; they didn't bother us. After shellings, the fields were littered with dead cows, which smelt powerfully and took dozens of gallons of petrol to burn.

On 31st July we fought our first battle. The objective was Hill 309 near Caumont. Our tank attack was with infantry and, despite a lot of mortar and gunfire, we advanced several miles and captured the top of the hill – the dominating feature for miles around.

Because of shelling and attack by rocket-firing Focke Wulf aircraft our infantry were unable to keep up with us and we had to sit alone on top of the hill for more three hours. We were caught in the fire from both sides, and it was uncomfortable. Eventually, as night fell, our infantry moved up to our tank positions and we were able to withdraw from the crest for the night.

By then I had spent 16 hours in my tank with only occasional forays out either to extinguish fires on the back or, after moving through orchards, to sweep away the fallen apples which were obstructing the exhaust.

Thereafter there was no let-up and during subsequent weeks we had several minor skirmishes. One day, for example, while travelling down a wooded road beyond Caumont I saw a German soldier about 80 yards away, peering out from behind a tree and pointing an anti-tank gun at us. I ordered the gunner to rotate the turret and shoot him, which he did. We kept moving, and met no further close opposition that day.

Next day our troop supported the infantry in an attack in open country and was successful, but other tank troops were not; so after an exchange of fire with enemy tanks, machine-gun bullets rattling on the side of our tank and one of our tank crew being wounded by a sniper, we were ordered to withdraw.

Surrounded by mortar fire we moved slowly back a few hundred yards in the dusk through no-man's land; but soon it was so dark that we halted and drew ourselves into a laager for the night. We pointed the four tanks outwards to the points of the compass and mounted a double guard.

That night, armed with first aid kits, we tried to help the wounded. They were in a bad way: one with both legs off, one with both kidneys punctured, others with broken legs and lacerated throats. I gave six morphine doses and a lot of chloroform. Although there was much blood the men behaved well, including a German prisoner who helped me even though he was badly hurt in the stomach.

We had nine stretcher cases. I stayed awake throughout the night with them and also visited the sentries. Off duty, each of the men had half-an-hour's sleep at a time. Meanwhile we kept trying to wireless the battalion for help but we failed to get through.

Dan Meinertzhagen, who was in command of one of the tanks, went off in the dark to try and find further help for the wounded. At 5am he returned with some jeeps.

They showed our infantry the way back to the squadron and took off our dozen or so wounded but they wouldn't take the dead, which now numbered three. So, when we moved we put our dead on our tanks. The men were good about this, but one NCO refused to lift a body and I had to do it for him. At first light we pulled out, and eventually found our way back to the squadron, and left the dead with the padre in the cemetery.

Two weeks later, on 12th August, I was wounded. We were travelling in line along a road when my squadron commander telephoned telling me to signal to the scout car behind to move forward. As I put my head out of the top of the tank a large shell landed on the bank to my left and I found myself at the bottom of the tank with a signaller shouting that I had been hit. There was a lot of blood. I jumped out and lay on the side of the road while my driver got a shell dressing.

I was taken by scout car to the Regimental Aid Post and by

ambulance to the Field Dressing Station further back. At the first I got tea and at the second morphine, which eased the pain, and I fell asleep. By air and train, and for the most part unconscious, I reached a general hospital in Cardiff, where at one stage I came round to find a Catholic priest bending over me, praying. I had been logged as "George Carr, RC" instead of "R.C. Carr-Gomm". But no last rites were necessary and the side of my face healed.

I was back at the front for the Rhine crossing early in 1945. Using a pontoon bridge we led the push through Germany and drove hard night and day, at first with American paratroopers as infantry to help us. We were successful, but several days later there was stubborn resistance, and the elation we had felt earlier turned to dogged pushing-on backed by exhaustion and hunger.

3. 4th Battalion in Munster, April 1945, with troops from the American Airborne Division

Attacking a village, my tank was hit and I was taken blindfolded from the front. At the field hospital, a few miles back, my eyes were checked and washed and some burns and scratches dressed. Two days later, I could see again, so walked from the hospital and hitched back to my battalion at the front. It was Easter Day 1945 and I went to communion in an orchard.

For my part in these various actions, I was lucky enough to be awarded the French Croix de Guerre and gain a "mention in dispatches".

Belsen

Hana Greenfield, a woman slave labourer in Belsen, later wrote:

> Whoever lived through the experience of Belsen lived through his own death. Death was everywhere. It stared at us from every-one's eyes. The pitiful walking dead bodies no longer knew where they were walking to or why.
>
> Everyone was searching for non-existent food. Our tongues were swollen from lack of water. The little water that was available was contaminated with typhoid. Some drank it, not caring any longer ... At night, we heard the guns of the advancing armies. How much longer can it take before they reach us? How much strength will it take to stay alive until then?
>
> And then it happened. The first British tank rolled up and we heard the sweet words we had waited for so long: "YOU ARE FREE ... YOU ARE ... FREE ... YOU ARE FREE ..."
>
> Those of us who were still alive – while thousands lay dead, no longer having had the strength nor will to live – became free. And so April 12th, 1945, will forever remain engraved in my memory.

Continuing our advance from the Rhine into and across Germany we drove through Celle and on 12th April, 1945 found ourselves the first troops at Belsen concentration camp.

4. Belsen

We were still in the lead of the main British thrust and facing opposition. We began to notice prisoners of all nationalities on the road, some of them thin and staving, wandering alone in light, striped prison clothes; some were carrying fellow inmates to a civilian hospital.

The gates to Belsen were open and we stopped long enough to learn that the people we had seen around Celle had broken out of it, and another concentration camp nearby, and had looted a flour mill. They were weak from starvation; some, these former prisoners told us, had been beaten and several had died that day. Even though a few of them had managed to smile, the atmosphere all round was unpleasant and there was talk of typhus in the camp. The citizens of Celle, the nearest town, were terrified of these wanderers and kept their doors locked.

We couldn't afford to stop and take over the concentration camps because fighting was still going on. On the outskirts of Celle, a carrier was hit by a bazooka and we had to send a troop to clear the road. Civilians, too, were reported to be fighting against us, so we burned down houses which might be shelter for them.

Later, at Rhalestedt, near Hamburg, after the chase was over, we came across another concentration camp where all the German soldiers – 300 of them – on the staff were lined up in the square to surrender. A hard-faced SS man commanded them. While my senior officer inspected the troops and accepted their surrender, I noticed a truck driver unloading its cargo into one of the buildings. Wearing concentration camp uniform he, with just one hand, was lifting live bodies as if they were bundles of bedding.

I went upstairs and saw the barrack rooms. They were half full of victims lying on filthy bunks with only a few feet between each layer. One man had so little flesh on him his bones stood out sharply, stretching his skin. He was so thin he could hardly move or speak. To wash him, later, his clothes had to be cut off; he had gangrene in the groin. Others did not show elation at their freedom, shows of emotion had been the cause for beatings and death threats from their Nazi guards.

I arranged at once for the temporary civilian staff to be brought in to see what had been going on. They came through in single file and stared at the louse-ridden, thin and unshaved victims. Some civilians, though, I had to hold while an interpreter explained my words to them; they hid their eyes and stood there shaking their heads.

A week later I entered yet another concentration camp and saw the gas chambers, gallows and incinerators. These last had coffins in them and nearby were the metal stretchers which had been used for pushing the victims into the furnaces. In the middle of it all, quite alone, stood a pretty Polish girl.

Although the memories remain I didn't take in, at the time, the enormity of the crimes the concentration camps represented. We had not been warned about them and, until we saw them, did not know that such places existed.

Bob (Robert) Runcie – then in the Scots Guards, and with us when we arrived at Belsen – made a point during the Eighties when, as Archbishop of Canterbury, he said publicly: "I was at Belsen. Being there then convinced me that a war, which closed Belsen, was worth fighting."

Victory in Europe

By VE Day on May 7th in 1945 we had advanced across Germany and reached the Elbe where we met the Russians.

5. RC-G cartoon, Schonboken, May 1945

After the armistice I was detailed to take some men and capture an enemy train. It was a command train, that is to say it was semi-permanent in a siding and HQ of an engineer general. When we surrounded it, the General and his staff, some civilian, surrendered without a fight.

I divided the prisoners into groups according to the number of available sentries and crowded them into the train's few carriages. I then moved the train to Flensburg, about 80 miles north on the German-Danish border. Handed over to the military police there, the General waited to go on trial; Himmler, too, had recently been brought in, though by his suicide he would avoid trial. My General was a nice man, worried mostly, and needlessly, about the future of his son who was acting as his prisoner father's ADC.

Before our German prisoners had disembarked from the train, I told them they could take with them only what they could carry and wear whereupon men and women alike undressed and proceeded to don several sets of underclothes before adding numerous layers of outer clothing. Some were so overdressed and weighed down they could hardly walk from the train. Our men were most amused at the spectacle. We, too, then left the station and returned to our barracks by truck.

Bravery and fear

Some say one must be brave and fearless to fight on the front line, but the really brave man is the one who knows he is afraid. During the war I, by luck, was simply not afraid. Perhaps it was due to a lack of imagination and not thinking ahead, but I never ever thought or talked about fear. I found real fighting very like exercises on Salisbury Plain – exciting and acceptable rather than terrifying. The sight of the wounded did not revolt me and I did not mind the dull food or sleeping underneath my tank and such like. I accepted things as they came and certainly had no doubt that our actions in this war were justified.

It is the man who returns to the fight having been wounded several times and knows what it feels like to be hurt who is brave. Anyone who has felt punishment or torture and chooses to face it again, or the person who offers life or limb, knowing what that loss will mean; they are the really brave. I was never brave like that nor did I experience such challenges or trials. For me, the episodes of war in which I was involved did not produce thoughts of bravery or fear, that is, until the very end.

On 4th May 1945, three days before peace was declared in Europe, I was really afraid. After a day's fighting one tank was needed to drive about a 1,000 yards down a straight road in the gathering darkness. It would thereby open a road link between two villages, both of which our infantry had already occupied. A German self-propelled gun or Tiger tank was thought to be hidden in a farm building halfway along the road and that one of our tanks should drive down the road to draw its fire.

The plan seemed foolhardy and our squadron commander, Major Mark Milbank, tried to get us out of it. When he couldn't, he said he would drive along the road himself. All we junior officers felt then that we ought to volunteer and did so; it was, therefore, necessary to draw lots from a hat, and that – having been several times wounded – was the moment when I felt fear.

The lot did not fall to me. The tank which did go got there and back safely; there was no enemy in the farm buildings. It was with a great sense of relief that I then set about recovering a blown-up tank in the dark.

Sometimes we shared a kind of telepathic prophecy about death, but even this didn't spark fear in me. Two brother officers called their soldier-servants one morning and told them exactly how to divide up their belongings if they didn't come back that day. Their tank troops were then called to do battle and both officers were killed. In a letter from a guardsman to his parents, penned just before an action in which he was killed, he wrote that he was going to die and thanked them cheerfully and strongly for the loving upbringing they had given him. These were prophecies, not death wishes; as tank crews we worked in groups of five and never, as a consequence, could individuals influence their own wounding or death.

A guardsman's war in verse

A general account of our war and tank experiences is summed up in a guardsman Tommy Lynch's poem:

>Have you ever commanded a Churchill
>When it's going flat out on the track
>And your eyes are red through lack of sleep
>And staring, when nights are black?

>Have you ever commanded a Churchill
>Over hills, through ditches and streams,
>With no time even to think
>Of your home and all that it means?

>Have you ever commanded a Churchill
>When the shells whine their way overhead,
>And the Spandous and Besas are spitting out
>Death and destruction – hot lead?

>Have you ever commanded a Churchill

With the gunner's head gripped t'wixt your knees
And the driver's been hit by a splinter
And the engine has started to 'wheeze'?

There is no time to stop to examine
The attack must go in right or wrong,
The objective has got to be taken
And it's already taken too long.

Have you ever commanded a Churchill
When Tigers and Panthers are near,
And your hair stands on end with excitement
But your brain is ice cool and quite clear?

The lads in your crew are dependant
On you and the orders you give
For they trust you and know that your judgement
Will decide just how long they live.

I've commanded a Churchill
With the finest lads on earth,
They fought all day and half through the night
But were never lacking in mirth.

I remember at Overloon fighting
When my tank blew up on a mine,
And the mortars were coming down heavy
In our special part of the line.

Said the gunner 'Hey sarg, what hit us?'
A mine or a bleeding SP?'
The driver said, 'it makes no difference,
Get cracking with that brew of tea'.

And that's how it goes in this fighting
And that's why we're going to win,
For no matter what odds are against us
We also find time for a grin.

Through France, through Belgium and Holland,
To the land where the trouble began,
The SS and Hitler are scared now
Of the guts of our fighting man.

Well anyway, have one with me mate,
OK then I'll have one with you,
And, when this lots done with, we'll be proud to say

'It was hell' but we got through.

To Paddy, Defiant and Moleskin Joe,
I hope that you get through.
Tommy Lynch, that's me of course,
Pays his respect to you.

Good luck Mick,
There's a good time coming
Though we may never live to see it.

6

"WAKEN ... THE BLUE MEDITERRANEAN"

With the coming of peace in Europe we handed over our tanks, disbanded our 4th Battalion and I returned to England to join the 3rd Battalion. It was the summer of 1945 after VE Day (May 7th) and we were to prepare for fighting in the Far East. It was planned that on our way there we would go to Texas to train for an assault landing on the Singapore beaches. It was fortunate for us that the actual operation never took place, for it transpired that the Japanese had, in fact, twice as many soldiers defending Singapore and on our beach as our intelligence had estimated.

6. RC-G, 1948

Peacekeeping in Palestine

When the Japanese collapsed and the whole war ended formally on September 2nd, our destination was switched to Palestine where I remained from 1945 until 1948. The Jews, declaring that VJ (Victory in Japan) Day for the world meant D Day for them, took up arms against the British and determined to rid the Holy Land of them. They wanted to create an independent state and make a corner for Jewry in the heart of Arab territory.

We in the battalion knew little about Palestine at that time and less about the political situation there. We had only three weeks hurried preparation before leaving the UK but, during that time and the 17 days at sea out of Liverpool, a good deal of fact-digestion went on. By the time we arrived at Haifa most of us were pro-Jew.

However, such was the behaviour of the Jews during the next two-and-a-half years that by the time we left in 1948 almost all of us were pro-Arab. Many had become so anti-Semitic that when the battalion returned to England and was posted to Aldershot, the Hebrew symbol of a star was torn off the synagogue nearby and the officers, burning it, danced around the funeral pyre. The feeling prompting this action submerged, temporarily, our more unbiased and dispassionate feelings at a time when sympathy for the Jewish people was growing with the unfolding awareness of the Holocaust which was only just beginning to surface.

It was perhaps inevitable that the Jews could see only their side of the conflict (in the Middle East – they seeking return to the fatherland while the Arabs saw it as their birthright. We soldiers, on the other hand, had to see both sides for we were in Palestine to back up the administration of the mandate which our country had been given after the First World War.

However, even though the Arabs did not like it, there seemed to be an unavoidable movement towards the creation of a Jewish State. There was a biblical as well as a historical background for this, and liberal Jews were prepared to leave it to the passage of time and the conscience of the world to bring it about. Indeed, the more liberally-minded Jews did not even envisage a Jewish State becoming a politically separate country.

During the 1920s, Uganda had been proposed as a national home for the Jews and, oddly enough, this idea was revived by the Jews in 1972, although at this time it would have been, for them, a second base to Israel and have provided them with a good launch-pad for a pincer-movement on unfriendly Egypt. In 1945, however, political Zionists were not content to wait for what they considered was the liberation of Palestine; they wanted quicker action, and it was with them that we, mainly, had to contend.

Extremism: certainty and doubt

The terrorist section of the Jewish army, the Haganah, was called "The Stern Gang". Of these, those considered the best fighters went under the name of the Irgun Zvei Lumi (IZL). Sniping and stabbing, the men and women of the IZL fought an underground war. They never came out into the open and used every form of deceit against us.

The country life of the ordinary Jew was concentrated around the kibbutzim. These were villages built, usually in compact formations, surrounded by barbed wire and usually without a synagogue. One day we had to go to one of these settlements to arrest some terrorists. Once we were inside, the Jewish men gathered themselves into a group then surrounded themselves with their women facing outwards from the circle. The women, in turn, put their children in front of them. To get to the guilty men, the guardsmen first had to put aside the children, then ward off tearing and scratching women, who also used high-heeled shoes as weapons. Eventually we got the wanted men hiding in the centre.

On another occasion, we were about to search a diamond factory for two of our missing sergeants. Afraid they would loot it, the Jewish mayor asked our brigadier if the guardsmen would not enter the factory, and he gave his word that our missing sergeants were not in it. His request was granted and the search continued elsewhere.

A few days later the sergeants were discovered, dead, and it transpired that at the time of the search they had been alive in that same diamond factory. Their bodies were left hanging from trees in an orchard, and when the guardsmen went to cut them down a mine detonated by the falling bodies blew them up.

It was in these ways that we quickly came to know the Jews. Those of us who had been stationed in Palestine before the war had similar stories to tell of the Arabs. After 300 years of Turkish rule (until Allenby's campaign of 1917 cleared the Turks out), the Arabs had longed to run their own country and as a result resented our presence in it. Hence, from 1917 until the coming of the Second World War in 1939, they, too, had resisted us.

But in 1945 a partitioned state with each side having its own autonomy seemed an answer, for each race had a historical claim to a share of the land; however this suggested solution was not acceptable to the extremists on either side.

My experiences and the incidents that took place in Palestine between 1945 and 1948 gave me a special insight when reflecting on Israeli terrorism. In 1989 I read newspaper articles reporting that the now elderly Jewish terrorists still enjoyed reminiscing about their days on the run as killers. I include the following extract from one such article, although I cannot now recall in which newspaper it was published:

> The assassin of the Swedish UN mediator, Count Bernadotte, joked about his aliases. "I was Dan in the south, Ephraim in the north, Meir in Jerusalem, and many other names." A couple of hundred old stalwarts had come, many accompanied by their wives, for a reunion. They had come out from the shadows; first from the British, then for thirty years from the forerunners of their Parliamentary Labour alignment.
>
> Their political rehabilitation was finally achieved in the 1977 elections, that turning point in Israeli political life, when the former Irgun leader, Menachem Begin, swept to power, to be followed later by Ytzhak Shamir, also a member of the terrorist group called IZL (Irgun Zvei Lumi).
>
> As for their deeds, the old veterans were in no doubt in their minds of the legitimacy of their cause. "We were fighting to obtain the freedom of the Jewish nation," one old gang member declared.

In fact this freedom referred to in the article was, anyhow, on its way and the IZL's acts of terrorism served only to pave its way with unhappiness and hate. The Holocaust was only two years over and the United Nations already had Palestine on its agenda. The Stern Group melted on Independence in 1948.

It seems there will always be people who, like these terrorists, are prepared to kill illegally for their own ideological ends, and that makes attractive the idea of a constitution which would allow neither an unelected head of state nor automatic hereditary powers – both situations in which terrorists flourish. It would be based on democratic elections, referendums and sharing and would ensure that the proclaimed or secret schemes of leaders such as Idi Amin, Saddam Hussein or Robert Mugabe and of organisations such as the Irish Republican Army (IRA), the Taliban or Al-Qaeda would be rootless and, therefore, wither. There would be no monopoly of rule and evil would be more difficult to perpetrate.

Thinking on these lines, I recall something I heard about Richard Meinertzhagen (Dan Meinertzhagen was a fellow officer with me in Normandy). He had been a legendary intelligence officer during the First World War in the Near- and Middle-East and it was in Palestine that he had dropped the famous false message from Allenby misleading the Turks.

Before that he had spent most of his time fighting colonial battles. As a soldier he had followed whole-heartedly what was known in India as the "Punjab Principle"; a shot in time saves nine, that is to say that swift and drastic punishment is the best way to ensure peace.

This, of course, is what General Dyer maintained when he made his colossal blunder at Amritsar in April 1919, killing 375 Indians and wounding another 1,500 while they were taking part in a peaceful demonstration. During 1946-48, while I was in Palestine, I wondered whether we should have tried the "Punjab Principle" there. But we never did and received no credit for not doing it.

Michael Hollings was a brother officer and holder of the MC from Italy fighting days. (He was, later, on the very short list to become Archbishop of Westminster) While he was with us in Palestine, Hollings wrote a prayer from which the following is an extract:

> Lord, my thoughts are going round and round in circles. All the activities of the day crowd into my mind and jumble and jostle each other. I am far from peaceful and am quite uncomposed for sleep. Could you, please, calm me, the way you did the storm, saying quietly "Peace, be still".

Lord, give me your peace, your deep peace, so I may sleep restfully and get up tomorrow refreshed and ready for another busy day.

And, again in Palestine, he wrote:

> There always seems to be a war going on ... but you Jesus, promised that you had come to give peace. So what am I to think? Why doesn't your gift work? They say you are powerful and loving. Surely you would not promise something you couldn't give?
>
> It's the kind of time I sit down and think, and look around, and see the chaos and fighting and hatred. Then I think – Jesus, you promised peace! It goes round and round in my head and I find myself saying: 'You must be joking Lord.' But then I think you said you would give peace 'not as the world gives it'.
>
> So I am in a muddle about what that means. Is it deep down inside me, not outside? Will you help me to be quiet and at peace, even though the world is at war? And will you help others to be like that too? I find it hard to believe and understand, so perhaps, Lord,

You will make me see and hear, if I am still and listen. Anyhow I am going to try that now.

All of us in Palestine at that time felt like this; his words mirrored our feelings and reactions.

Bible stories

History was visible all round us, some of it recent. During the Mandate the British had put up square, hollow-shaped forts, and the roads and railway tracks reminded us of Allenby's campaign and of Lawrence of Arabia during the first Great War. The Crusaders, too, had passed that way and left their castles. Mainly, however, it was the places familiar from the Bible which we saw.

From our camp on the Plain of Esdraelon we could stand and see many holy places: Mount Carmel; the Brook Kishon where the ravens fed Elijah; Megiddo (or the fields of Armageddon) where, it is foretold, the last battle in the world will be fought; Nazareth and the Rock of Precipitation from which Christ was nearly cast when he revisited his old home – and all around were the cornfields in which he walked.

I visited Masada, the rock fortress beside the Dead Sea where the Romans, in 72 AD, thinking that the resurrected Christ lived there, besieged the town and built a rampart from which to storm it. The next morning, when they did storm the town, they found that all 953 residents had committed suicide during the night.

I visited Tiberius, Capernaum and Jerusalem, and on Christmas Eve 1947 I took part in a service in the fields outside Bethlehem. There, I could look up and see the star we were singing about in the carol. The effect was spoilt only by the guardsmen's bad language as they stumbled back through fields in the dark. At midnight I attended communion in one of the churches in Bethlehem.

Some towns and other places which Jesus visited and which were now built over had, to me, no atmosphere of holiness: Jacob's Well, the house at Cana where Jesus turned water into wine, Bethlehem where outside the Church of the Nativity is a tourist shop called the Holy Manger Stall, Jesus's parents' home in Nazareth – all these places have lost something of Christ in the alterations made to them by man. I even felt this about the Church of the Holy Sepulchre in Jerusalem, and preferred instead the garden tomb nearby which was discovered at the end of the last century by General Gordon. This place is thought by many to be the real site of Golgotha, where Jesus was crucified, and where his tomb lies.

With all the routine and difficult days we spent in Palestine, few others remain in my memory as being carefree. Some of these were spent duck shooting on the lakes, partridge-shooting in the stubble fields near Gaza or chasing gazelle and capercaillie on the salt lakes near Amman. There were days spent sightseeing, and days just bathing and sunbathing.

Once, some of the officers held an eating competition in a beach café. You scored a point for each dish on the menu you ate and I was winning, until another officer realised that you also gained a point for each roll of bread. Concentrating on these, he pipped me at the post.

Globetrotting

The long holidays which one gets in the army should be one of the best incentives in recruiting. Their purpose is not that they should be periods of idleness, but opportunities for travel and gaining insight into the customs and life-styles of others. Most unmarried officers used their leaves in this way and benefited greatly from their experiences.

From the very earliest days when I went on holiday to Appin in Argyllshire where, with my parents and three brothers, we stayed in a couple of railway carriages converted into caravans, I had loved seeing new countryside and staying in unusual places. This was a pleasure I later enjoyed bringing to holidays with my own family. Susan, however, and not unnaturally, never liked the less comfortable side of camping or caravanning, and none of our children seemed keen to repeat those excursions which had included some discomfort. But for my part, as a result of all the outdoor living on army exercises and holidays in unusual places, I enjoyed roughing it and was very happy tenting and bivouacking.

During the three years (1945-48) I spent in the Middle East, with occasional sorties back to England, I took full advantage of long periods of leave using them to travel and explore. Holidays spent in Cyprus, Turkey, Tangier, Jordan, Iraq and elsewhere were a mix of comfort and roughing it, and as various as climbing into the romantic Hilarion castle in Cyprus at sunrise to an inspection of the area in Istanbul walled off for prostitutes.

I saw the coronation of King Abdullah of Jordan in 1945 and the same afternoon had tea with Glubb Pasha, who was commanding the Arab Legion. His house was high on the hills of Amman, and as Arabs in the town below celebrated the coronation by firing their rifles in the air, many of the bullets fell, fortunately harmlessly, in the Glubbs' garden. His children were going through a stage of free development which included an interest in encouraging rabbit production. Everywhere we sat in his sitting room seemed to hide a baby rabbit. They popped out of chairs and cushions, but no one appeared to mind or even notice.

Out for a duck in Egypt

I went duck shooting in 1946 with our Ambassador in Egypt, Sir Miles Lampson, later Lord Killearn. The shoot was a most impressive affair. We motored from Cairo through miles of desert with Egyptian soldiers, each posted at various points, as markers along the empty route. When we arrived at the shooting area we were sent off, with a loincloth-clad bearer, to our various islands where we waited for duck to fly over. Having failed to hit anything I became so ashamed of my performance that I offered my gun to the bearer; he came out of the water near naked and shot every duck within range.

When it was time to return I proudly (though guiltily) produced all his duck without confessing who had shot them. After paying for the cartridges we drove back to Cairo. No-one was allowed to get in the way of the Ambassador's car; traffic lights were ignored and everything had to move aside to let us pass. It was embarrassing.

All points of the compass

In an effort to cover as much ground as possible on my travels in the Middle East I, and usually with friends, set off each time in a different direction: to the east in Iraq was Baghdad and its airport, Habbanya; to the north in Syria was le Crac des Chevaliers, the world's finest Crusader castle standing high and isolated in a desert of scrubland; there were the towns of Aleppo and Homs, with duck-shooting along the Orontes river which flowed between them, and I visited Antioch and Shughur to the east.

In 1947, I travelled north to Asia Minor, where the wolves howled beside the train out of Syria and we had to borrow an extra engine to get us over the Taurus mountains and into Turkey. The children in the countryside were shoeless yet the railway station at Ankara was magnificent; this, recently-built, capital city was opulent and lush. The ambassador (Sir David Kelly) and his family gave me lunch at their lovely house beside a boulevard.

On journeys nearer Palestine I visited the beautiful city of Damascus, where I sported a fez in the curiously named "Street called Straight". And I enjoyed Beirut which in the Forties was modern, safe and cosmopolitan. Baalbek, the ancient Roman city, lay nearby and it was close to here that I got lost in the mountains and was taken in by some kindly Druse villagers who fed me and let me sleep the night on the floor of one of their mud-packed houses. I later skied in the mountains among the cedars of Lebanon, and visited the towns of Tyre and Sidon on the Mediterranean coast.

Again to the east, but closer, I went to Amman and the excavated Roman town of Zerqua nearby. I lay down to sleep that night in a dry wadi, but around midnight there was a thunderstorm and if I hadn't woken quickly would have been swept away by the torrent that soon flowed through it.

Petra: half as old as time

I travelled twice to Petra in the south: "the rose-red city half as old as time". Since being deserted in the 7th century, Petra fell into oblivion until it was re-discovered by a Swiss traveller in 1812. To reach it we had to walk or ride a mule through a chasm too narrow for a vehicle. In Petra we wandered around the houses and temples built into the red sandstone cliffs around the edge, and foot, of a giant, cliff-sided saucer. The original, almost pre-historic, village and homes had been built in this vast hole at the end of a single narrow passage, well protected from pirates and robbers.

South of Petra was the beautiful Gulf of Aqaba, full of porpoises. In the late Forties, the town itself had not yet been developed and along the shore there was white, white sand and clear, clear water. The fishermen had glass-bottomed boats from which we could watch the incredible underwater life – crystals and fossils and hundreds of multi-coloured, delicately shaped fish and marine animals, small and large.

In the Sinai I drove for days through the Valley of Sin (Zin) following the path which the Israelites had taken when they left Egypt some 5000 years before. My party and I went to the far (southern) quarter where we visited the monastery of St Catherine. It was from this monastery that the Russians stole the, possibly, oldest (4th century AD) copy of the Bible in existence, the Codex Sinaiticus (codices took over from scrolls in the 2nd century and then became manuscripts and books). In 1923, Britain bought it from Russia and it's now kept in the British Museum.

On our visit in 1948 we first made contact with the monks by raising and lowering a basket outside the monastery wall, although when they did, eventually, admit us it was through a modern door. They were very hospitable. I don't remember if we spent the night there, more likely we put up a tent on the mountain slope – not too far from the supposed site of the "burning bush".

On several occasions, I took parties of officers and guardsmen from my company to the white sands of Athlit and to the shores of the Gulf of Suez. In both these places we were completely out of touch with any other human life and it was remarkably peaceful, with nothing to do for days at a time but walk, read, swim and play the inevitable games of football on the sand.

Things that go bang in the desert

Then there was the time I rehearsed, with the whole company, the defensive squares which were used at the Battle of Waterloo, and at many others. So open was the land in Jordan, and uninhabited, that I was able to form up the men on four sides of a square, facing outwards and with three ranks: one lying down, the middle rank kneeling and the third standing. I then gave orders for each rank, or side as appropriate, in turn, to fire. We used live bullets and nothing and nobody was hurt or killed. My contribution was to fire straight up into the air with my duelling .22 pistol as a signal for each start.

The noise was so tremendous that orders to fire had to be relayed by an officer or NCO touching the men on the shoulder with swords or pace-sticks; this they did by standing beside or behind each flank of rifles – or smooth bore muzzle guns or muskets as they would have been at Waterloo. With one rank firing while the other two reloaded, we were able to keep up a continuous barrage of fire in any direction, or in all at once. The exercise proved the formation very strong and effective.

Gloves off in Cyprus

Cyprus is an island which I have come to know quite well having visited it on a number of occasions, both with army friends and on family holidays. It was even in the early 1950s when I first went there, racked by internal troubles and civil war. The Greek Church unhappily (and at the beginning, perhaps, unknowingly) had allied itself with the Communist Party and cried loudly for a union (enosis) with mainland Greece to which Cyprus had never been united.

The Turks, to whom the island did justifiably belong up to 1874, had a far greater claim to sovereignty than the Greeks; the Turks' numbers, though, were small and their mindset, until decades later, not ambitious.

Political actions followed the lines of a remark made by Oscar

Wilde: "Whenever a man does a thoroughly stupid thing, it is always from the noblest motives." And that is how both the Turks and the Greeks seemed to set about trying to gaining control of the island – with badly timed complaints, embarrassing failures to negotiate and bomb attacks and ambushes which rarely worked.

But, for us, in the early Fifties it was a lovely place for a holiday. I could ski in the Troodos Mountains in the morning before motoring down in the afternoon to sunbathe by the sea at Larnaca or Limasol.

It was in Cyprus that I challenged a drunken guardsman to a barefist boxing match. I did it within a circle of men urging us on to fight but it was a wrong thing to do, for an officer should in no circumstance ever hit a guardsman. I had forgotten how to box – not since my prep school days at Mowden had I done it, and then not much. However, I hit him hard enough that he stumbled and fell. Although he was drunk he got back up, but we decided not to continue and were friends afterwards. No-one told senior officers of the match.

7

EGYPT TO ENGLAND

In 1952 I spent two years in the Canal Zone in Egypt. On the way there I stopped at Tripoli in North Africa, and stayed with a battalion finishing its tour of duty. I managed a lot of sightseeing along the coast of North Africa during my two months there. I saw the Roman towns of Leptis Magna and Sabratha, gambled in the casino and ate endless sticky cream buns in the bonbonniers (sweet and cake shops) in the villages and shoreside cafes.

Militarily my most difficult task during this particular tour was to carry £5,000 in notes from England to Trieste for the Pay Corps. It was thought that, as I was taking a routine train journey, no-one would notice that I had this extra package with me. However, all the other officers travelling seemed to know about it and they amused themselves trying to pinch this large wad of notes off me. I had to take it everywhere: to the bathroom, to bed and to the table during meals. Once I looked round to find a friendly King's Messenger crawling on hands and knees to sneak it off me.

Idle hands

During the two long years which followed, mostly in the Canal Zone in Egypt (and with periodic returns to the UK), we moved around various tented and hutted desert camps surrounded by barbed wire. There was little to do; we used to have races and swim from Africa to Asia – across the canal. Our presence with 79,000 other soldiers was to act as a deterrent to Egyptians who threatened to occupy the zone which we held under United Nations Charter.

We were there to ensure not only the free passage of ships through the Suez Canal but also the safety of British residents in Egypt generally. There were, for example, 10,000 people in Alexandria who might have needed evacuating and this figure alone showed the size of the problem. However, until there was a crisis we were to keep quiet and do nothing militarily other than put up roadblocks or do local patrols. Often, we could not see the point of doing either.

The General Officers told us that we were "a show of force" or "a hidden might". We were also, they told us, the "mailed fist in the velvet glove", but even this contradictory encouragement did not cheer us.

Our morale sunk still lower at the time of the Queen's Coronation in 1953. We were told that, according to tradition, we and all the other units in the Brigade of Guards would return to London for it. They then thought again and decided we were needed more in Egypt – apparently in order to discourage the Egyptians from doing anything war-like on Coronation day.

Perhaps they were right. Everything was very quiet and our bored indifference to the event seemed to be shared by the Egyptians. There was a complete lack of enthusiasm for the celebration parade, and at the evening party on Coronation day the sole aim was to get drunk and forget about it. This we did, and even those who fell into the canal as a result floated.

To occupy my time I thought I would try and become an author. I had always kept a full diary so now I tried my hand at short stories and script writing. In 1952 I took a correspondence course, and sold my first story to an Egyptian paper, the *Gazette*, in Cairo. I also started an interest in scrap and photograph books but filled them much too full too quickly, of events such as earthquakes and tidal waves, and soon had to cut them to a more manageable size.

On Sundays the men would not go to church, although the padre was good and the small chapel pleasant. A choir, which I was allowed to join provided I didn't sing, was started but they never attracted a congregation of anyone other than the officers and senior NCOs. One officer, however, later confessed that seeing the others going regularly and happily to church had made him want to go again himself, and this he later did. Perhaps in this sort of way the officers were a good example.

Escort duty: one month on tour in the Middle East

Towards the end of my time in the Mediterranean I bear-led a group of senior officers of the armed and diplomatic forces on an Imperial Defence College (IDC) course around 21 countries in the Middle East.

It was a great bit of luck in the first place that I got the job. As I explained earlier, I had hoped to return and parade in London during the Queen's Coronation in 1953 but with this having been cancelled, and when things were quiet and the coronation alert in Egypt over, I was offered the IDC tour as compensation. A brother officer, Charles Wynne-Finch, and I were appointed to take charge of the group and were sent to Malta where we met the 12 distinguished officers from the army, navy and air force on the course, who arrived from England in their own aeroplane.

We kept this aeroplane and, for the month or so that the tour lasted, I was virtually in command of it, responsible for deciding when we would start, where we would go and whether we would fly high or low. It was a rare luxury to have an aeroplane at my (our) disposal to fly around Asia and Africa.

The idea of the tour was to give these officers and diplomats, who had been studying Imperial Defence for six months, the chance to see what their plans would look like on the ground; it would also give them the opportunity to talk to local representatives about their special subjects. Wherever we went the top people entertained us and we stayed one or two nights in each location. The senior member of the party would be put up in the Governor's or Commander-in-Chief's house while the rest of us would be posted around, coming in for meals, drinks, receptions and so on.

Wynne-Finch and I merely tagged along but we were in the pleasant position of having no axe to grind and were thus free to ask questions and be inquisitive. We could listen in whenever we wanted and learn what people were talking about, hear what questions were being asked, and judge how capably we thought – without a twinge of humility on my part – the officers in our charge were answering them.

When, for example, some particularly pertinent questions about Middle-East defence were asked of a Commander-in-Chief I, being a Regimental Officer on the ground, felt, presumptuously, that I knew more about it than he. I even assumed that I, rather than he, had the right answers. How conceited can you get?

The tour included Aden and its Crater district, Egypt, the Canal Zone, Cyprus, Turkey, Iraq, Jordan, Bahrain, Muscat, the Arabian peninsular, Aden and Africa with various points of call all over Southern Rhodesia and Nyasaland including Bulawayo, Livingstone, Rhodes' Grave and the Victoria Falls. Next came Uganda then Sudan, north and south Tripolitania and Malta.

Whistle-stop Kampala with the Kabaka

In Uganda I was given my first introduction to the African palace of my friend Freddie, the 35th Kabaka of Buganda; coined "King Freddie" by the British press he was later to become the first President of Uganda. We had first met in 1948 when he was serving as a Grenadier and I was at Caterham. Together we had gone to the Horse Show at Aldershot and, mixing with the same group of friends, we had met on various social occasions, including formal dinners when I was on guard in 1950. Freddie was outgoing and interested in everyone and, with our inquisitive natures in common, our friendship was undemanding.

He was much liked in the Grenadiers and they had wisely given him an old soldier as a servant so that whenever he had found things hard – the Sergeant-Major had shouted at him or the Adjutant checked him – he was able to retreat to his room and have it all quietly explained.

The IDC tour had reached Kampala and we were visiting an agricultural college when I was whisked away by the Kabaka's ADC on the back of a motor cycle and taken to Freddie's African palace; I arrived a good deal out of breath. One of the first things Freddie had told me was how his grandfather used to throw unwelcome guests to the crocodiles after dinner. I now had the opportunity to see the lake, below the palace walls – it was still called the Crocodile Lake but the last crocodile had, in fact, died just before I arrived.

Freddie took me for a drive around the capital and to the Kasubi Tombs, the ancestral burial grounds for all the Kabakas which, of course included a vacant place for him. This was the first time I'd seen an autocratic sovereign among his people; as we passed through the streets everyone bowed and anyone Freddie stopped and spoke to knelt – forearms on the ground. His ADC drove me 30 miles back to my hotel in Entebbe where I offered him a drink; the barman refused to serve an African so I ordered two drinks for myself, gave one to him, and thereafter the barman refused to serve me.

Meeting the Mahdi

In the Sudan we stayed in Khartoum but crossed the Nile to Omdurman to see the site of the battle fought there in 1898. We went to a reception given by the Mahdi. He was then fighting an election which would determine the country's ruler on the departure of the British in four months time; as a Nationalist, he failed to get in.

He was a fine figure of a man with a bushy white beard and steely eyes but a cherubic face. He was large and had a commanding stature – though being dressed in Arab robes and a turban helped. The rank of Mahdi had a sort of magical ring about it.

I knew that the earlier holder had been the opponent of General Gordon and Field Marshall Lord Kitchener and that he figured largely in the Sudanese battles of the last century. This Mahdi was the grandson of that earlier warrior and to meet him, as a holder of that title, was something in itself, to find him an ordinary human being as well was better still.

We had arrived in his country while it was in political turmoil and I had expected, naively, to see people rushing about, looking worried, whispering politics and intrigue. Perhaps they were elsewhere, for what we found was peace, with the Mahdi completely settled, serene and seemingly in control of the situation and interested as much in us as in talking about his own country.

He gave a large lunch party for us at his palace –very ornate and decorated with much gold but also very uncomfortable, cold and draughty. But there were masses of servants – one for each of his 60 guests. Our lunch was really a sort of high tea and he talked throughout with a chuckle and a glint in his eyes. He was very friendly, but he was sitting on a political volcano as if he were sunbathing.

Following our first meeting with the members of the course, Wynne-Finch and I had written down exactly what we thought of each of the officers: whether they were going to be easy or difficult to work with, friendly or unfriendly, helpful or unhelpful. We had kept our papers in sealed envelopes until the end of the tour, during which we lived cheek-by-jowl with the subjects of our analysis.

When the officers had returned to England, we sat in a hotel in Malta and, over the breakfast table, took out our confidential envelopes, opened and went through them to assess the accuracy of our first impressions. We had been wrong in every single case; the poor ones had turned out trumps, and those we'd thought powerful had collapsed later on. So much for our hasty judgments.

Slow train home

When I was posted home in the summer of 1953 I was told that I could make my own way back to England. I was in Malta at that time and decided, instead of catching a boat and going straight back past Gibraltar, that I would cross by night-ferry to Syracuse in Sicily then make my way home slowly, by train and ferry, stopping wherever I chose in Italy and France.

My train ticket from Syracuse to Bordeaux cost about £10 and it was valid for one month. I stayed in Taormina in Sicily – surely one of the most beautiful places in the world – and in Pompeii, Naples, Rome and Florence, Bologna, Venice, Milan, Genoa and many other places besides.

Being late summer it was warm enough to sleep out at night, and to travel without a coat. I journeyed as a tramp: not shaving, sleeping where I could, eating scraps bought from shops which sold cheap food, and washing at public water taps. The sea served as my (occasional) bath but at smart places, such as Gracie Field's swimming pool in Capri (she was not there), I was able to have a good shower – with soap.

I lost a lot of weight travelling this way and, of course, saved a great deal of money. Because of its discomfort the tour ceased to be a holiday but it was a worthwhile experience. Some years later, when discussing this account of my travels, Susan, my wife, rightly told our friend Mark Amory: "Don't be sorry for him; he did it on purpose just to see what it was like."

I learned to keep the remains of the bread, biscuits or sugar I was served in restaurants and to eat them either before I went to bed that night, or first thing in the morning to get warm. Other useful ploys included obtaining sheets of lavatory paper from good hotels and using their soap and towels for frequent and very necessary foot baths.

I learned the care needed in laying down clothes to sleep upon and knew where to find discarded daily newspapers to read – usually in railway waiting-rooms or small cafes. Hotels invariably had numerous weekly papers, and comfortable chairs where I could sit and read until someone would wonder what I was up to.

And I learned how to get hold of an inexpensive bed for the night. This led to my sleeping in a variety of unusual places: in the toe of Italy, for example, I slept in a beach hut. That night, most of the other huts along the row were swept away by a storm, but mine was all right and the beach chair under which I was sleeping kept me fairly warm. In Florence I slept in a cinema, but as my bed was on the balcony I couldn't sleep until the last showing of the film was finished – in Italy this is very late.

I spent nights in a warehouse and a monastery, on three (very uncomfortable) padded chairs in a railway waiting-room, in a borrowed tent and in a brothel. The brothel was in Rome, where I had searched fruitlessly for accommodation; finally I refused, in a thunderstorm, to leave a pension to which I had been directed unless I was allowed a bed. This they eventually promised me – on the sitting-room floor and providing I didn't return before midnight. Innocently, I accepted this offer and it wasn't until the early hours, listening to "comings and goings" and remembering the sly and rather curious welcome I had been given on my return, that I realised what sort of house I was in. In such a house, however, nobody wanted to get up in the morning and I was able to creep out with the minimum of fuss while everybody slept late.

The pumps and fresh-water taps in Italy were a great boon. I used water from them to drink, wash in, clean my teeth, rinse the fruit I had bought and cool down. Every village, town, railway station and beach had one, and they were all in constant use by everyone. How in England we get by with so few I don't know.

I had elected to travel as an inquisitive person looking at things not normally seen, but I also saw the sights as much as any tourist – the ruins of Pompeii, the bathyscope of Professor Piccard at Castellamare, the slums and back streets of Naples, the Coliseum in Rome, St Peter's into which can be fitted six football pitches, the Vatican, many grand hotels and several unhelpful British travel agencies.

With my clothes unchanged, my beard ragged and my shoes worn I did look like a tramp, so it is not surprising that in no place did anyone seem pleased to see me. During all my travels through Italy the only time someone was kind was when I was in Venice; I was almost penniless and unable to buy a proper meal, but an Italian in a restaurant told me what to eat, paid the bill and even gave me a British newspaper to read.

Travelling was often lonely. Away from my family (except during leaves) since the beginning of the war, I had been one of a set of six or so brother officers – friends who generally made up parties between us. I had also enjoyed the companionship, forged through shared work, hardship and boredom, between all ranks inside the army. On this journey I had neither family nor friends. Although I am better at getting on with groups than with individuals, here I had neither and I missed them.

"Cottolengo": a turning point

I saw more unkindness to animals and hardship to children during my tour than I had ever seen in England. The Italians did not look a happy race; the rich were obviously very powerful and the poor very poor, there was a pervading sense of dishonesty and a lack of patriotism, with many Italians pulling strings to get out of conscription. There were a lot of Communists and armed police about.

At the end of my travels in Italy, I visited the Little House of Divine Providence, more usually called "Cottolengo", in Turin. I might never have discovered it had I not, on my way to visit the Cathedral – and to see the Turin Shroud – noticed an unusual mix of poor and rich people in a smart street nearby. An English-speaking passer-by told me that more than 100 years ago a priest, Joseph, had found distressed people living isolated lives in ruined villages throughout the countryside and brought them here for companionship and care.

I was intrigued enough to visit and "Cottolengo" made a deep impression on me. Run by an Order of Sisters in a Christian atmosphere it was a home, or really a small town, in which some 8,000 people lived – young and old, some orphaned, some mentally or physically handicapped.

I walked around the wards and dormitories, the living-rooms and chapel. I saw deaf and dumb children trying to speak and the deformed playing football. I saw the aged lying in their beds at the foot of a crucifix and madmen walking about declaiming. Visiting parents and friends allowed their children to roam freely and see all, including the almost animal-like behaviour of the deranged: "It is not infectious," they said, simply – and perhaps that was the right way to look at it. However, I was appalled both at what I saw, and that the children visiting "Cottolengo" should witness such sights.

In Britain we were relying on the Welfare State to care for our poor and our unwanted, but after visiting "Cottolengo" I began to think that some people might be left out. I wondered what happened to them.

8

DOUBT AND DOUBTING

I was 31 years old when I returned home and for my remaining years as a soldier I served mainly in and around England. In the winter of 1953 I joined a battalion in Wellington Barracks, Westminster, and was soon involved in public duties. These take up most of a Brigade officer's working time in London but, for me at that moment, the most important thing was to decide whether, or not, to continue my career in the army.

My thinking about the future had changed; it was seeing all those in need at "Cottolengo" that did it. I had never had any definitive sort of ambition but now I felt I wanted to help people, although I didn't know how. Gradually I was beginning to see that a start for me could only be made by leaving the army.

I had had a wartime commission (the only one on offer at the time) and when that ran out, about 1948, I had to make a decision. I had considered taking up a civilian profession and the only attractive one then, for me, was the Diplomatic Service. I had obtained support for this from my brother Roddy's godfather, Edward Grigg (later Lord Altrincham), who was at that time a senior diplomat.

I did not, however, pursue this course for I was enjoying being a soldier and somewhere within me lurked the ambition to bring a second Field-Marshal's baton into the family; the first having been my great-great uncle Field-Marshall Sir William Gomm. So, putting thoughts of civilian life behind me, I had signed on and been accepted in 1948 for a regular commission with the Coldstream.

National Service had just been introduced but was not available to me as I had already served for a compulsory period during the war. My only options were either to accept demob from being a conscripted soldier or sign on voluntarily for peace. I chose to become a "regular" and thus continued, as I had begun, being an ordinary soldier – though, since 1948, disguised as a captain.

Nationally, the compulsory call-up was an excellent thing – not only for the obvious international and defence purposes for which it was designed, but also for all that it did in the way of character building and teaching basic discipline to all who were caught up in it.

The training for National or Regular Service started at military depots with the simplest things: recruits were shown ordinary hygiene practices such as cleaning teeth daily and brushing hair, then polishing boots and making beds, sewing on buttons and washing-up, standing when addressed by seniors and minding language. Although, while few regretted their enforced service as conscripts, some regulars did feel that the money spent training these temporary soldiers would have been better spent on modern arms, transport and equipment for the "proper" army.

As for National Service, there had been public support for its continuation but its abolition in 1960 was nevertheless welcomed as a sign of confidence in world peace and national well-being.

Reflections on pacifism

I was never worried by the questions raised by conscientious objectors and never considered, nor questioned, the Christian principles involved in legalised killing – that is to say, in war. I had accepted that a democratic nation has the right to call upon its people to fight. Throughout my career in the army I never concerned myself with the morality of imposing Britain's will on another race or country. War, other than honouring treaties, was to stand by your allies, to resist invasion or/and to preserve the British way of life.

Having joined the army during the war and then stayed on as a regular soldier, I was never to question my right to kill or dominate those whom my democratically-elected Government designated as enemies or subjects; nor did I question my role in teaching other races what to do and how to do it. Such is blind obedience.

It was five years after the war ended that I first seriously considered that a man might be both a pacifist and a patriot. A young officer told me that, much as he enjoyed being a soldier, he would not apply to become a regular officer when his National Service finished. He said he could not reconcile the teachings of the Bible with a military career and learning how to kill.

I didn't accept his argument: I believed that Jesus looked upon the profession of arms as an honourable one; I also believed in the concept of the "just" war – that is to say, war used as a last resort against a dictatorship; and then using only the weapons necessary, and with limited, concise aims involving no element of revenge.

In addition, I believed in capital punishment as a just sentence for murder. And, certain that if threatened with violence I would react forcefully and with a clear conscience, I could never see the sense in advocating surrendering to a burglar; a burglar I would resist, a potential killer I would not hesitate to kill, and in any future war I would want to fight. I am considerably less sure about all of these things now, and I am no longer in favour of capital punishment.

Until I left the army I never identified with conscientious objectors, since the various translations of the Sixth Commandment on which they base their stand can be interpreted in different ways; for example, does it read "do not kill" or "commit no murder"? I would interpret the latter to mean that killing in a legal war is not murder. And it is this "commit no murder" translation which allows soldiers and public executioners to do their jobs, for it separates killing from murder.

I now see strongly the point held by conscientious objectors, that if killing in war was banned, disputes would be settled instead by diplomacy, but I doubt if I would stand against public opinion and join them. However, I do respect them if their stance is on religious grounds and they volunteer for non-combatant duties.

A reluctant spy

Only once was I lucky enough to be sent on a course near to my parents' house in Hassocks, Sussex. It was an intelligence course at Maresfield, and there was something very pleasant about sleeping in one's home bed each night.

For those in the army who wish to obtain a high rank it is now obligatory to pass through the Staff College then serve on the staff. In my day it was possible to get around this by going on the Intelligence side, and this I had begun to do after failing the staff college examinations for the third time; I had passed all the papers, but never all at once as was necessary. Although privately I had begun to think of leaving the army, in 1954 I accepted the offer to go on an intelligence course as a possible way forward. However, I soon discovered that spying was not for me.

Nevertheless, at Maresfield we were pumped full of semi-secret information about MI5, spies and Communist tactics. It was fascinating to learn of plans to try and maintain such international peace as there was.

Espionage is an essential part of Intelligence and I was told at the beginning that I must be prepared to bury my principles and not be squeamish: "the end justifies the means", they said, and no holds are barred to defeat an enemy. They are right, but I didn't want it enough to do it as a career.

Twice for Military Intelligence, I was asked to photograph military objectives on the Continent under the pretext of taking holiday snaps; this seemed to me innocuous, but I had no inclination to take on jobs in which I would have to make friends in order to get information out of them and then, unknown to them, pass it on. So when I was asked to allow my name to go forward for an undercover role, which would have included wearing disguise on the other side of the Iron Curtain, I declined. And that was the limit of my experience in the Intelligence sphere and Susan's view is that anyhow I would have made a rotten spy.

Of guns and drills

I have always enjoyed shooting guns and this aspect of soldiering was one I carried consciously into life with our children many years later. I had looted various pistols, rifles and guns throughout the war, and when our sons Adam and David came along, I enjoyed shooting with them at old electric-light bulbs, tin cans and empty bottles; I kept an old long-barrel .22 duelling pistol for this very purpose and even our daughters Anna and Elizabeth had a go.

The most interesting drill movement with the rifle is the reverse arms done by guards of honour or at funeral parades. There are 12 distinct actions of the hands, feet, head, and rifle or sword – all executed without a single word of command beyond the first. The movement is rarely done now; in fact it can't be done with the new short rifle and is kept, therefore, for purely ceremonial occasions, such as memorial services around catafalques, when the old rifles are available.

It was with this now old-fashioned rifle that I used to shoot on Bisley ranges. At Bisley's "mile range" in order even to see your target you need a telescope – aiming was hazardous and I always felt lucky just to land a shot on the target; I never expected a bull's-eye.

I acquired a rifle of my own while serving in Europe; it was Canadian and had been sold originally by international gunrunners to Middle Eastern terrorists. Its particular advantage was that it fired British army .303 ammunition, but with much of the woodwork taken off, the butt planed down and the sights altered, its weight had been reduced and yet its balance not impaired. I relished the pleasure I derived from using it when stalking deer in Scotland, and of course it was much lighter to carry over the moors. Bullets with their heads nipped off made good dumdums for stalking and ensured a quicker and more humane killing of the stag. Now I have reservations about such field sports and apart from the obvious necessity for culling in the animal world, I am glad that opportunities for me to take part no longer arise.

While I was a soldier I never questioned the rightness of killing animals. I went stalking, shooting and wild-fowling quite happily – although more for the pleasure of being out in the countryside than through any serious dedication to field sports. That these occasions often included weekends enjoying good company in comfortable houses with a ball and dancing thrown in obviously held an added appeal.

London, the Oliviers, my first car, a Franciscan retreat

Army life in London from 1953 to 1955 was interspersed with a mix of oddities and chance meetings: finding myself in a public lavatory next to the sculptor Jacob Epstein, for example, and, determined to speak to him, saying "Excuse me", or something like that, which he acknowledged. I also met the author Graham Greene on his way to the Far East to report on the French fighting in Indochina. He wanted to learn how to fire a machine gun and I had to teach him. He told me that he regularly took opium to gain clear-sightedness, as did high-level Chinese to increase their mental agility. This later made me wonder whether we shouldn't accept the situation more in this country and acknowledge a reasonable legal taking of drugs.

Twice while in London I motored down to Stratford upon Avon with Tarquin Olivier, then doing his National Service in the regiment, and saw his father and, then, step-mother, Laurence Olivier and Vivien Leigh, on stage there. I had never before seen such fine acting. The couple lived in Notley Abbey near Thame, not far away, and I drove them there after the last of two tiring performances of "Coriolanus". Between performances, Leigh had to fight with the restaurant staff before they would serve Olivier a steak – the cooks were off duty; Olivier remained calm and got his steak.

Seeing Olivier and Leigh on stage then spending the weekend and meeting them at their home made me think more about my own role as a traditional soldier: in full dress I was not an individual but a symbol of history and tradition, something the public wanted to see, something they liked and which entertained them. It was not me on parade but the uniform, and all the pomp and glory that went with it. I was not creating parts, I was just filling them – and probably not all that well.

I was 27 years old when I first owned a car. Petrol rationing and the army having provided my transport had, until then, negated my need for a car. However, once I had my Humber Hawk I clocked up many miles roaming all over the countryside in it. It wasn't long before I had added both wireless and heater, and then, with sandwiches to eat, I felt totally at home.

Thereafter I rarely journeyed by rail; my car was always there and it seemed easiest to use it. But not without incident, for I was held up for speeding and wrong parking dozens of times; sometimes I had my license endorsed. My most worrying casualty was a child I knocked down in the street; tossed by the bumper when she dashed out from behind a parked car. She lay unconscious on the road and I took her to the local hospital, fearing the worst. However she was not badly hurt and was soon allowed home, fit and well. Fortunately her parents did not contemplate charges.

Too often I killed some animal while driving – big ones such as dogs and cats, small ones such as moles and rabbits. This always sickened me, and all the more if I had to back over the animal to finish it off rather than let it survive maimed and in pain.

I am lucky in not being keen on drink, over-drinking has never been a problem for me so there is for me no virtue in abstinence; in fact it makes me a bit naive. Once, in the middle of the night near Sunningdale, I found a drunken woman by the roadside. I carried her to her caravan nearby and her husband took her in.

Friends told me I had been foolish, I might have been accused of robbing or assaulting the woman. I'm sure they were right and their comments reminded me of the natural feelings and reactions of the priest and Levi to leave well alone, avoid trouble and don't walk into a trap or get involved. But this doesn't make me a good Samaritan, I was simply unthinking, unsuspecting and, possibly, a little curious and stupid.

Meanwhile army life in peacetime continued at home and abroad: parades, lectures and military exercises, routine meetings, conferences, emergencies and rehearsals. During the early Fifties I was even sent to Courmayer, near Lake Geneva, to spend a few weeks with the elite French Regiment, the Chasseurs Alpins. They were very kind to me and didn't seem to mind that I couldn't ski. I slid around and had an enjoyable time at their barracks before appearing before their Colonel, the Prince Napoleon, on a parade. There he kissed me and pinned their Regimental badge on my chest.

I was, however, beginning to think more and more about changing my career and in 1953 spent a retreat weekend with the Franciscan friars at their friary at Cerne Abbas, Dorset. I slept in a comfortable cell and had what felt like endless time to think and read.

We passed most of the time in silence, although one of the Friars read aloud during meals and at set periods we guests helped in the garden or workshop. We were free to attend the services in chapel whenever we wished, and for me this was often. Apart from the primary spiritual side, I enjoyed the intoning and chanting of the Friars. Here, given the opportunity to meditate I again felt a clarity of vision and a peace, feelings very rare for me. The following year I helped the Franciscans run a weekend mission among the hop-pickers in Kent. We slept on piles of straw in a cowshed which we christened "Bethlehem" and did more hop-picking than mission work.

From 1953 to 1955 the mix between London ceremonial duties and field training in the English countryside and abroad helped keep me busy; my hours, days and weeks were full and never tedious.

9

PUBLIC DUTIES WITH THE COLDSTREAM

The Coldstream Guards attracted men with a wide variety of backgrounds and abilities and it was a very happy regiment to be in. To me it gave, among much else, opportunities to meet a very wide cross-section of people – often when carrying out public duties, for example. These comprised the parades with which the Guards Division is associated – at the Bank, the Tower of London, Windsor Castle, and the Queen's Guard at Buckingham and St James's Palaces – as well as guards of honour lining the routes on state occasions and Trooping the Colour as well as other less well-known official occasions.

In good weather the Bank of England guard (12 men) always marched to the Bank from Wellington or Chelsea Barracks but if it rained, to keep their uniforms dry, they wheeled into the London Underground station, where a guard in ceremonial dress made an unusual and impressive sight. The officer on guard at the Bank was given half a bottle of port with his dinner and the other ranks a pint of beer each. It was only an overnight guard and, being inside the building, was done wearing tennis shoes with, otherwise, full dress uniforms. Since it was policing and completely unceremonial it was discontinued altogether in the late Fifties.

One of the most unusual public duties I was assigned involved taking some men to test the acoustics and ventilation of the new House of Commons in 1950. We drove up in red double-decker buses then, exchanging their boots for gym shoes, the 635 men – one for each Member of the House – entered the new House and sat in the debating Chamber. The name of the recruit in the Prime Minister's seat was Tom Chicken; the assembled journalists had their headline: "Chicken, Prime Minister for the day".

We came into the Chamber under the rugged Churchill Arch, and it was easy to imagine that the days of Cromwell were back and that the army was once more in power. Lord Morrison had been given the job of talking to us and said that he was glad that the country had, at last, come to its senses and elected a sensible and intelligent parliament. While Lord Morrison spoke, the technicians experimented with the acoustics and air flow, switching the air intake and exit from side to side seeking a flow and temperature which would keep us alert;

whether or not this procedure succeeds with present Members I do not know.

7. House of Commons 1950 (only time - on Opposition front bench)

Guarding the Tower of London and Windsor Castle are both traditional duties and Harrison Ainsworth's books on both describe them perfectly; the wind whistling round the ramparts and beating the trees against the walls. At Windsor we were able to go and pray in St George's Chapel, joining in the daily Evensong which is held by candlelight. As duty officer there I was twice summoned to fill the numbers at a royal ball.

On the first occasion the equerry, Peter Townsend, detailed me to dance the last dance with the Princess Royal (Countess of Harwood) and her tiara kept catching my chin. I led her to say goodnight to the King and Queen, which even between brother and sister was a lengthy, dignified affair of bowing, kissing and curtsying. The King was wearing black suede shoes with his dinner jacket and I'm sure he wore make-up. On the second occasion – on which the wine and beer ran out – I found myself beside the Queen (the King, her father, had died) watching the fireworks from the terrace; they were very good.

On guard at Chequers 1943

During the war there was the guard at Chequers, the Prime Minister's official countryseat. This guard had earlier been in attendance on the

Royal family to escort them out of London if there had been an invasion. It was called the Coates Mission, named after its Commanding Officer, Jimmy Coates who was in my Regiment. After the end of the Battle of Britain in 1940, when imminent danger of the Royal Family's capture was over, the guard switched to the Prime Minister – Sir Winston Churchill – on country breaks, usually at weekends. So secret was the guard's new role that no-one was allowed to mention the word "Chequers" but to refer to it as the "Special Area" – which, with hindsight, must have raised suspicion if overheard.

Our billet and mess was in the Gate Lodge. Churchill used to invite the officers of the guard into the house on Sunday evenings to watch films with him and his family. These films in the picture gallery never began until about 11pm and, after a full day's work, most of us by that time were more ready for bed and sleep.

We once watched a Russian war film and during the final scene Russian soldiers were rushing forward in a wild victorious attack on the Germans; Sir Winston leant forward in his chair and enthusiastically cheered them on. The film always finished about 1 o'clock and then, with a cheery wave, and a less cheerful secretary behind him, he repaired to his study to work.

When we walked around the garden at Chequers making security checks, or simply for pleasure, we would see Churchill in his study practicing speeches at his lectern. Otherwise we rarely saw him or his family, except when guards of honour were mounted occasionally for visiting dignitaries. My only memory of these formal guards was when the Russian ambassador visited. He had arrived at dawn and was doubtless feeling sleepy when he got out of his car and, seeing a lot of soldiers standing with their hands out presenting arms, shook each one of them in turn.

Entertaining on Queen's Guard

Soldiers on Queen's (King's) Guard can invite anyone they choose to join them for a drink or a meal. The form is simple: the Ensign is ordered by the Captain to invite the most interesting person he can think of to join them in the officer's mess at St James's Palace at a particular time: 1pm for lunch, at which both men and women are allowed but must leave before afternoon's rounds at 3pm; tea-time, best for children; and 8 pm for men to eat – women may be invited for a drink, but earlier, for they must leave before 7.30pm. A formal letter of invitation is issued and usually delivered by hand.

For dinner, the whole evening is conducive to good conversation, all the arrangements lead to it – formal evening dress and Regimental Blues uniforms, candles, port, polished tables, cigars, a log fire in a book-lined room and coffee from a silver pot, served by a well-trained mess waiter. There are always four officers on guard, five if the Horse Guards' officer from the Household Cavalry has come up from Whitehall, and perhaps a few male guests.

When I was on guard I met several people in this way one of whom, Lord Moran (Churchill's doctor) was the best raconteur that I have ever listened to. In ordinary life, discussion across a wide range of subjects, whether serious or witty, seemed rare. Even in a pub, club or over the port at All Souls College, Oxford, the conversation was rarely instructive or constructive. The tendency to have one's thinking done elsewhere – on radio, television or in the newspapers – was probably the cause, but on guard this was not the case.

It was certainly there that I met and learnt the practice of conducting general conversation: of listening; of encouraging the shy and less talkative to be heard; of seeing, when leader, that the subject was kept to and, at the end, summarised and where possible a conclusion drawn.

We enjoyed the company of many and varied visitors, though not that of actress Virginia McKenna who we did invite but her mother would not allow her to come unchaperoned. A procession of entertainers did, however, include the actress Muriel Pavlow, the pianist Leslie Hutchinson ("Hutch"), a striptease dancer whose act had intrigued me at Ciro's Club and the pop star Johnny Ray. Other memorable invitees included the Queen's dressmaker Norman Hartnell – drinking beer and looking like a rugger forward – and Bishop Wand, who came for a drink after preaching next door in the Chapel Royal, and also Lady Harding, wife of the King's secretary, who talked about her favourite subject, moral re-armament

Sir Malcolm Sargent

Sir Malcolm Sargent was not only a brilliant conductor, but also a brilliant raconteur who came several times on guard and fascinated us with his stories. Once, when explaining how he had helped control the music of a band on a state occasion, Sir Malcolm was challenged by an officer on a musical point. To prove that the officer didn't know what he was talking about, Sir Malcolm made him – in the middle of dinner – sing, or rather falter bravely through, the National Anthem. Sir Malcolm then handed the officer a signed score on which the tune he had intoned was transcribed as little more than a single note.

Humbled but unbowed, the officer tried to stick to his guns but his argument was lost.

Noel Coward

Noel Coward, the famous playwright, dined with us in 1954 and, as with Lord Moran, we just sat and listened to him talk. I noted how interested he was in others and how few personal anecdotes he told. He wanted to know what we were doing and what we were going to do if and when we left the army. Coward recorded that evening in his diary: "a perfectly sweet evening. Three very young officers and one slightly older one. Lovely manners and good old, shabby, traditional glamour."

Godfrey Winn

Godfrey Winn, another great raconteur and public figure, dined with me on guard at the Bank of England in the City of London. I met him when playing country house cricket with family friends (Cosmo and Rosemary Crawley) in Sussex. Incidentally, Camilla Crawley (later Worthington), one of the Crawleys' beautiful daughters, liked to remind me (I hope jokingly) that I was asked to play for the village as I wasn't grand enough to play for the house party team.

Winn told how he had found that writing for and about women could earn him £15,000 p.a. and so he had made a career of it. He became the highest paid journalist of his vintage – a stark contrast to his wartime days as an Ordinary Seaman. His best book "PQ17" tells the hardships and dangers met when serving on convoys making Arctic crossings of the North Sea carrying supplies for Russia.

Billy Graham

The American evangelist Billy Graham wrote in an article in 1989 that he had always admired the Coldstream Guards. It was an unusual remark for a great preacher and pacifist to publicise, and for the regiment to have attracted such a statement from him was to its credit.

When Billy came from the USA to England to conduct a Crusade at Haringey in 1954 we invited him to lunch on guard. He accepted, but asked if he might bring two reporters from *Life* magazine who were spending 24 hours with him. We didn't want the reporters and so the date was cancelled. I was on guard one week later and invited him and his wife Ruth to a luncheon party for 12 people.

My interest in meeting Billy was encouraged by his celebrity rather than his spirituality. The Grahams hesitated at first to talk about themselves – perhaps because the press had been so much against them – but we professed such interest that they opened up and spoke simply and effectively about themselves and the Crusades which he was about to conduct.

They wanted to know all about St James's Palace and the Guard, so I took them down to the guard room to meet the men, who were then cleaning their uniforms.

The following week I, my servant and some of the NCOs and men on guard went to Billy's Crusade at Haringey. I took my parents, brother Roddy, a brother officer and a Roman Catholic friend. I immediately liked the mass singing and found Billy's preaching meaningful. There is, after all, nothing new to say about the Bible but his way of saying familiar things stuck.

I felt a sort of rededication of my faith, which was, anyhow, broad, middle-of-the-road Anglican. Billy's preaching produced one of those few moments in my life when I felt at one with God and able to plan my future with clarity, and it led to my going forward and making a re-affirmation of my faith in the spirit of "stand up and be counted". After Haringey, many of us who had been there met regularly for prayers and bible study.

On his next visit to England in 1955, Billy was invited to meet the Queen and preach in the private chapel near York House in Windsor Park. He lost his sermon notes and had to preach extempore; he couldn't remember what he'd said but gathered it had been well enough received.

On Billy's next visit in 1957 I asked him to speak privately to a group of friends. He dined with a few of us in a private, tent-shaped room at the Belfry Restaurant near London's Belgrave Square. Then in the beautiful Wren Room of Chelsea Hospital he spoke completely off the record for more than an hour to some 120 Brigade officers and their friends. Again, he only said what we already knew, but in such a way that many found a new depth and interpretation in the familiar passages.

At the end of Billy's first tour in 1954 a farewell dinner was held at London's Dorchester Hotel with Lord Luke as Chairman. After dinner Billy spoke for about 20 minutes; when he sat down there was little clapping and nobody moved. Lord Luke rose and said: "I don't feel I can say anything after what we have just heard." There was complete silence; everyone seemed mesmerised by Billy's words. After many minutes Lord Luke suggested we rise from the table and walk around and it was then that Sir Malcolm Sargent asked me to introduce him to Billy.

Johnny Ray

When Johnny Ray came he half expected to find Princess Margaret having a drink as well and he spent a lot of time gazing from our window to the back of Clarence House where she lived; apparently he was disappointed that she had never been to hear him sing.

The following night, Ray invited me to the Palladium to see his show. I was taken to the front of the auditorium to watch his act.

It was extraordinary, with a magnetic element which Ray himself didn't understand; a psychiatrist told him that it came from the peculiar notes in his voice. Whatever it was, it drew screams and howls from the young audience and, despite a cordon of men across the front of the stalls, his fans managed to get to him.

At the final curtain he had to retreat to the back of the stage with fans, clinging like limpets to a rock, being pulled off him. It all looked genuine – none of it planned, the emotions not contrived.

At the end of the show the fans besieged the theatre. From his dressing room, Johnny took me up the fire escape onto the roof and we gazed down on the mass of fans screaming their heads off. A taxi, with its engine running, was drawn up by one of the theatre's side fire-doors and off we sped, but not without having to dust a few girls off the bonnet.

I was terrified when, to stop fans in the road climbing in, the taxi-driver took to shooting the lights. As it was, fans following in cars drew alongside and thrust pieces of paper, including money notes, into the window for Ray to autograph. He seemed genuinely worried for the crowd's safety but he was also very frightened. A solid mass of hysterical people is extremely un-nerving.

We went to his suite at the Dorchester Hotel for a stage party of which I remember little, except the actress Beatrice Lillie sitting on my knee asking why I was the only person in white tie and tails.

Buckingham Palace "under attack"

Two of the privileges on guard at Buckingham Palace are being allowed to walk in its gardens when the Royal Family are away and to play squash at the RAC Club. Both are good exercise. The gardens are the largest in London and include a small lake, tennis courts, cricket net and garden houses; beside them is the Royal Mews, into which we could also stray.

Playing squash at the RAC entails walking with bearskin and sword along Pall Mall to the Club – your racquet and gear follow separately. After a game of squash you can swim in the pool then return to the guard room for crumpets and coffee cake with your family or anybody else you might invite. While waiting for you they can see the hoof of Napoleon's charger, Marengo, swords of famous officers, a TV set given by Queen Mary or a screen with pictures of ladies dressed and undressed on it.

During the war, as officer-in-charge of Buckingham Palace, I had to defend it against a mock attack. I sited machine-guns in various rooms and at windows around the Palace with the best moment being when I stepped out onto the centre balcony very early in the morning and placed a machine gun trained down the Mall. There was only one man in sight and he was somewhere down towards Trafalgar Square with his back towards me; this didn't stop me waving to him.

When the "attack" started in the afternoon I was lunching at St James's Palace. I hurried over to find all the gates locked against the "enemy" and had no alternative but to climb over the railings, which are very high. I managed to do it, watched by the sentries and police under cover of the Palace. The police said they had never before known anyone climb down from the railings without finding a pair of handcuffs waiting for him.

Hurrying into the Palace I found that a battalion of the Irish Guards had been driven into the gardens through a back garden gate and, debussing from their trucks, they had been left in the middle of the lawn pretending they had just dropped by parachute and were about to attack. Fully deployed they advanced slowly on the Palace. My men, stationed at their posts, stood firm, and as the first of the "enemy" put foot on the terrace the umpires came out and stopped them. It was, no doubt, due to my good siting of the weapons that the battle was won and I could return to my meal at St James's Palace.

Ceremonial duties

Three times I took part in the Birthday Parade or Trooping the Colour; once keeping the ground. This means standing round the edge of Horse Guards, the parade ground, and it is almost harder to do than being in the middle with one of the guards, when the monotony is at least broken by marching.

On the Parade, the longest you have to stand to attention or properly at ease is 20 minutes, and this is a long time. Once in practice, and there was a lot of practice, I fainted and was reprimanded. I had fainted because the war wound on my face caused my blood to flow more slowly and was thereafter given special injections of heroin to get me through any big parade.

Another constant duty is street lining for state occasions. I was doing this in the Mall when a horse escorting the Queen's Coach trod on my foot. I winced and the Queen saw it and smiled. I also lost my spur as I walked around with my sword hanging at my side and, next morning, all the papers carried a picture of my spurless foot; it was, unhappily, recognised by the Regimental Adjutant who wanted an explanation.

My ceremonial duties with the Foot Guards so accustomed me to wearing and seeing others in full ceremonial dress that it did not surprise me in the least when, for example, although I was wearing civilian clothes a gold State Coach and horses drew up and the footman, in breeches, tunic and wig, jumped down to chat; we had once been in the same company. Nor did I think twice when, wearing bearskin, sword and scarlet tunic, I cashed a cheque at my bank. On another occasion, in full dress I was marching the Queen's colour from the Palace to Wellington Barracks. A woman darted across the road between me and the ensign carrying the colour. A lawyer told me I could have cut her down with my sword (which was, anyhow, unsheathed) had I thought her dangerous – attempting to steal the colour or kill the escort, for example. And I rather wished that I had, perhaps just to prove the point.

All these peculiar happenings and highlights in no way reflect the endless military job of repetitive soldiering. What made that fun and bearable for me was that not only was it part of a good, satisfying and worthwhile job, but also that it included the friendship of so many people who went with it. We all knew each other, rank did not really signify and talk in the barrack room or canteen was as easy and enjoyable as in the Officer's Mess.

10

1955: A YEAR OF TRANSITION

Soldiering had by 1955 been my career for 15 years. It had filled my time since leaving school providing me with a full, varied and entertaining life. I was now, however, at a questing stage of my life, wondering about the future.

The only regret I have about my time in the army is that I spent it all on general duty and never held a proper staff job. On the general staff side I never got beyond doing small staff appointments – adjutant for a few weeks on a troopship, temporary staff captain, conducting officer for VIPs, and a hammock officer on board the aircraft carrier "Illustrious".

During the war, when my medical grade was lowered after my first wound in August 1944, I was offered the job of ADC to General Sir Willoughby Norrie, later Governor General of Australia. I didn't want to leave the war but I had accepted the post. However, I was then immediately medically upgraded and send back to my fighting battalion.

In 1953, Field-Marshall Alexander interviewed me as a prospective ADC to him. I would have liked this appointment very much – because of him and because of the chance to see Canada. I think I would have made a good ADC, but the Field-Marshall had also interviewed another officer and decided on him for the post.

It was true, I suppose, that by 1953 I had lost ambition. At one time I had wanted to be a Field-Marshall; now, somehow, that didn't seem important. Failing the staff college had been a shame though it may have been one reason for my change of direction. But basically, I had just never wanted enough to be a soldier. I had never had any thirst for command or sufficient driving power for higher positions.

However, in 1954, with no extra-Regimental jobs on offer and no promotion offered, I had time to think and try and plan my future.

A question of religion?

From my parents I had learnt about religion; they were practising Christians, and had taken us regularly to church on Sundays. Sometimes I used to object to the regularity of it but my mother insisted that it was a good habit and she would not accept excuses. On reflection, I think she was right. With a conventional baptism and confirmation behind me I never doubted my belief in Christ or the presence of God. I took them for granted and, self-conscious as a child, was in church far more concerned with how I looked than being sincere about my worship.

When still soldiering after the war I did worry about possessions; reading the story of Studdert Kennedy, who gave up a fortune and an English cricket cap to live in poverty and do mission work in China, made me wonder whether that was what I ought to do. Fortunately, the battalion was in the cure of a very sensible padre, John Dunne, so I asked him about it, and particularly about the bible passage recommending a rich man to give up everything and follow Christ.

Dunne explained that Jesus was speaking to a particular person and probably was not generalising or intending that the passage be taken literally by everyone. Dunne also said that shifting the responsibility which goes with ownership of possessions (or talents) to someone else might not be right. As an officer, had I not been trained to carry responsibility rather than abandon it? He also pointed out that treasures on earth had no value unless they were held lightly for ourselves but seriously in the service and for the good of others – wasn't this perhaps more to the point for me?

I never had any difficulty accepting the existence of all religions; it never occurred to me to question whether there was any rightness in Christianity as opposed to wrongness in other faiths. To me, the only real religious crime was to deny that God existed. Once you accepted that God did exist, or at least thought that He might, it was logical and right to try and discover, through the medium of your particular belief, who God was, and then to act on his teachings: "In my house are many mansions"; another person's mansion might be very fine.

Christianity was right for me, and the commandment to go out and preach it to the entire world was binding. If Muslims, Hindus or those of any other religion saw something in Christianity to change their own faith, well and good, but to those who had no faith or denied God, then Christianity must be seen working even within the hollow vacuum of their reasoning. Then they could – or might – accept it and find the way to God.

My mother held strong views on the ecumenical issue, and one of her last "causes" – she was a great "cause" undertaker – before she died was to write letters stirring up interest in the building of an ecumenical church at Hyde Park Corner in London. She wanted this to be used by all faiths, and for each denomination to be responsible for certain parts of it.

The Church of England has always been my denomination; it is a simple and straightforward way of worship, which answers my needs. While staying in Cambridge in 1948 I went to the early service in King's College Chapel, and as I was going forward for my communion I saw that the person waiting in the queue behind me was the then Archbishop of Canterbury, Dr Fisher. It is good to belong to a faith in which no person has precedence over another.

I have found help in religious discussion groups, and for a long time helped run one which Bishop Hugh Gough used to lead. During the late Forties I attended bible rallies, Quiet Weekends and retreats (sometimes with the Franciscans), finding the latter particularly helpful. Prayer twice daily, meditation weekly and sometimes fasting became a natural part of my life, and their value to me is not only spiritual but also reflective in that they, collectively, remind me of the presence of God and the wish to say "thank you" for something before asking for more. I found I needed this for I don't remember being a thinker as a teenager nor in my early 20s. Although the army lets you do so if you choose, it doesn't make you think, and responding automatically to discipline tends to let the brain become rusty.

Soldier or civilian?

When I was in the army I used to go home to Hassocks for holidays and occasional weekends, and it was on one of these occasions, in 1954, that I finally told my parents that I might leave the army and work in Bermondsey, the decision I had been working towards since visiting "Cottolengo" in 1953.

In his diary, Harold Macmillan quotes Winston Churchill: "Between the baton and the bowler [hat] there is no middle course". These two politicians, of course, served as Ministers during both war and peace and saw themselves operating with, at one extreme, the baton and, at the other, the bowler.

However, in my experience the social worker follows a middle course which recognises, yet is not bound by, extremes; a course between the doer and the thinker, the realist and the idealist. Only now, in retrospect, do I realise that the experiences I had and the people I met during my home, school and army lives were not only hugely influential but also invaluable to me throughout my subsequent career in social welfare; they helped me to maintain a sense of balance and proportion

According to one soldier, I had ceased by 1952 – my last year in the Canal Zone – to be a "hard officer" (though I hope I had always been fair) and had begun to be more individual-minded towards the men under my command. This had been a year during which I had thought and wondered very much about the future; I had not had a religious experience during it but it had certainly been a time of prayer.

While working both abroad and in England I had wanted more and more to get out of the army and work among people in need. I didn't know what their "needs" might be, only that I wanted to do something practical to help them. As some of it was our family property and I therefore knew the area a little, Bermondsey seemed an excellent place to start.

Since 1948 I had been visiting houses in Bermondsey with our family's agent and used to look in at Bede House, an interdenominational settlement which ran, and still runs, clubs for all ages and provides digs for students. One of Bede House's buildings was called Lady Gomm House for, formerly, it had been the cottage hospital built by my grandparents about 1880.

I had sometimes taken elderly or handicapped people from these houses for drives in my car and visited others in their homes and clubs. Over the four or five years up until 1955 that I did this I came to realise that far more was being done for the young than for the aged. Wherever I travelled in England I saw elderly people, alone, on park benches, looking out of windows, coming out of public libraries or walking, it seemed aimlessly, on the streets. I stood on a busy street in Brighton and counted the passers-by; two-thirds of them were over pensionable age and many walked with difficulty.

I learned that of the 55,000 people living in Bermondsey in 1955 more than 12,000 were pensioners. It seemed to me that there must be many who couldn't get to clubs, even if there were clubs to go to, and many perhaps who wouldn't want to go to them anyway. But in either case they were probably confined to their own homes and, most likely, to their own company. I wanted to know more about them and see if there was anything I could do to help – if they wanted it.

And was it really only the elderly who were on their own? What about the young, the sick, the mentally or physically handicapped, the ex-offenders, children from broken homes; were they just as isolated? Rather than bury my feelings, leave the questions unanswered or deal with them half-heartedly, I decided in the autumn of 1953 to work seriously towards resigning from the army and going whole-heartedly to live with those in need.

The only practical contribution I could make would be as a home-help. The scrubbing, cleaning and general usefulness involved required no training and there were always vacancies. The practical nature of the work also suited my mood. In April 1954 I wrote to the home-help organiser in Bermondsey, Miss Marie Monk, asking if I could join. She ignored my first two letters thinking I wasn't serious and, anyhow, men didn't apply. After my third letter, however, she interviewed me and told me I could join her organisation once clear of the army.

I had talked to several people about leaving the army and especially to clergymen because my decision was more a spiritual matter than anything else. Billy Graham, for example, thought I was wrong to leave; whatever their profession, he told me, everyone was called to do their best and serve their conscience, thus I should stay a soldier and get on with it. After I had left the army he rang to ask about my work in Bermondsey; thereafter, whenever he himself couldn't visit, his wife would come and see what we were doing there. The Grahams have helped me in many other ways ever since.

But by Christmas 1954 I still hadn't completely made up my mind whether or not to leave the army. I was lucky in that I had little to give up materially and few responsibilities to forego. I was without responsibility for parents, a wife, children or property and able to do what I felt was right in the light of my own experiences. And, though not rich I was financially sound and independent with an annual income from the family Estate and from investments of about £1,500 and a capital of £3,000 to £4,000. In Bermondsey I felt out of place, in the army something was missing – there was an emptiness.

Arguments for leaving the army grew. If I tried to live full-time in Bermondsey I might grow to feel less out of place and I might find there what the army lacked for me. But outside the army I had no skills to offer. I had experience as a leader but none as a servant. I was uncertain what to do.

No doubt "God helps those who help themselves" but not everyone has to be a leader, there have to be followers, too, such as butchers and bakers and candlestick-makers. I could quietly get on with doing things at the bottom and see where I went from there.

Most of my contemporaries followed a career path along the Thames Valley, which starting from birth in Hampshire or Gloucestershire, led to preparatory school at Ludgrove, the Dragon or Summerfields, then on to Eton, Winchester and Oxford University. Next came the Brigade stations at Pirbright, Windsor, Chelsea, Knightsbridge or Wellington Barracks and from there they went to the City and worked at Lloyds, the Baltic or stock exchanges – all on or near the Thames.

It is possible to have too much thinking and analysing. In the early Fifties, a neighbour told me how he had always admired beauty and nature, both freely and unthinking, until he attended a series of lectures entitled "The Appreciation of Beauty". From then on his appreciation of beauty was taken from him, because he'd heard it docketed, labelled, split up and dissected.

To paraphrase Oscar Wilde, the full enjoyment of beauty cannot be shared. Knowing even subconsciously that someone else is with you detracts from full concentration on the beauty before you appreciate it fully. However lovely something is, you cannot appreciate it if you are not in harmony with yourself.

I felt a bit like that – I didn't know what my unease was and I couldn't explain it to myself. It must, I reasoned, be some innermost thing to do with the soul. I began to notice in older people's faces that those who seemed to be at peace with themselves and happy never appeared ugly but that those who were bitter, hateful or resentful couldn't help showing it.

I was gradually getting into an awful muddle. I knew that if I went on thinking, praying and wondering about it any more I would become as confused as my neighbour had been about beauty. I had had a surfeit of it all – of study, thinking, wondering, debating and arguing with myself and others – almost to the point of mental and spiritual indigestion. Stop. Forget yourself – think about others, look after them, I said to myself. And I did.

Clarity: prayers answered

I continued to pray until, alone in the Guards Chapel at Chelsea Barracks on April 22nd, 1955, I knew in a moment that it was right to resign from the army and try to help others. My prayers had, always, been short and simple enough: "Tell me what you want me to do", and at that moment in the chapel I knew. From then on there was no uncertainty.

Preachers preached that service to others should come before self and security; this I certainly didn't practise although fine music, good prose and splendid sunsets made me feel that it was true. Being in Cairo where poverty and riches were so clearly defined, my visit to "Cottolengo" *(Ch. 7)* and to Bermondsey, my feeling that I had become but a symbol in military uniform – all this had contributed towards my growing awareness of hardship and need in society.

Visits to soldiers' family's, too, broadened my view of others' lives. In Burnley, Lancashire I visited a guardsman's mother and family. I have a happy memento of this in a calendar marked: "Dear Friend, always welcome in Lancashire." Burnley, in 1949, was a typical industrial town with its downtrodden park, small shops, a market square, many public houses and street upon street of back-to-back houses

Such towns were home to millions, but I knew nothing about them nor had I thought much about the lives lived in them. Cosseted and limited by my own sheltered, secure childhood, and being unimaginative, it just hadn't occurred to me that this basic, ordinary existence was how so many people lived. I found it magnetic and wanted all the more to live and, if I could, be of use, help and work in such an area.

My plan came as a shock to my mother and father. The thought of my chucking the army and going to live in Bermondsey to scrub floors was "really too much" and my mother cried. My father didn't question my decision but was against the move to Bermondsey. The family, he felt, as landlords, employed people to manage our affairs there and it would be an embarrassment for them to have me around; my brothers felt as he did.

Resigning, or "handing in your papers", from the army takes time – there are no actual papers to hand in, only a form asking the Monarch to accept your retirement. I resigned in April 1955 and was released in September with a gratuity and having been promoted to the rank of major.

Africa beckons ...

As I was driving out of Chelsea Barracks bound, with my suitcases, for Bermondsey I was handed a message telling me to go to the Colonial Office. So, instead of turning left across the Thames I turned right to Whitehall where I met the Minister of State.

After more than two years in exile the Kabaka of Buganda (my friend Freddie) was about to return home to Africa, would I go with him? My role would be a combination of Master of the Household, Personal Advisor and ADC. I would stay on the army's pay-roll, my commission would be re-activated and I would go as a soldier but would also receive a salary from the Kabaka.

In the summer of 1953 when the British Governor in Uganda, Sir Andrew Cohen – Britain then held Uganda as a protectorate within the Commonwealth – had exiled the Kabaka, I had gone to see him at the Savoy Hotel as soon as he had arrived in England. He was sitting in his suite, surrounded by Baganda and looking very lost. He had been summoned see the Governor who had told him, to Freddie's astonishment, "you must now leave the country"; a plane was waiting. All Freddie remembered was wondering whether to fire his pistol at a light bulb or throw it through a window. He had wanted to do something dramatic but in the end all he could think of was to insist on going to the airport in his own car – this was not allowed.

Oliver Lyttelton, the Colonial Secretary had just told the House of Commons there was no chance of the Kabaka ever returning to his country. The only MP who had stood up for him was Fenner Brockway, known for backing lost causes. It was a sad occasion but he was dignified throughout. What's more, on his arrival in England he had heard that his favourite sister had died of shock.

After 20 months in England, during which time we met frequently, he was recalled and returned to Uganda. The night before he left he had invited me to a cocktail party which Oliver Messel was giving for him; Freddie had made many friends. He had been living at a flat in Eaton Square, paid for by the British Government, filled by Baganda with no sense of time or hurry they would talk late and sleep whenever they felt inclined. Into this relaxed place had come all sorts of people, members of Parliament and of the Follies Bergeres, photographers, dress-designers, Brigade Officers and others. Freddie was welcoming to all, but decided that if his exile was ever to be permanent he would rather spend it in Tangier than in England.

We went once to a concert at the Albert Hall during which he taught me about drums: "This is a mournful note, someone is dying; this is a vigorous beat, someone is in love." He always held that the tribal customs of his people must be maintained, wanting them to take tradition into developing sophistication.

The decision for the Kabaka to return had obviously been taken several months before and Ronnie Owen, like the Kabaka an ex-Grenadier, had been earmarked to go with him. Owen, however, couldn't go and so the offer had come to me. I asked for time to think.

It was an attractive prospect but I had reservations: shadowy figures behind thrones are doubtful assets to any monarch; with Bermondsey on my mind I would be unable to devote myself fully to the post, and the language barrier would need to be overcome – I am very bad at learning languages.

Ultimately, however, to go with the Kabaka would mean remaining a soldier when I now knew that it was Bermondsey I wanted, and I wanted to get on with it. So I declined to the Minister and went ahead with my move to Bermondsey.

11

TWO MONTHS IN BUGANDA

I describe in Part II the full story of my work with the lonely, from my early days as a home help in Bermondsey in 1955 and the start of the Abbeyfield Society in 1956, to my subsequent association with it and the Carr-Gomm, Morpeth and affiliated societies– all and always inextricably linked to my personal, family life.

My first year in Bermondsey (Ch. 20) had been exciting and wonderful – so much had been achieved – but it had also been tiring, so when Freddie, the Kabaka, invited me to Buganda for two months I accepted immediately. It was October 1956 and an ideal time to take a complete break. My visit would coincide with celebrations marking one year since Freddie's return from exile in October 1955, his 32nd birthday in November 1956 and opening a new parliament building in December.

But the Kingdom of Uganda is a fairy tale. You climb up a railway rather than a beanstalk, and at the end there is a wonderful new world. The scenery is different, the vegetation is different, the climate is different and, most of all, the people are different from anything elsewhere to be seen in the whole range of Africa ... a tropical garden.

Under a dynastic King, with a Parliament, and a powerful feudal system, an amiable, clothed, polite and intelligent race dwell together in an organised monarchy upon the rich domain between the Victoria and Albert lakes ... able to read and write ... have embraced the Christian faith. There is a Court, there are Regents, and Ministers and nobles, law, discipline, culture and peace.

... I asked myself whether there is any other spot in the whole earth where the dreams and hopes ... have ever attained such a happy realisation.
"My African Journey", Winston S Churchill, 1907

Uganda is large in comparison to England – 230,000 square kilometres against England's 130,000, but with only one quarter of the population: Buganda comprises approximately one third of the land and is sub-divided into counties, divisions, provinces and sazas, while the remainder of Uganda is largely made up of three neighbouring kingdoms; Ankole, Bunyoro and Toro. Kintu, a wandering priest from Sudan, an Arab country in the north, founded the Buganda kingdom and race – a mix of Arab and African peoples – in the 14th century; its population, under five million in 1956, had risen to more than 14 million by 2004.

8. Uganda

The royal Rolls-Royce was waiting for me at Entebbe airport. At the palace in Kampala a teeming throng was dancing and singing before the Kabaka and his Queen (Damali) in magnificent celebration of their king's return from enforced exile a year before. There were also some 1,500 invited officials – including neighbouring kings – many sporting top hats and carrying shields and spears; they, too, were dancing, beating drums and blowing horns. The dancing over, I went into the palace and met the Kabaka and guests who had come to pay their respects to him.

Paganism retained a hold across half the country and one year to the day since the Kabaka's return people called *Mourners* had chosen to celebrate the original founding of their country – something Freddie was trying to overlook because at this time of harmony it tended to stir up inter-tribal discord. Dressed in bark cloth and singing, dancing, drumming, and mimicking the calls of wild animals they approached the palace. The Kabaka declined to see them, but they kept coming back until he relented. The *Mourners* worship trees and believe in magic, ghosts and spirits in the traditions which existed before Christianity was introduced.

When they appeared before the Kabaka they gave speeches, which I suspected were anti-British, then danced to drums, rattles and castanets. Some of the dancers became so frenzied that they fainted, others so hypnotised by the drumming that they danced on after the music stopped until they were brought back to consciousness by a rap on the head administered with a severed cow's tail by the medicine man. The Kabaka, aware of such mesmeric states, thought at first that they were acting, but afterwards said that he had never seen anything quite like it.

9. The Kabaka Mutesa of Buganda with Sarah and their two sons Richard and Ronnie and one of his daughters

Christianity had to battle hard against paganism's wide grip but I sometimes wondered if missionaries were right in saying that to convert pagans one must assume that they hold no belief; they did, in fact, believe in such wholesome things as a god, a tree or the sun and that, surely, was something on which to build.

Here in Buganda as a temporary member of the Kabaka's family I had no worries and only the greatest enjoyment. He, however, had considerable responsibilities – to his country, of course, and he also had 120 relations to support. He saw a good deal of his immediate family and Sarah Kissosonkole (his favourite wife and Damali's sister) ran his home life for him. Polygamous relationships meant that he had fathered many children – for whom he ran a school within the grounds – but his two sons in prominence at the palace were Ronnie Mutebi, named after his godfather (and my great friend) Ronnie Owen, and my godson, Richard Walugembe.

A kind of "ADC" to the Kabaka

I was housed in a wing of the new palace which stood in front of the old one. From a hut between the two drums beat day and night when the Kabaka was in residence and, by the main gate a constant flame burned to show that he was alive.

I took breakfast alone in my suite and wanted for nothing: at my disposal was a fleet of Rolls-Royces, whisky and champagne flowed and meals were large. I would join the Kabaka at his office each morning where anyone could, and did, come to him with anything from official business to domestic arguments. The first case I attended, for example involved a man seeking compensation because a young girl had bitten off his ear. The Kabaka's prime minister would discuss affairs of state then the family would come to plan their day. There were letters to sign, projects to talk about, and so it continued, each day full of variety.

There was a welcome for Princess Margaret when her 'plane briefly touched down at Kampala and a visit to the Kabaka's new country palace at Bamananika, there were cruises and canoe races on Lake Victoria and a jungle safari – on which I shot an elephant – and a multitude of dinners and official engagements. I even helped arm the Royal Guard with 100 new rifles and ammunition; I only realised later that they were Uganda's only organised army and therefore had there been any uprising against their colonial masters, the British, they would be first targets.

On Baganda's National Day – me in morning dress, the chiefs in full tribal ceremonial robes – we attended a jubilant Thanksgiving service, on Armistice day a service in the cathedral and at the Cenotaph, and an investiture at the old Lukiko, the parliament building where the Kabaka, cloaked in gold and black and wearing his high gold hat, sat on a throne atop a carpet of 12 lion and 12 tiger skins.

Freddie's birthday saw a small private service in the palace chapel with his birthday celebrated officially the following day – and with such enthusiasm the crowd overpowered police and thronged into the palace grounds. Drumming and dancing continued into the night; it was a marvellously festive occasion with grand guests in attendance and public events including parades and a football match. And, further among my varied duties, I – temporarily made a Major-General by the railway staff to give me dignity on such a big occasion – represented the Kabaka at the official opening of the East African railway extension. Begun in 1896, the railway had connected Mombassa in Kenya to Kampala, and now went as far as the Ruwenzori Mountains (the Mountains of the Moon – 16,000 ft) and the Kilembe copper mines. The Kabaka cut the tape as the train left Kampala, and the Governor drove it the last few yards to its mountain terminus where the Omukama, King George of Toro, unveiled it.

A tour of the copper mines revealed stark contrast in the mines' camps between the Africans' low, squalid, one-room huts, their small school and poorly-paid teachers, against the spacious, well-equipped houses with small gardens and good amenities for white workers; separate eating halls and buses, too for black and white. "Don't worry," said the Omukama, "one day soon all will be put right," – and it was; five years later when the country gained independence.

I returned to Kampala for more ceremonial duties with the Baganda including the final formal ceremony I was involved in – the opening of the Bulange, the new Parliament building in Kampala. This was a great event with all the trappings befitting such an event: a Guard of Honour, a band, trumpets, drums and dancers. The Colonial police – sadly, as they were wont to do – treated the royal party with little respect.

Conversations with Freddie

My conversations with Freddie were many and varied, although sometimes it was difficult to spend time alone together. We talked about the future of his country; the British would soon be pulling out and a new, independent Uganda would be created. The Baganda people were wary of the proposed federal status and hoped for a constitution which would acknowledge that each of the tribes followed various faiths including Muslim, pagan and Christian. Insular in outlook the tribes seemed not to concern themselves much with world affairs and the Kabaka himself received no digest of national or international news from his staff – although the people I met wanted to know all about England, and especially the East End of London where I was working.

The Baganda were, with justification, a proud race who longed to self-govern. Unable to accept either an East African federation or any political links with neighbouring Kenya and Tanganyika, they could, however, just about accept federal links with Uganda's other kingdoms and, ultimately, seemed to believe that a tribally mixed population would triumph. They were suspicious of white men while realising they also needed expert help from the West in order to modernise: the Owen Falls dam needed technicians; Makerere College needed teachers; Mulago Hospital needed doctors and nurses and farming practice needed skilled review.

We talked, too, about social problems in relation to changes within Uganda: the drift of the young into towns, leaving the elderly neglected and lonely in the villages; the shift from polygamy to monogamy allied with prostitution, illegitimacy, unwanted children and venereal disease; the increase in mixed-race marriages in a world still prejudiced against this; unequal justice between black and white and the potential damage from alcohol, increasingly available and affordable.

During my stay I hosted several cocktail parties to which the Kabaka's family came then, before I returned to England, they gave a European-style dance for me. Guests included three monarchs, the Kabaka's Prime Minister and his Chancellor of the Exchequer with music for dancing by a South African swing band. We partied joyfully until 2 am then – true to the Baganda style – we sat down to dinner.

I had delighted in this wonderful break, fascinating and enjoyable on so many levels, and returned to Bermondsey January 1957 refreshed and ready to get back down to the serious work in hand.

12

WEDDING BELLS AND FAMILY LIFE

I had been living and working in Bermondsey *(Ch. 20)* for just over two years when I married Susan Gibbs on October 21st, 1957. We had first met three years earlier when I was in the army, stationed at Windsor and Susan's brother, William, was in my company. We had been left to keep an eye on the barracks while the rest of the battalion went on an exercise and William brought his sister into the mess for a drink, but she didn't stay long. Then, 18 months later we were working together for the Abbeyfield Society in Bermondsey.

Brown-haired, tall and very attractive, Susan was natural with all people and everyone felt at ease with her. She had an intuition and composure which drew friends to her and acted as a balm in all our community crises. In fact, I think she worried about things as much as the rest of us but she was better at not showing it; we all used to turn to her with our problems.

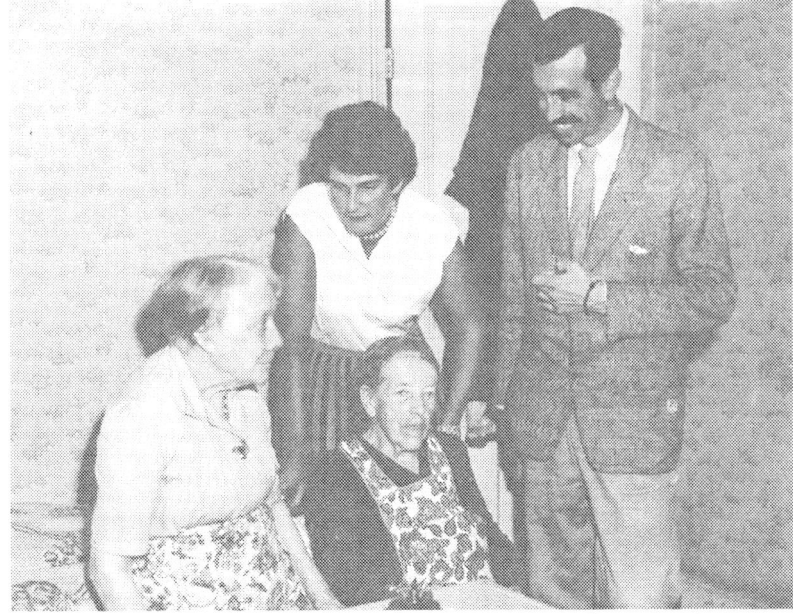

10. Susan and Richard – an engagement photograph, October 1957, with Mrs Rouse and Miss Gilbert

Within six months I knew that my problem was that I wanted to marry her. When I told her this, she said no and flew off to Ibiza in the Mediterranean to think. A week later she returned and, at Lynton Road in Bermondsey where I was housekeeper, she said "yes". We made plans for a wedding in Gloucestershire where most of Susan's family lived. It was organised by her elder brother, Peter, since both her parents had died (her father only very recently). Then she changed her mind and put me into a depression and others into a muddle. The breaking-off announcement in the newspaper looked bleak.

Soon, though not all that soon, Susan changed her mind again and we married, quietly, having made no formal announcement, in Manor Methodist Church, Bermondsey on October 21st, 1957. The minister was Leslie Timmins at whose house in Abbeyfield Road, London I was then lodging *(Ch. 21)*.

Though I was by now aged 35, I had never thought of not getting married; but it had never crossed my mind that it would be a wedding like this. On the morning of our wedding about a dozen people were hurriedly assembled, I wore an ordinary suit, we used a curtain ring for the wedding ring and we had no time to organise a photographer.

Ad-hoc honeymoon

We had no honeymoon plans; Susan and I, with our guests, just drove from the church in a mini van, first to the Savoy where we lunched with our families, and then to tea in Crawley on our way to supper and the night at a hotel on the front in Brighton.

Next day, we drove to Salisbury where there was a fair going on. As we arrived I heard myself on the wireless, in a pre-recorded interview; it all seemed very strange. We then dove west to Dartmoor where we stayed in a stately home called the Moretonhampstead Hotel.

Still in a state of newly-wed surprise, we nevertheless knew that we couldn't afford to continue staying in such a grand hotel and found a small guesthouse hidden in one of the valleys of the Moor. Then, as later in life, our different approaches to situations showed – Susan would look at the shorter term, the immediate situation, I – in idealistic terms, and not when it came to paying the bills – the long and possibly eventual solution. Susan would notice the flowers and the Moorland ponies, I the panoramic view and sunset; all were nice for us.

As a result of our muddled engagement and surprise wedding our future was completely unplanned and we had had no time to organise ourselves, let alone work out where we were going to live. And, of course, by our rushed and secret wedding we had deprived ourselves of wedding presents. So, back at work, we spent our first few weeks of married life living in a room at Gomm Road – one of the Society's Bermondsey houses. We did, however, start house-hunting and thinking it an error to live too much on the job soon found a delightful little house at the World's End off the Kings' Road in Chelsea.

"This is Your Life"

During our honeymoon, while we were staying at the Moretonhampstead Hotel, Susan's brother, William, had been telephoning asking her to arrange to "produce me" for the television programme "This is Your Life". I was too unenquiring to ask what these calls were about and their purpose therefore remained a well-kept secret.

Susan had told me we would spend the last evening of our honeymoon with both our families at a party in London, which would include being part of a live audience watching a television play. A chauffeur-driven car collected us from Abbeyfield Road and we were driven, very fast, across London to Shepherd's Bush, where (having arrived ahead of schedule) the chauffeur pretended that the car had run out of petrol. We waited while he pretended to fill up then drove the last 300 yards to the theatre.

The show started and, as I had never seen it before, I was not suspicious when Eamonn Andrews went around the audience introducing various honeymoon couples, who "just happened" to be in London that night; these included us, and Susan remembered to say that her name was Carr-Gomm and not Gibbs.

I still didn't know what it was about when he returned to me and said, "Richard Carr-Gomm, this is your life", and led me onstage. I didn't hear a word he said after that –it was all so bewildering. I didn't think about the cameras, it was just great fun seeing our Bermondsey helpers, Lavinia Keppel (favourite "Deb"), our first and other residents, my squadron Sergeant-Major, a sympathetic neighbour from Sussex, friends, my mother and other relatives, but sadly not Freddie, the Kabaka – they'd decided it would cost too much to fly him over.

After the show more friends and family came down from the balcony, where they had been hidden, and we enjoyed a splendid drinks party courtesy of the BBC. Adrienne Allen, the actress, had seen the show and invited us to a late theatre party she was giving in Hampstead so, off we went and continued to party there in a high and happy state till the early morning.

Several nights later I awoke with the realisation that 12 million people had seen me on television; I felt shivery and rather frightened. The programme produced a great response from people all over Britain and the interest it aroused both in Abbeyfield and in me lasted for many years. The mailbag was heavy and, despite the help of Eamonn Andrews and the BBC, several correspondents impatient for replies to their offers of help cancelled them before I could get round to replying.

There were offers of caravan holidays for the elderly, pen-friends, tickets to strip clubs, interest from official organisations and a Christmas party invitation from a Rotary Club. Sadly, all offers of full-time help were withdrawn once the spontaneity had worn off but we were sent several hundred pounds, all in small amounts, and one man left us a legacy. A rag-and-bone man offered a half-share of his takings if he could collect on our behalf and someone promised a cut from his slot machines on the Brighton piers if he could use our name on them. To almost all of these we said no, but we gratefully accepted the donations.

One of the more unusual gifts came from the comedian and author Spike Milligan who offered us a barrel of beer he had been given to help him train for a tiddly-winks match between the Duke of Edinburgh's team and a Cambridge College; we accepted the offer but the beer failed to materialise.

More than 40 years later we discovered that our daughter in law Ros's father (Bob Holness) had also been a subject on "This is Your Life". When the TV company's invited Bob to its party celebrating 1000 of its subjects in 2000, Ros (our son David's wife) reminded them that I, too, qualified (they had forgotten). So Susan and I went with Bob and Mary Holness and together we had a great evening surrounded by well-known faces and familiar names.

House-hunting
Since we bought it in 1957 Susan and I had continued to live at our Chelsea home. Anna, our daughter had been born on August 12th 1958 then, with the imminent arrival of our second daughter, Elizabeth, we needed more space. Born and bred in the country Susan longed to return, so we began our search for a house in Sussex. We trailed endless country lanes looking at, to my mind, unsatisfactory farmhouses and isolated cottages – "Nonsense," Susan would say: "There were three or four and some were nice." It was a weary business and, to make matters worse, I became ill and had to have an

emergency operation to remove one kidney. While I recovered at the Middlesex Hospital, Susan was in the Lindo Wing at St Mary's Paddington giving birth to Elizabeth by Caesarean Section on 18th October 1959.

That year, we took a flat in Brook House, a large country house in Ardingly, Sussex where we, and a nanny for our daughters, settled comfortable for the next two years or so. A significant amount of my time was now taken up by travel –commuting to London, going to and fro between Abbeyfield's central office and its houses in Bermondsey, visiting new Societies and attending meetings – so I stayed in London during the week, although it wasn't much fun leaving the family behind in Sussex. In 1962 we decided to move closer to London and, by luck, found a large Victorian house which we both liked at 15 Ulundi Road, Greenwich. This was an excellent location from my point of view as I could travel easily to central London and reach Bermondsey, even on a bicycle, in about 15 minutes. The house was both ugly and cheap so we were encouraged to spend on altering and decorating it to our liking.

13

IN THE WAKE OF ABBEYFIELD

Following my dismissal by Abbeyfield in March 1964 (Ch. 24) I needed to reflect and consider my future. Recalling happy memories of a holiday in Buganda with the Kabaka in 1956 I decided to revisit him there. Susan, pregnant with our third daughter, Harriet, was unable to travel so I went alone for a three-week holiday.

Three months prior to my visit Uganda had ceased to be a British Colony having gained independence as a Republic incorporating its four erstwhile kingdoms: Buganda, Bunyoro, Ankole and Toro. Freddie (who was also Kabaka, or King, of Buganda) was now President of the new Uganda and Milton Obote was its Prime Minister. The British had honoured Freddie with a knighthood and he had been given honorary lieutenant-colonelcy in the Grenadiers.

But there were problems. Uganda's first President had to set the style for leadership and he and Obote were not natural bedfellows. With the British no longer in charge, Uganda had to contend politically with politics on the international stage at the same time as setting an agenda to deal with the complex issues facing Africa as a whole alongside bringing together the various tribes and former kingdoms under the Ugandan Republic.

Despite holding the Presidency Freddie felt ignored by Obote and other Ministers who seemed to be wielding the real power; he hoped the people of Uganda were behind him but was certain of loyalty only from the Baganda (about one sixth of the total population). I quoted Napoleon's quip on hearing the cheers of the crowd: "They would do just the same for my execution."

As for the hold of Christianity in Uganda: few Africans were coming forward for priesthood, few Europeans attended Christian church services, many Ministers of State had been excommunicated and Obote had threatened black magic against the Archbishop and his Church. While on a personal level, Freddie's problems included running five homes, educating ten children and living apart from his legal wife, Damali – he could not accept that until he sorted out his private affairs he could not expect any official Royal invitation to Britain. Hardly surprising then that he sought solace in alcohol.

When I visited in 1964 I was Freddie's first European guest at State

House – formerly Government House – in Entebbe. The building retained all the trappings of its recent colonial owners from the fixtures, fittings and paintings to the liveried footmen.

I was given the royal suite: four bedrooms, two bathrooms and a private balcony, overlooking the lawns towards Lake Victoria; no wonder some had thought it the most beautiful of all Government Houses. Life there was extremely comfortable although Freddie, who lived 20 miles, away said he found it a lonely place.

Hunting in the "lost counties"

Soon after my arrival, we went to a camp at the small town of Ndaiga in the "Lost Counties" – an area taken from the Bunyoro by the British and given to the Baganda and which Bunyoro now wanted to reclaim. Metalled road turned to rough track as we neared Ndaiga; I was housed on the royal compound in a small hut with a tin-box shower behind. The fertile country around this hilltop town was not only fertile but also had a potential for rare mineral-mining, so the Baganda obviously wanted to keep it for themselves and could see no reason to give it up just because the Bunyoro had asked for it back.

In camp we felt completely cut off from the outside world – neither wireless nor telephone worked – and I was pleased to be the only non-African for miles, although I enjoyed the guard turning out at sunset and the bugler playing the "Last Post". Margaret, an African girl pregnant with Freddie's baby, lived on the compound and she would fall asleep on the bed or the floor while we talked in his tent.

We went hunting in a long line – some 48 of us in all – led through the bush by a man with an assegai. We returned empty-handed but, next day deep in the Great Rift Valley around Lake Albert I shot a buffalo. This caused tremendous excitement and there was much cheering as spears, pangas and more shots were aimed at my (already dead) buffalo. Expert butchery left few remains for the circling vultures and my African companions put me to shame as they, - carrying great haunches of meat on their heads, trotted effortlessly out of the steep valley back to camp. I had been given the buffalo's tail as a memento and just that and my rifle were almost too much for me. Breakfast had been a boiled and we'd slogged for nine hours; I was exhausted. Lunch was brought to my hut at 5 pm, I poured liquid into and over myself and lay down. The Kabaka sent a leopard skin to reward my kill. It had been an adventure, but I think I would have found it just as exciting to have shot the beast with a camera as a gun.

Mutiny in Jinja

Then, following an earlier revolt by the army in Zanzibar, rumour reached us of another in neighbouring Tanganyika. Freddie didn't believe such things could happen in Uganda but he complied with Obote's request to return at once to State House at Entebbe.

Back in Entebbe we heard that Ugandan troops in Jinja were in revolt, planning to kill their white officers and loot the town's Asian shops. Obote, by 'phone had assured his President that all was well, but half-an-hour later we heard that he (as had Kenya) had requested help from British troops which would arrive in two hours' time. Furious that Obote had not told him, Freddie asked me to go to the airport and report back to him.

Having been warned that the airfield might be in the hands of revolutionaries the troops came in with rifles held high, shooing people out of the way and took up strategic positions on the rooftops. They, generally, behaved in a very aggressive fashion, even brushing aside the official welcoming party of dignitaries. I realised and resented the horror of being occupied by foreign troops. Freddie, even as President and his army's commander-in-chief, had still been told nothing of the situation by Obote. Troops flew in throughout the night; Freddie stayed up late, drank too much and about 2am made an unfruitful call to Obote.

Over the next few days I acted as a sort of runner for the President. While most politicians and the military commanders wanted to keep him and his office in the picture, effective circulation of Intelligence was almost impossible while Uganda's infant chain of command remained unorganised and inefficient. Meanwhile, British troops disarmed the mutineers in Jinja and the rebellious battalion was disbanded; the ringleaders were court-martialled and the rest put on buses, driven off and left in the countryside near their home villages. The white officers – disillusioned and dismayed by the actions of their soldiers – were posted elsewhere and, as a general measure thereafter, units were put under the command of Africans. Idi Amin, then a major and showing a gift for leadership, was promoted to colonel, morale was restored, shops reopened and a more peaceful situation developed. Ultimately Uganda hoped to deal with its own internal problems but, for now, the country began to invite and accept much needed help from individual British specialists and companies.

While he was establishing the authority of his Presidency and getting to grips with the new politics at large, I helped Freddie concoct a personal letter to the British Queen thanking her for his Grenadier colonelcy and together we planned regular lunch meetings to which he could invite Ministers and anyone else he needed to get to know better and how best to use State House for official entertaining.

Tours and celebrations

During the remainder of my unexpectedly eventful holiday James Lutaya, chief of the Ssese Islands, took me to visit these peaceful landfalls on Lake Victoria and I managed to fit in a short visit to Toro which coincided with the Omukama's celebration for the 35th anniversary of his accession to the throne. In Fort Portal, the Toro capital, flags were hoisted and streamers flew. Overlooking the Ruwenzori Mountains a new circular palace was being built; it was rumoured to have rooms for concubines radiating from its central bedroom. I had arrived in time to attend a private service in the church with the Omukama and his sister and, at the next day's public service I was able to join in a hymn – the Buganda's national anthem as it transpired – sung to the tune of "Swannee River". Freddie and the monarchs of Bunyoro, Ankole and Toro joined the celebrations and, because the waiter had to kneel to each one he served, meals lasted for a very long time.

I returned to England and gave the Foreign and Commonwealth Office and the War Department my account of the military crisis at Jinja and the political situation as I saw it. Another African interlude was over.

Greek island idyll

Back in London and with – as far as I knew then – Abbeyfield over for me I worked again, briefly, as a home-help. But it was time too, I felt, for us to get away on a family holiday.

In spring that year (1964), I suggested to Susan that we should disappear for several months to a Greek island. Our third daughter, Harriet, was born on 9th May 1964 and was only two months old when Susan proposed Corfu; she had read about the island which was said to be green and full of butterflies, tortoises, lizards and birds. So, Corfu it was – but first we had to find the money.

My parents had died recently – both in their 80s, and within two years of each other. My mother retained her full vigour until after a long and painful illness she died at their home at Hassocks. True to her temperament, she had composed her own funeral service, including a joyful anthem she had written especially for the occasion;

she also had us sing "Fight the Good Fight". Soon after my mother's death, my father had slipped quietly into senility.

Just before her death my mother had given me an old glass-fronted showcase containing various pieces of china and glass; nothing, according to insurance, of any worth. However, when Christie's were valuing our house and contents, the only thing which excited them – and rather to our sorrow as we thought we had a few other good things – was an early Meissen china tea set in this cabinet. It failed to reach their reserve at the first auction, however they persisted and split it into two lots which sold in excess of their original estimate. This made possible a three month holiday in Corfu.

We answered an advertisement on the front page of *The Times* and took a beach house on the unfashionable side of the island at Glyfada, just below Pelekas. The house was delightful, matchbox-like, and almost totally isolated at the end of an earth track winding down a cliff face. It was hardly the place, however, for a brand new baby but we hoped for the best and cut Harriet's hair to keep her cool.

The beach, one of the few sandy beaches in Corfu, was half a mile long and often, at least at the beginning of our stay, completely deserted. The weather was good, though once it rained and sometimes the wind got up, but mainly it was a blue, blue sky and lapping water. After a month of going nowhere except to shop, we climbed to the top of the hills behind our bay to watch the sunset: a wonderful sight with the sun like a red ball dropping into the middle of the sea. I soon lost the taste for reading English newspapers and didn't welcome letters. I developed a face-rash and, to avoid shaving, grew a beard, which I have kept ever since.

Anna and Elizabeth (then aged six and five) collected beetles, grasshoppers, butterflies, frogs, toads, crabs, sea snails and tortoises – we kept three and called them Gli, Fa and Da – after the village. Anna had a birthday party on the beach and we invited all our new friends – the taverna owner's family, campers, villagers and various foreigners who owned houses or land nearby. Greek, English, German, Swiss and Swedish all celebrated together with chicken and chips (the children's favourite) barbequed on a charcoal fire.

We swam at midnight without bathing dresses and, once, Susan swam so far in the phosphorescence of the moon's path that we thought we had lost her. She, however, reappeared and we all walked back up the hillside, Susan tearing her nightdress and me breaking my wooden sandals. The mountain view from the top was magnificent, but it was light when we got back – and Harriet decided to wake early.

One day Anna cut her hand on a fizzy pop can and a local man put cigarette ash on it. Susan and her sister, Mary Macdonald, were shocked and washed it off as soon as he had gone; but perhaps nicotine really was good for it. Next day the children dropped cold-water washing-powder down the drinking well. Our landlord was rightly furious and Raymond Hylton, a friend who was staying with us, kindly went down to clean it; three times the well had to be washed out before its water could be safely drunk.

On our last evening the village gave a fiesta for us; we danced in the street until midnight, they gave us presents and we drank a lot. Showing great warmth and friendship they lined the route next day to wave goodbye and some even came to the ship to say farewell. The family flew back from Brindisi but I, with my nephew, Ian Macdonald, motored home in our car; the straight journey through Italy, Switzerland and France took us one week.

Beyond the ordinary tourist attractions, I remember the bad guidebook in Monte Cassino, the ten cardinals praying in the Chapel at St Peter's in Rome prior to the Vatican Council, the aliveness of Michelangelo's "Last Supper" figures in Milan, and a small chateau we stayed at near Lausanne, which turned out to be the last bed we found until we reached Boulogne – a long drive.

Captivated by Corfu, we visited two years later (in 1966) and, with borrowed money, bought nearly an acre of land on the island, including an olive plantation running down to the beach. Becoming property investors involved a period of uncertainty while we made sure our minds were made up, saw the land, found a Greek nominee, went through complicated conveyencing and planned layouts with the architects. We had occasional qualms about the wisdom of it all and needed plenty of time to deal with it all – which we had.

Return to England and reality

When we returned to England in the summer of 1964 I began to think once more about Abbeyfield and the home-helping I had done earlier in the year.

We toured around visiting relatives; Susan, being a Gibbs, had a host of relations mainly living in the West Country, several of whom had served with me in the Army – on his entry form for the Coldstream her brother, William, was able to put down that he had 43 relations connected with the Brigade of Guards. I enjoyed coming into such a large extended family, my own comprised relatively few; we four brothers, our wives and families, an aunt and one first cousin –

none of our grandparents or parents were living. To go to a Gibbs gathering of 100 to 150 people was great fun and it didn't seem to matter that I hardly knew anybody's name. Susan's widowed eldest sister, Mary Macdonald, and her four young children had all stayed with us in Corfu and we often visited her lovely large house in Yorkshire where our children had a happy time with ponies, rowing boats and treetop houses.

Two things had become obvious: I couldn't stop doing and thinking about the work in which I had previously been involved; and I had to earn some money. It was at this point, in the autumn of 1964, that I, slowly, revived my earlier concerns in working with the lonely and, with the advent of first the Carr-Gomm Society in 1965 followed by the Morpeth Society in 1972 – and ultimately others besides – I picked up again the work which meant so much to me.

Our family grows and grows

Susan and I had always wanted a large family, but a combination of stress over strains within the general management of Abbeyfield in the couple of years preceding my dismissal, and because for all three children Susan had needed Caesarean sections – which, her gynaecologist said, was the limit – led us to decide to adopt. Coming from a family of four brothers I wouldn't have minded if we'd stayed with girls, but with three daughters already, Susan opted for a boy. So, through the Adoption Society, Adam joined us aged just a few months. To give us time to make up our minds, we were left in a room alone with him but we needed no time at all and said at once, "Yes, please, we want him".

By 1967, now with five children – Elizabeth, Anna, Harriet, Adam and David (Susan, after a safe interval, having had David by Caesarean that year) – we were settled in our Greenwich home where we remained for 13 years. Nanny Coombes and, sometimes Eileen Parish as governess, helped us, and we employed several European *au-pairs* some of whom became life-long friends. Sometimes, too, we took paying guests to boost the family finances.

Because some of the Society's residents who visited us at home were often eccentric and occasionally hysterical, our friends suggested that, to avoid any adverse influence, it was unwise for our children to meet them. Susan and I acknowledged this, though without great conviction.

We did welcome some rather unconventional visitors but I don't believe our children have suffered as a result. For example, a man going to live in one of the Society's houses after being released from prison wanted to live, and therefore arrive at the house, as a woman. He came to our home to change his clothes, hoping to avoid confusion among the residents if he arrived at the Society's house in his new gender. The children saw him go upstairs dressed as a man and come down dressed as a woman. It surprised them and had to be explained but I don't think it was of more than passing interest to them.

They were more likely to be bothered by men exposing themselves in the park or pursuing them in the street than by hearing of an occasional scandal in the Society. At one time – when their average age was about six – they seemed to think of nothing but death and plaster-casts, counting injured people in the street and asking houseguests how soon they were going to die. This was certainly influenced by their Society contacts but they soon grew out of it. Since all their grandparents were dead, the elderly in the Society's houses provided a counter-balance to their contemporaries with whom they more usually mixed.

There has never been any question that the family is the most important thing in my life but I soon gave up the idea that they might become part of my work; my family came only to Christmas parties or, occasionally, on an outing with the residents. Susan always wanted to keep a clear gap between her involvement in the Society and mine, and had been perfectly right to dissuade me from wanting to live in Bermondsey after we married – the children would have become over-involved. Indeed, Susan, sometimes as a volunteer, always has been involved in the various Societies' work, often knowing far more than any of us about everything and serving longer on committees.

When Anna and Elizabeth were in their early teens they began to take a genuine interest in the work and on their own initiative helped in decorating houses and office work as well as getting to know residents and colleagues and joining parties, outings and so on. Harriet and the boys later did the same but none, rightly and sensibly, take it too closely into their lives unless it, somehow and sometimes, fits for them and those with whom they are involved to do so.

From student to social worker

Following the advent of the Carr-Gomm Society in 1965, in order to increase my knowledge our committee (Edward Palmer, John Stitt, and Juliet Bingley) insisted in 1967 on my undertaking a three-year, part-time sociology course at south London's Morley College. Morley combined a friendly, informal atmosphere with a high standard of teaching for mature students. I enjoyed the course and learned a lot; I couldn't face taking the exams but recorded everything of particular importance to the Society's work for reference and to pass on to the office.

While taking tea in the refectory with Barry Till, who had been in my regiment and was now Principal of the college, someone said that of the 5,000 adult students attending Morley a large number would have registered for reasons of loneliness. It was suggested that I sit in as a consultant for a term for any students who might want to discuss non-academic problems and, from this, we could determine whether the college should employ someone – lawyer, psychologist, doctor, priest – permanently to help them. Six months later, the idea of a student adviser was approved by student representatives.

Two people, both elderly men, wrote at once: one had problems facing retirement and the other an unidentified problem. Then a young wife wrote wanting to help lonely women by enhancing the status of women in society, and another man with a retirement problem. My interviews were supposed to begin with the new term but one couldn't wait and came to see me in Bermondsey and I put him, by mistake, on a bus, in the rain, heading in the wrong direction.

A foolscap sheet was pinned on the college notice board so that people could mark a cross against the time they wanted to see me. There were no crosses at first and I just waited in a small room to see what would happen. On the first night, I discovered later, the man with the unidentified problem hovered around but did not come in. On the second night I found the man whom I had last seen heading in the wrong direction on the bus waiting for me.

That night I fell asleep waiting – life was peaceful – then the Principal sent a note around the classes reminding them of my role and people began to seek my advice on matters as diverse as difficulty making friends and whether a firm which had delivered a harpsichord in imperfect condition could charge rental for the period until they returned to collect it.

After one term as Adviser I stayed for another – then another. Crosses for interviews came steadily but there was never a rush; some wrote, others talked to me in the refectory or elsewhere – there was not always a specific problem to start with but, often, one would emerge. People came mainly for advice on personal problems ranging from loneliness to accommodation to alcoholism – often one interview was enough, but occasionally more were needed. I gained considerable experience in the multitude of problems that beset people and I continued my role as an adviser for ten years until a tutor running a course on advisory services took over from me.

Retreat to Somerset

I always tried to spend as much time as possible with Susan and the children and – although Susan longed to live in the countryside and keep ponies – this was made easy from 1962 when we bought our home in Greenwich, so ideally situated for my work. With the children in bed by 6.30pm, I could attend evening meetings at the Society's (Abbeyfield then Carr-Gomm) various Bermondsey houses on Tuesdays and Wednesdays and committee meetings on Thursdays. All my other evenings were free to spend with Susan – at home, at the theatre, or dining out.

Money was a constant issue and we never had much more than our basic needs required. Fortunately, neither of us had expensive tastes. Susan had a small private income and was very careful with the housekeeping. We lived mainly off investments plus the small income I received from the family estate and, from 1968 my very fair salary from the Carr-Gomm Society. I made donations, in the spirit of tithing, from my net income, not the gross, although many feel the latter is right – to God first then the State.

Combining State and private education enabled us to save money for holidays and to buy a country house in 1973 at Mells, near Frome in Somerset, to which we could escape.

The village of Mells is much admired, settled in itself and with an air of eternity. It has a lovely church with a clock which plays a carillon every three hours, a dignified war-memorial whose inscription justly includes " ...raised to us in the home of our delight" and a 17th century Lock-up. The three-mile walk along the river bank to Frome must be one of the loveliest in England and, in addition to its rural charm, the village benefits from many practical, modern amenities – a regular bus service, a good pub, a shop and post office. The barber, dressmaker and gunsmith have gone, but fresh milk, turkey suppers and a Daffodil week remain part of village life.

In the early 1600s the village was in the hands of the Abbot of (nearby) Glastonbury and its history includes connections with the Horner family – immortalised in the nursery rhyme "Little John (more commonly "Jack") Horner"; John, who "pulled out a plum" was Henry VIII's chancellor who while overseeing the dissolution of the monasteries for his king kept the one at Mells for himself.. The famous First World War poet Siegfried Sassoon lies buried in the village graveyard; Jennie and her son Sir Winston Churchill visited Mells and a First World War chancellor of the exchequer Reginald Mckenna lived there.

The necessary rash of limestone quarries after 1945 has subsided but some of the eastern foothills of the Mendips are still worked. However, the noise, dust and heavy road vehicles associated with them is balanced by advantages such as a reduction in rates, better road surfaces, jobs and spending power and active involvement in charities in the surrounding villages and towns – particularly noticeable at times of village events such as flower shows and sales of work.

14

THE KABAKA: LIFE AND DEATH IN ENGLAND

By the end of May 1966 the political situation in Uganda had destabilised completely. The royal residence at Mengo had been stormed by Prime Minister Dr Obote's special forces – under the command of Colonel (later Field-Marshall) Idi Amin – and the President, Freddie, had been forced to flee for his life; first to Burundi near the Congo and from there to England.

Ronnie Mutebi, his eldest son, was at public school (Bradfield College) in England and Richard Walugembe, my godson, was at school in Kenya. Being out of Uganda these two were safe but Damali, Freddie's queen, and his favourite wife Sarah had been imprisoned in Uganda.

In June, Freddie having reached England, I met him at Ronnie Owen's Chelsea home. He asked after my family and, hearing that we had recently adopted Adam, told me that Margaret, the African woman I had met at Ndaiga in 1964, was pregnant with his child. He talked of his other children and how Obote had let one of their mothers out of prison, and of his escape: how he had seen Damali with his sister and others being led away then hearing a burst of fire had assumed (fortunately incorrectly) that they must be dead. In the melee of shooting and burning huts he had heard a soldier call out, looking for him; realising his life was at stake he had shot the man and felt exhilarated as he watched his intended assassin fall.

At Freddie's request, a few days later I arranged a meeting between him and Billy Graham, who was in England on a mission at Earl's Court. While we waited for Billy at the flat Freddie had been loaned at Albany in Piccadilly, we read Psalm 27. While Billy and Freddie talked, Ronnie Owen, his wife Ardyne, George Wilson (Billy's aide) and Katende (Freddie's bodyguard) waited together until Billy called us in and said a short, sensible prayer thanking God for Freddie's safe delivery from his enemies: he asked God's help for Freddie's family, people and country; for wisdom in future developments; for return to health and to be conscious of, and heed, divine guidance. Later, Billy also offered to talk of Freddie's plight with President Johnson of the USA.

As the months went by Freddie began to build up an ordinary life in England, this despite his many problems; among other things, he learnt that all the women in his family had been released into what he believed was a hostile countryside (in fact, the Christian community had helped and protected them as much as they could). He had also been told that Obote remained keen to kill him and, failing that, was conducting a smear campaign against him. Thus, while he remained in London, officers from Special Branch officers guarded him round the clock and he became excessively security-conscious. During 1967 Freddie, with Katende and an air-hostess friend, moved from London to a delightful rectory on Bill and Toni Spowers' Sunningdale estate. His Special Branch protection was withdrawn because it was felt that he could now settle into normal life.

Settling down in Bermondsey

The following year, just before Easter, he and Katende left Sunningdale and moved into one of our family flats, Orchard House in Bermondsey. Freddie's people, the Baganda, had collected £65 towards furnishings which Damali had sent over secretly. Local children helping to carry in his belongings were calling: "Where's the King? Where's the King?"

The DHSS's regional manager discussed with Freddie how much public assistance he would receive; no favours could be pulled and he was, therefore, entitled to about £4 a week and his rent (also £4 a week) paid. Although supposed to sign on in person every week, Katende was permitted to sign on Freddie's behalf if, for any reason, he couldn't attend.

Following a "hyperactive episode" one evening for which sedation had been needed to calm him, Freddie was admitted for a few weeks to the psychiatric ward at St Olave's hospital; a dull unwelcoming place where he kept to his room until he was discharged.

Once out of hospital Freddie offered to help with our social work and, while I went on holiday, he visited potential residents and did odd jobs. Good at borrowing from neighbours and happy to come to house prayers, Freddie was shocked that some relatives in Britain would not care for their elderly or disabled – this, he said, was not the case in Africa.

Freddie shared my office at Gomm Road while he undertook his principal job with us – re-editing the book of songs, hymns and carols which we used at singsongs. Showing more his tact than sense of rhythm he change "nigger" to "Negro" in "Polly-Wolly-Doodle" and we would hum and sing to each other as we worked. He expanded our favourite house tunes to include Tin Pan Alley songs, and posed for publicity photographs which he hoped would raise money for printing; they didn't and it was Billy Graham and his wife who kindly gave us the £400 necessary to republish the book. He did, though, and with great success, crown the Happy Hearts Queen at Mablethorpe, Lincolnshire.

The DHSS were trying hard, without success, to find a job for Freddie. He had hoped to rejoin the British Army but the Chief of the Imperial General Staff turned down his application. His greatest helper in trying to resolve his various problems were Ronnie Owen and Alan Boyd (Lord Boyd of Merton) who had been Colonial Secretary at the time of his return from exile in England to Uganda in 1955. During his stay in England, although surrounded and supported by friends, Freddie was subject to both racial and personal prejudice, as well as simple misunderstandings. All this he took in good part and dealt with slights against him with tact, humility and good humour.

"Number 10"

In January 1969, began a series of ultimately unproductive meetings to try and improve Freddie's financial and work situation. I met an old friend, Michael Palliser, – at that time Secretary for Foreign and Commonwealth Affairs – at 10 Downing Street, to ask if the Foreign Office would persuade Obote to distinguish between Freddie's Presidential status (which he was prepared to resign) and that of Kabaka, or king (from which he was not). If Obote would accept Freddie's resignation as president, he might also release his private money allowing him to plan his future, be that in Uganda or England. But the outcome of this and subsequent meetings was, for Freddie, no money, no job and no grace-and-favour residence. Sad but philosophical Freddie remained good-humoured and an excellent companion.

Visiting "Number Ten" was interesting, though. I met Michael in the White Drawing-room overlooking Horse Guards and the lake in St James's Park; 18th-century oils from the Samuel collection hung on parchment-like wallpaper. Michael showed me other rooms: two further drawing rooms, and a small and large dining room – the Cabinet room was occupied so I didn't see that but I thought the house friendly and warm.

Death of the Kabaka

On 20th November 1969 Susan and I invited Freddie to dinner at

Ulundi Road with Jenny Gibbs, Susan's cousin, and Mark Amory, an old friend and one-time tutor to Freddie's eldest son, Ronnie; he drank little and was on good form. We talked on the telephone the following afternoon but when I telephoned him that evening, about 7.30 pm, I thought he sounded odd. Later that evening Katende found Freddie unconscious on his sitting room floor and, assuming he must be drunk, we agreed it best to put him to bed and let him sleep it off. He was due to celebrate his 45th birthday the following day and, suspecting he had been drinking his presents, we were not unduly worried.

At midnight Katende rang me at home to say that Freddie was still out cold, but by the time I reached Freddie's flat that night a doctor had already pronounced him dead (he had, in fact, died at 10 pm.) The police were informed but no foul play was suspected and an undertaker removed the body. There followed the sad and inevitable string of telephone calls to and from relatives and friends, press inquiries and legalities to be organised, in all of which Susan and I played a part.

At Freddie's small flat some 30 Baganda had come to pay their respects – singing African songs or asleep in chairs, with more waiting on the stairs outside. Sarah was in a Kampala hospital having collapsed on hearing news of her husband's death. Damali had arrived and Susan and I took her home with us. Obote wanted Freddie's body returned to Uganda for full ceremonial burial: Damali and the Baganda elders were determined this would not happen. Why should Obote give him glory in death? One telegram from Ugandan supporters read:

> Do not bring the Kabaka's body to Uganda unless it is agreed to return him as Kabaka not ex-Kabaka of Buganda. Here the plan is when the body arrives in Entebbe it is to be taken to a place where it will be burnt to ashes. We are not prepared to see this action, so you are asked to insist from what I have told you NOT TO BRING THE BODY TO UGANDA: It is very sad.

Argument about the Kabaka's final resting place continued: Ronnie Owen, Freddie's solicitor Martin Flegg and I attended a secret ceremony with Baganda elders at which Ronnie Mutebi covered his father's body and the coffin with a big sheet of bark-cloth, a necessary tradition before burial and to name the new Kabaka – he who covered the body. Ronnie's assumption of the title was announced publicly the following day after lunch at the Owen's. For the Baganda, Sarah –

Ronnie's mother – became the most important person in the land.

Funeral in London

On 4th December 1969 the Kabaka's memorial service was held at the Guard's Chapel at Wellington Barracks after which his body was buried in Kensal Green Cemetery. The Chapel was filled to overflowing with an international congregation and a full coach-load of friends he had made in Bermondsey attended the service.

At the Coroner's inquest the verdict had been death caused by alcoholic poisoning but some of us had doubts about this and soon theories that death might have been caused by voodoo – he died on the same day and at the same hour as his father, 10pm on 21st November – or poisoning began to circulate. I told the CID of suspicious events of which I was aware and took a Baganda chief to the police to tell them the theories then held in Uganda. We had hoped that the police would continue to investigate but New Scotland Yard refused to accept that there was anything in our suspicions and they considered the case closed.

In May, Ronnie Owen and I went to Kensal Green to see Freddie's grave. We went to the catacombs under the chapel and saw his coffin, draped with flags in an alcove on its own. Concerned about security should anyone want to steal it, we were glad this coffin was an empty dummy; the real one was elsewhere in the cemetery hidden anonymously in a large family vault.

Some of us continued pressing to re-open investigations into the cause of Freddie's death. With Ronnie Owen, Mark Amory, Professor Camps and others we compiled a detailed timetable of Freddie's last days which, we felt, included evidence inconsistent with the Coroner's findings. Alan Boyd and I took this to the Commissioner of Police at New Scotland Yard who, by the end of our meeting had agreed to consider our suspicions.

The Commissioner did, in fact, order new investigation in England and in Uganda into the Kabaka's death. For several months thereafter inquiries continued, more statements made, more people interviewed. But ultimately, with insufficient evidence to satisfy the police that death had not been the result of alcoholic poisoning the investigation petered out. Idi Amin later set up his own investigation but this, also, foundered.

Dispute

Meanwhile the Baganda tribe's Katikoro (Prime Minister) and elders started meeting Ronnie Mutebi in the Orchard House flat to talk over their problems with him and teach him his country's history and traditions. The flat was maintained as a centre for Baganda meetings and the Kabaka's room remained unchanged and locked. Katende became its custodian and the Katikoro and others stayed there whenever they needed to.

In late January 1971, we heard that Obote had been overthrown in a revolt led by General Amin. There was talk of returning the Kabaka's body to Uganda and much jubilation in Kampala when political and royal prisoners were released. But morale plummeted when Amin stated that, while the Kabaka's body and Prince (Ronnie) Mutebi could come back there would be no restoration of the monarchy.

President Amin then ordered the return of the Kabaka's body for a state funeral with a date fixed for it in six weeks' time. The British High Commissioner reported peace and a general acceptance of the idea and the British government, then, encouraged it. Our Queen and Prime Minister were invited to attend.

The Ugandan High Commissioner asked Ronnie Owen and me for our co-operation and help in the ceremony but knowing Freddie's wish not to return until, at the very least, there was a Head of Tribe – thereby, acknowledging tribal existence and restoration of their dignity – and hearing from Uganda that the Baganda were not restored to any form of tribal dignity we, politely, refused.

State funeral, Uganda

The British High Commissioner then arranged a meeting in Uganda between Ronnie Owen, me, and President Amin and some of his Ministers: we discussed the proposed state funeral and Amin outlined security arrangements for Ronnie Mutebi saying he would take personal responsibility for the boy's safety in Uganda. He told us the traditional ceremonies of the Baganda to be carried out at the Kasubi Tombs and that Bamunanika, the country palace, could be re-occupied by the Baganda Royal Family.

All this seemed to indicate that the Baganda would regain some status. But at meetings with the Baganda arguments over the return, or not, of the Kabaka's body raged on.

The Ugandan High Commissioner's application for an exhumation order had already been granted by the British Home Secretary thus Britain had determined to return the body and so appease Amin; the body would go, whatever we thought or said. We told the elders, therefore, that probably their own and certainly their country's interests would be best served if the body came back and the funeral took place, a decision supported by most members of the Baganda Royal Family.

Then back in England came a week of hectic preparation for the return of the body while Uganda went into a week of national mourning. Throughout the week were numerous changes of plan, decisions about who should attend the state funeral and so on; three of Freddie's Bermondsey friends – Doris Sayer, Doll Haydon and Jane Harington (later Whitteridge) – were told they had not been given any of the 130 free flights allocated by the Ugandan High Commission. This was resolved after much pressing over a neurotic weekend at home – not, though, before Susan had put me on to tranquillisers and sleeping pills. Susan and Ronnie Owen's wife had rightly and wisely elected to remain at home because of the security risk. A message came from the Baganda: "Don't bring the body until the monarchy is restored," but by now it was too late.

Finally, we flew to Uganda. It had been agreed that the full traditional Baganda ceremony should be completed, with the exception of the final act – the beating of a drum by the new Kabaka – because this could only be when the monarchy was restored. Ronnie Owen kept up with all the details and seemed to understand superbly their intricacies.

The Baganda traditions were carried out to the letter and, in an all-glass coffin the Kabaka's body lay dressed in British military uniform. Generous presents and ceremonial animal skins were given to us and hospitality seemed unbounded. The ceremonies, parades, grand dinners and parties, dancing, drumming, processions and all the magnificent pomp surrounding the state funeral on 4th April 1971 were overwhelming and lasted seven days. The crowds were huge beyond belief – some cheering, some softly crying.

Mutebi's investiture as Ssabataka
When the drums announced (Ronnie) Mutebi's succession there was so much other noise I doubt whether many heard; but they went on beating, the pipes played and some danced. Mutebi was invested formally, not as Kabaka but as Ssabataka (head of the clans) outside the main gates of the Bamananika palace. Here, he was robed with five bark cloths, a lion skin, bracelets, a dagger, two spears and a shield, then he was carried, shoulder-high, to the palace where thousands of cheering and happy Africans started a party which would go on for

days. And the flames which burn at the palace gates to show the Kabaka is alive, were re-ignited.

Back in England there was a quiet period; nobody wrote and only a few sent photographs of the week's events. A letter did come from one of the elders, Muganda:

...you have deceived me, you didn't bring the actual body back. Not a single person was allowed to touch it according to Kiganda custom. We are not satisfied. Is my Kabaka still with you?

The people of Mablethorpe, remembering the Kabaka's visit shortly before he died, received permission to send flowers annually in remembrance. I had left my hat, coat and diary in Uganda, but the only thing which worried me was that my presentation antelope skins were missing.

Some of us remain doubtful that Freddie was not murdered, and we did all we could at the time to press for full investigation. Politically, subsequent events brought much change and misery to the people in Uganda, and its relations with Britain fluctuated. I knew little more than the papers told but my antelope skins, mislaid on the aeroplane, did reappear.

15

HESITANT COUNTRY-DWELLERS

In early 1974, with the work of the Carr-Gomm, Morpeth and other societies under way, I developed bronchitis and gout. As I'd coughed through every winter of our marriage Susan insisted I underwent a complete overhaul during the course of which shadows were found on both my lungs. Following one major and two minor operations tuberculosis was diagnosed and routine treatment prescribed: rest and antitubercular drugs. Since the early Fifties efficient preventative measures had brought about a sharp decline in infection from tuberculosis in the UK; fewer than half of one per cent of deaths were now due to "consumption" as this infection had once been known. This brought me little comfort as I lay in Lewisham's Grove Park Hospital and was given the choice of halving my workload or suffering the consequences.

(Later that year my tuberculosis was re-diagnosed as chronic sarcoidosis – the lung X-rays in both cases appear similar and some physicians believe the two are related – an uncomfortable but readily treatable condition.)

I went to a healing service which made me wish such things could be a normal part of worship and family communion. It seems natural to ask God for healing, whether physical or mental or emotional, and the result depends on His wishes and our efforts medically and by prayer; the laying-on hands, signifying a corporate action of healing by God and man, ought to be as common as giving communion from a chalice.

Over the next four months my only activity was to attend a Buckingham Palace garden party held within two weeks of my largest operation; the Not-Forgotten (an ex-servicemen's charity) party given annually the party given annually by the Queen offered all hospitals two places for old soldiers. From pyjamas to a smart suit, I, my confrere – a next door bed-mate – and our male nurse were chauffeur-driven in an Austin Princess from the hospital, via a detour around the sights of London, and received by a General who had served with me in the Guards Division; both he and Field-Marshal Templar were kind to me on my crutches. The Field-Marshal telephoned my old regiment to tell them of my illness and later wrote to wish me well. We enjoyed a good meal followed by music-hall entertainment in the party marquees but I was glad to return my hospital bed that night.

Convalescing at Mells

Our family holiday that year was spent at Mells, and when Susan and the children returned to London for the new school term I stayed on to convalesce and lay the foundation for two centenary preparations in 1978. One centenary was that of the Carr-Gomm name which had been promulgated by Royal Warrant in 1878. I wrote alerting the family and my brothers and I laid plans to celebrate in a subdued but seemly way; we had thought a family biography booklet, a medallion and perhaps a large gathering of our relations but, overtaken by some financial problems we could do none of them: instead, my brother Tony's wife, Jeannie, and a cousin made some centenary pottery for us. There were three Carr-Gomms in 1878, one hundred years later we numbered 19. I wondered if this was the average rate of growth of the human race or were we slow (or quick) in reproduction.

The last battle of the Zulu wars, the battle of Ulundi, was the other centenary I was keen to mark. Ulundi was the name of King Cetewayo's kraal but it was, perhaps, politically unwise in the 1970s to remind people of Britain's Colonial wars. Anyhow, since Susan and I were then living in Ulundi Road, Greenwich, we wanted to remember it; there was considerable local interest in marking the battle and a street committee took on the planning, although by 1978 we ourselves were now living permanently at the Stables in Mells.

I also spent my convalescence at Mells collating an anthology of poetry to use during Carr-Gomm Society evening house meetings and writing a biography (unpublished) of John the Baptist. I was intrigued to trace the connection between the Baptist and the St John Ambulance Brigade member, who takes his name. It was an interesting exercise as John the Baptist's life is not well documented.

There is a link between St John and a medical first-aider, for both are concerned with the wholeness of man; the Baptist through repentance and baptism leading to Christ and the St John Ambulance personnel who administers first aid within the framework of a religious order of chivalry. The Order of St John traces its story from 1099 in Jerusalem (which is near to the final burial place of the Baptist 600 years earlier) when the Knights Hospitalers became rulers of that city and of the countryside around it. This area, in the Near East, was named Palestine at the end of the First Crusade. From there, through Cyprus, Rhodes and Malta, the history of the Order was continuous through their creation of both Roman Catholic and

Protestant organisations – both religious and medical – which spread throughout Europe and to the USA.

11. Ceremonial procession, The Order of St. John, 1985

The research was an interesting and peaceful diversion for me. It was, however, interrupted by Susan ringing up to say a battle between two visitors had been fought in our house at Ulundi Road; the fight was a personal one between them, we only provided the battlefield. A jaw had been broken, police and ambulances had been required and there had been more than £400 of damage to our house. Needless to say this had some effect on those of the family – Susan and a relation, not the children – who were in on it. David, aged seven, who had slept through it, saw the wreckage in the morning and made Susan promise that the next time we had a fight in our house would we please wake him.

Family finance and property

That year (1974), Britain's economic crisis had complicated my own finances. In order to convert the Stables at Mells into a home I had had to borrow extensively from the bank and, at the same time, our family estate had recently branched into property development and found itself owning an expensive piece of land in Exeter which it was unable to re-sell. Mismanagement by the auctioneer did us out of an immediate sale and we went through too many years of painful exploration of the land sale market with mounting interest charges and no dividends being paid.

My brother Tony led us through this and other ventures and we learned the hard bargaining and ruthless side of speculative land exchanges. Both our architect and our lawyers were changed midstream and we took (and later dropped) legal proceedings against an estate agent. The unhappiness which such things engender should have been enough to keep us away from this sort of enterprise, however money became the pace-setter and we got so far involved with advisers and bank managers that going to court was the only way forward.

So there were no dividends, a heavy bank overdraft and, because of my illness, a cutback on my earning capacity, as well as the worry of maintaining our houses at Ulundi Road in Greenwich and at Mells. On top of this, the company which was supposed to be letting our tumble-down villa in Corfu had paid no income and then went bankrupt and, to complete the misery, the Isle of Wight house which I had inherited from my cousin would not sell because its sitting tenant refused to move. I was overdrawn and my income barely covered my bank charges.

To add to this, our expenses were increasing as the children grew older and successive appeal courts had turned down my temporary sarcoidosis sickness benefit claim from the DHSS because I had omitted to apply within the first six weeks of the onset of my illness and this deprived me of the first six months' benefit; later they paid benefit for the half-weeks I was not working Finally, the investments which Susan and I had were doing badly on the stock market and our income from them was therefore reduced.

With all these problems it made financial sense to sell a house: the larger one, Ulundi Road in Greenwich, would make most money but there was much against it, added to which moving isn't much fun unless you want to and most of the family didn't. But financial pressures over-ruled and our Greenwich house went up for sale in 1971. It took 18 months to find a buyer, by which time we were on the verge of changing our minds and put Mells up for sale instead. Then, while Susan was painting a wall at Ulundi Road a more than keen man turned up on the doorstep and without a survey was prepared to buy. The bank strongly suggested we accept his offer, which we did, and the Stables sale-board came down.

We also, in 1991, relinquished the small flat we'd kept since 1961 in a block called Orchard House in Lower Road, Bermondsey; we had given it over for a while to different people and to the Kabaka during the latter half of the Sixties. When we had first taken this flat my mother had been appalled, writing:

> About the Orchard House flat. It sticks out a mile how unpopular you will be – and Susan and the babies and dogs and the nanny – if you go and keep a *pied-a-terre* in Orchard House. Poor young people have been waiting in a queue to get a decent flat there for years – and you sail in. Privilege. Hateful word and for goodness sake think twice before you take it. ...I suggest an Evening Standard advertisement "wanted 1 large bed/sitting room with breakfast in someone's completely furnished house in the Kensington District to be kept for and used occasionally by lodger and his wife".

I hope and think we were right to go ahead and take the flat; in fact, because we were soon living in Chelsea, we rarely used it and, apart from Freddie (the Kabaka) who lived there during the latter part of the Sixties, it was generally filled with either friends or paying guests who wanted to live and work in the area – which would have pleased my mother.

Fond farewell to Ulundi Road

Before we moved to Mells in the late summer of 1975 we gave a farewell street party at Ulundi Road, and we went on holiday to Denmark. First the party: we built it around the annual Carr-Gomm Society garden-parties at our house, which customarily preceded the Society's annual Thanksgiving and Re-dedication Service at St Alphege's Church in Greenwich. As well as the gathering of the Society's people from Bermondsey and Thamesmead and those from the Morpeth Society and East Grinstead, we invited all our Greenwich neighbours and London friends. Susan produced more than 700 sandwiches and lots of people brought homemade cakes, jellies and the like.

But the special attraction of the day was the Corps of Drums of the First Battalion, Coldstream Guards, in full ceremonial dress, Beating Retreat and later, during the service, playing hymns. They even wrote a special anthem – based on "The Lord of the Dance" – and enjoyed playing it so much that, I believe, they now play it on guard mounting in the forecourt of Buckingham Palace. The Regimental Adjutant had written out of the blue that they had never helped the Society with a band and would one be of any use? I explained that the Society's next outing would be at our house, and this was the most wonderful result. The police closed the street so that we could use it as a parade ground and the weather was fine. I feared that changing in our garage and the comparatively small crowd size might depress the bandsmen but they showed no sign of it and this encouraged us enormously. It was a great occasion.

12. The Corps of Drums playing in Ulundi Road, Greenwich, at the Society's annual garden-party, 1975

Two days later we motored to Denmark for a two-week holiday. The journey out ended in a moonlit forest at what appeared to be a magic cabin; it just appeared. The cabin was warm, comfortable, big enough for all 12 of us – the family and five friends – and had electric light and all modern conveniences. There we stayed – looked after largely by our Danish hostess – and did little but bicycle the two miles through the forest to the beach where we lay and swam with hundreds of nudists. It took us a while to feel comfortable about this, but our clothes soon became superfluous and thereafter I ceased to worry about nudity, whether swimming at home or sunbathing.

We move to Mells

Back we came to the move and the enormous eruption that gave to our lives. Three large vans and six removal people took three days to do the job. They were new to the work but did it well; they slept on the sofas or in the vans and, at midnight, found welcome relief in our swimming pool at Mells.

Friends across the road kindly lent us a dry but uninhabitable cottage for our overflow furniture, and for months we were bringing from it packing cases, cellophane bags and furniture as our house shook down and we had the energy to sort things out. Doris Sayer and Anne Anson (a helper from New Zealand who had become a great friend and, later, my invaluable secretary) were our greatest helpers; Doris was a special friend who during and after the War had been housemother to 13 unparented children and, after they had grown up, she lived mainly with us.

13. Christmas card 1978. Clockwise from top right: Adam, Elizabeth, David, Harriet, Anna

The move to Mells meant the upheaval of new schools and colleges for the children. In London, all the children except Elizabeth had a great start at a nursery school run by Doris Sayer. But money, again, was the chief decider; I was happy with state education, Susan was not, so we compromised – a bit of state and a bit of private for each. Anna, the eldest, after public school at St Mary's Wantage went to Frome Technical College before starting secretarial work. Elizabeth had a free place at a direct grant school in Blackheath and, after our move and failing to settle at Bath High School passed some A levels at Queen's College in London (with financial help from her godparents) and went to Bristol University but left after a term to work in London with a view to trying social work abroad.

Harriet started in state schools then moved, thanks to a relation's generous gift, to a local prep school at All Hallows, Cranmore and then to Croft House in Dorset. Adam having started in a private school in London also went to All Hallows then Frome College. This left David, aged eight, at the village school in Mells; later he went to Oakfield middle school in Frome before joining the others at All Hallows and finally to Warminster School in Wiltshire.

At times some of them had coaching at home and, at one stage, we had five children at five different schools – and these were only settled after at least a dozen others had turned us down and we had decided against another dozen; all in all a very tiring business. Meanwhile, the children survived; we talked it over with them and they, though they longed at times for different schools, all studied hard and accepted their various situations.

The Carr-Gomm committee had remained wonderfully understanding and helpful throughout the eight months I was virtually out of action and when I returned to work in late 1974 I did so in a part-time advisory role. I was allowed to keep a bed and an office at 11 Morpeth Mansions and, each week, I would have an early-morning swim at Mells on Tuesday, catch the train for London and return on Thursday night in time for my next swim on Friday morning.

At first, I kept a collapsible bicycle in the Morpeth flat for getting around London but soon a one-time Grenadier, John Agate, took time off from his farm in Wiltshire and together in his car we were able to visit a large number of local societies. Anne Anson, by now housekeeper at 6 Wyndham House, Sloane Square, continued as my secretary and from her flat meted out endless generosity to everyone, including everyone in my family.

It was strange to find myself in the middle of London within three hours of leaving rural, Somerset.

Upheaval takes its toll
While the work of the Carr-Gomm Society continued, life at Mells was not without its problems. The conflict between two individuals sharing with each other within a marriage was rearing its head, and it was all the more difficult in a new environment among new people.

My tolerance and liberal thinking in many spheres were almost totally unsuitable and unjustified within the marriage and family relationships. Indeterminate views on capital and corporal punishment, euthanasia and abortion, let alone more abstract practices such as politics and ecumenicity, were of little help when it came to solving the problems that went with family life. Our decision to move out of London had produced completely new situations and we had all suffered.

Nevertheless, in my new study – part of the entrance hall – I was able to do some work at home. And in 1975 I also began visiting new Carr-Gomm societies which were starting up not far away, including Frome, Bristol, Exeter, Plymouth and Salisbury. And, in 1973, at the nearby village of Ammerdown, Raymond Hylton – who had been a soldier with me and visited us on various holidays – had been turning part of his home into an adult study and renewal centre. Here I had an interest, for apart from our family friendship with him and his wife Joanna, it was a lovely, peaceful place to which anyone could go for talks, meetings and worship. It also became through its Hugh of Witham Foundation, a nodal point for research and action in dealing with the emerging problems of rural development.

Some of the older children went off to boarding schools and had their own social lives, while the others needed time to settle in to life in the country. Animals, all-important to Susan, came and usually stayed: rabbits took over the garden; a parrot, too noisy in our small house, was sent to Birmingham and a tortoise that couldn't face Mells was last seen walking back to London. All were loved, but I was seen as the hard one – relieved when they went for it meant fewer messes, less worry when we wanted to be away from home and less money spent feeding and caring for them. Despite this, animals have always been and still are an essential part of our lives.

The early stage of our move to Mells was an exhausting and not very pleasant time. All the children were homesick, Harriet particularly. Elizabeth didn't like the daily bus ride to Bath for school and ran the car into the wall. Three times we had the petrol siphoned from our car at night, the local children over-flocked the swimming pool and our swinging rope was stolen – though returned eventually one night.

But people were kind: they washed our laundry for us, lent us mowing machines, gave advice about shopping, mended the children's bicycles and chopped wood for us. It was a hot summer and a warm autumn so nothing in the pile of furniture left outside turned to rust.

Our relations and friends came to stay and, when it all became too much, Susan retreated across the road to sleep. The Stables was half the size of Ulundi Road so we had many things to give away. Our two Carr-Gomm Society charity shops were useful beneficiaries and the smart Morpeth Society flats provided welcome walls for our larger pictures and space for some of our furniture. Homemade bookshelves took most of the books but a sale to friends before we left Greenwich reduced their number and made us more than £100.

Anna opened a bank account, rode a moped and took car-driving lessons; the rector taught Adam how to shoot a shotgun and David took a leading part in the village Christmas play. When we first moved, we sometimes read poetry as a weekly family exercise to practice elocution and being heard in the back row of an audience; this proved so unpopular that it didn't survive long. We didn't sing collectively much either; this also was something we had once done whenever we could, usually in the car and before lunch on Sundays – awkward for Susan trying to cook at the same time; Adam in particular had a good voice.

On our Danish holiday Adam had led the other children frequently singing "Joseph and the Amazing Technicolor Dream Coat". Popular songs on previous holidays had included "Rocking, Rolling, Riding" in Ireland, "Johnny Todd" in Corfu, "Two Little Girls in Blue" on the Isle of Wight and "Emerald City" on the road to Yorkshire. We seemed drawn to holiday on islands: Ibiza, Jutland, Sardinia, Corfu, the Isle of Wight, Inch Kenneth and Mull amongst them.

The family shakes down

When I became Secretary to Mells Charities in 1978 Susan eyed me with suspicion for she saw it as a sign of digging in and, with me away half the week and all the children's school runs and, usually minor, illnesses life at Mells had sometimes been stressed and moving on was suggested. But once the house had been altered Susan felt happier about remaining. We created open-plan living areas and had began a kitchen garden.

Throughout our marriage Susan had borne the brunt of everything concerned with family home-life – and still does. At home, she is boss and at times (short times) I have felt my role confined to rolling up toothpaste tubes, replacing lavatory rolls, cutting grass and putting out dustbins.

Despite fierce arguments, plans and counter-plans we have always tried to work together and within the family; and after our move to

Mells we needed to – finding schools, doctors, dentists and so on for everyone was no mean feat.

14. Family group at Mells 1981. From left: Adam, Susan, James Macdonald, RC-G, Elizabeth, Gloria Hughes, Anna, Harriet, Niall Hamilton, David

Harriet returned to Greenwich whenever she could, Anna and Elizabeth spun like tops, while the boys built go-carts and skateboards. Living in the Stables' confined space all this gave rise to irritation and aggravation; fury and anger erupted, usually to subside when the telephone rang and there was a rush to reach it first. Living together so closely also, led to idiosyncrasies spreading: when Anna decided to sleep on a pile of mattress, all the children's beds were discarded and replaced with the same; duvets replaced blankets and when Elizabeth preferred to sit on the floor, cushions replace chairs; Harriet stuck pictures on the ceiling above her bed, so her brothers followed immediately with posters and when David took up cricket, so did we all.

The children would criticise each other's manners, accents and friends but be intrigued by their motorcars; they showed little interest in their relationships with one another but were very much aware of someone trying to avoid doing the washing-up. They were rude about the untidiness of each other's bedrooms but blind to their own. Happily laughing but capable of crying, they all seemed to be totally different.

By landscaping the garden and putting in a swimming pool at the Stables we owed the bank £20,000 – and then we had built some sheds and made alterations. Within two years we had sold Ulundi Road, but with five children being educated we were living largely on credit and, despite selling the villa in Corfu and the house on the Isle of Wight, I was back into debt by 1979.

When asked about my hobbies I glibly say "golf, painting and backgammon"; I enjoy them all but do none enough for people to notice – I suspect they are really an insurance against retirement. However, I cast these hobbies aside when I discovered the fun of dry building with bricks oddities such as family trees, giraffes and pyramids and now our garden is littered with these, not generally admired, creations.

16

OLD FAMILY FACES

Within 3 years of finishing my first autobiography "Push on the Door" (1978) we had decided to leave Mells, but were in no hurry. We looked for a house in the same area which would combine traditional architecture with new gadgets – something I had seen work well in old Avignon and at Elizabeth's new home in Provence. So, to Bath. On 3rd February 1982 we slept our first night at 9 The Batch in the village of Batheaston – almost a part of Bath in Somerset. In 65 BC Horace, the Roman philosopher, wrote:

> This was what I prayed for; a plot of land not too large, containing a garden and, near the house, a fresh spring of water, and a bit of forest to complete it.

After selling the Stables and renting a small house "Little Claveys", also in Mells, for five months we had a little money in hand. But there were storage and removal bills to pay and by the time we had settled in at Batheaston a year later, I was just £4,000 in credit. Buying a new car hadn't helped us financially but by 1982 my credit rating had improved considerably thanks to some sales within the family Trust.

I felt the same about our new "plot"; though without a forest, it did have a very large Wellingtonia tree which we subsequently cut down.

Susan's personal money was used largely towards the children's education and for household expenses – a wonderful buffer for us and given gladly by her. Our financial fortunes continued to go up and down throughout the Eighties. In the middle of that decade I was the unexpected recipient of the not very valuable runt end of a long lease on some houses in Streatham. This had been left to me by an old lady in Hove who, approving of my work, had been generous to me in her lifetime. With the profit from selling this legacy I was able to make large alterations to our house in Batheaston, including digging into a bank to make a water-filled cavern, with murals by Niall Hamilton, in which we could swim. Buying the adjoining strip of land for this was worth it and brought us the "fresh spring water" of Horace's quote. To be free of debt was a great feeling, although the pleasure and privilege of owning this lovely Georgian house took time to absorb.

The house, originally the end cottage in a row, was built in 1650 then partly rebuilt in the Georgian era. It is now a Grade 2 listed building with a lovely view south down the river Avon valley. The air is said to be lethargic and warmer in the West – Harriet and I are particularly pleased with that.

15. 9 The Batch, Batheaston

Settling in

We were lucky with our builders; Bob Little and his team virtually moved in for more than two years in order to add extra rooms and a balcony, move indoor walls, uncover alcoves and invent clever, concertina-style and sliding walls and doors. The gales in February 1991 blew down part of the garden wall and on rebuilding Susan added three small ponds for gold fish; my contribution was a magic tap which didn't work for long.

The Moroccan-style courtyard with its well and waterfall we decorated with African masks, Jamaican plaques and Ugandan flags. And, above it, the kitchen garden became Susan's pride and joy – and a productive larder with help from Harriet and with one of Doris Sayer's children, Peter John Langley, providing both expert advice and skilled labour. Finally, with sewage pipes to look like Roman columns we built a see-through garage, called, for planning purposes, a "carport".

I hesitated to use contemporary and technical household inventions, Susan much more; she actively discouraged their use, once even putting "out of order", when it wasn't, on the dishwasher. Her enmity to the dishwasher remained acute and she told it many times and unsuccessfully that it was broken and didn't work. Both of us had whiffs of Victorian austerity but, still, we bought various gadgets allied to modern living. We had radio, television and subscribed to a weekly magazine for news summaries when we discarded newspapers.

Subconsciously influenced by wartime shortages and restrictions – five inches of bath water, rationing, blackouts – I wore free National Health shoes and Susan seldom bought clothes for herself. We bought from second-hand clothes shops and Susan tried, but failed, to wean us off butter and onto margarine; she bought over-ripe fruit and ignored "sell-by" dates.

We took part in the village barter system; we exchanged our magazine with another family's collection, swapped rhubarb for the safe storage of a moped, furniture for a bicycle lock-up and exchanged chocolates or wall-posters for the use of a car. It was and remains a lovely village in which to live – warm, friendly and welcoming. At Bath Abbey Susan sang the "Hallelujah Chorus" with a massed choir. She was always available for family, children and grandchildren, she looked after our animals, she coped with crises and was delighted that her cousin Bridget, married to our vicar, John Perry, also lived in the village.

Throughout the years an artist, Jeremy Church, almost enrolled as a family member, visited us often with his daughter Isabel. His death in 2000 was a great shock and sadness; he was settling into a comfortable house nearby and taking up work again on his paintings. After a church service, we held a family luncheon in the Batch for his family and his burial followed next day in Scotland.

Mary Pactus also *(Ch. 27)* visited us and afterwards wrote:

Dear Susan,

I want to thank you so much for the most pleasant – and restful indeed! – weekend which you as the hostess provided me so kindly with.

The Room I slept in was bringing back all sorts of good memories – from the way I used to entertain my own children to that fireplace! I used it late into the night, and early in the morning – just watching the flames from my bed, and feeling so good and restful.

The Family gathering around the big table was also something we used to have – very, very long ago – when I myself was a child, and together with my 4 cousins and their parents we all would gather around the table where Grandpa and Grandma were presiding. You see – it's all the same around the globe, and everywhere children –

who then grow into the adults – must have these warm memories within themselves. I do – thanks most to grandparents (maternal ones) and such memories help me to survive and to face unpleasant things when these surround me at other times.

Family matters

I was intrigued by the former workhouse in the village which stands beside the main London/Bath road; now converted into offices it must have been noisy and grim in its day. These deliberately formidable buildings – run with Spartan regimes in the belief that this would benefit their inmates – reminded me of the old cry we sometimes met in the societies; that offering residents security, warmth and comfort would discourage them from standing on their own feet. We, of course, never saw it like that.

Not everyone wants to live with others. Our son David, for example, enjoyed being on his own and would sometimes ring to discover who was at home so that he could take avoiding action if he chose. His reaction to "push on the door" was "don't push on the door, it's bolted" and when asked in company why he was silent he replied: "I've switched off ... that's what you can do in a family. You don't have to try or make an effort." He also put a message on the answer-phone: "if we like you enough, we'll ring you back".

During the Eighties Susan's sister, Jane Gibbs, often lived with us. She was in her mid-Sixties and after breaking her arm then her hip needed extra help over three years or so. Aged 14, Jane, Susan, their brother William and a cousin had been evacuated to Victoria on Vancouver Island in Canada where Jane had suffered a breakdown – their mother brought the children back to England – rendering her unable to live alone thereafter; she had lived in Society houses, hospitals, nursing and residential homes and, in-between she stayed with us or other relatives. In 1992 Jane settled into an excellent private, residential nursing home in Bath. Susan organised a surprise 70th birthday party for her there in 1994 which, after a week of fury about it, she admitted how much she had enjoyed it. She died at the end of that year and we felt her loss particularly deeply –she had become so much part of our lives.

Although not always realised, a want for regular periods of quiet coupled with my need to read books continued. This led to meditating weekly – in our local churches or sometimes at home, or in a field or a friend's "quiet garden" in nearby Wellow; twice in a church, next to our house the priest who wanted to lock up ordered me out and sometimes I was disturbed by talkative villagers.

Such meditative times fitted in between more frequent energetic periods: visitors came and went, I swam most mornings and some evenings and would walk the three miles into Bath. The only drugs I needed were occasional anticoagulants to ease my gout and aspirin and hot whisky and honey if I developed a fever. Otherwise, daily exercises and walks in the beautiful local countryside kept me fit. I recall on one of these walks a topless lady, sunbathing in her front garden, invited me in and, unfazed by her lack of attire, showed me around her house; all above board, I rang Susan from the bedroom telephone (the only one in the house) to ask the name of a cleaning lady for my hostess.

Our children and our children's children

ANNA married Piers Newton (a marketing director in publishing turned management consultant) in 1985 and they have four boys – Sam born 1987, Aubrey 1989, Ollie 1991 and Punch (Miles) in 1995. In 1992 they sold their house in Balham, London and lived with us at the Batch for nearly a year until they found the house they live in now – a converted stable complex in the grounds of a large house in Keyford, Frome.

Anna started a very good, and much needed, children's clothes shop "Ruff and Tumble" in Frome and by the end of its third year she was able to pay herself a small salary; the shop continues to gather strength and Harriet helps out when she isn't travelling or working elsewhere.

The greatest wonder was how Piers, commuting to London for work, managed to keep at it after the IRA blew up the building where he worked on the Isle of Dogs. In his spare time, he produced wonderful leaflets and pamphlets for family occasions.

ELIZABETH married Jeffrey Kime (an actor working mainly in France) in 1986 – the wedding was in Chantilly with the reception nearby at Charles Milbank's horse-racing stables. After six years, with them living mainly in the south of France, we all had the very sad loss when Jeffrey died after a long period fighting leukaemia. Elizabeth and their children – Matilda born in 1987 and Emily in 1989 – stayed in France and we all spent that Christmas there together.

In the mid-Nineties, Elizabeth sold her house in Provence, brought her family back to England and tried different homes in London in Courtfield Gardens and Philbeach Gardens before she settled more firmly in a basement flat in Queens Gate, South Kensington.

Curiously, when I was a child it was from our home in the same Courtfield Gardens that I used to walk to my pre-prep school, Collingham. At our home there with my brothers one Christmas, we played in a theatre company we'd invented for the evening. "The Courtfield Players" performed a playlet which our mother had written for us to keep us occupied and quiet.

16. Modelling with granddaughter Matilda Kime in France for German IKEA

On the spur of the moment in 2000, Elizabeth bought a holiday house in Saignon, Provence; it was near Apt and close to both her old home in Menerbes and our holiday house in Maubec. After leaving a job in interior design, she joined the almost complete list of family temporarily unemployed around the Millennium. After awhile, she became involved in organising other people's houses for Jadis, the very successful initiative of our old friends, Simon Creese-Parsons and Neil

MacKay.

Simon and Neil stayed with us sometimes at the Batch before also establishing themselves in the antique and mural decorating world with elegant homes in Bath, Normandy and New York; with them, often and to our extra pleasure, came Chinese take-aways and visits to the multi-screen cinema in Bristol.

Soon after joining them in 2001, Elizabeth married Robert Parker, a classic car driver and farmer. Gaining a 99-year lease on a ruined shell in Belgravia, they built a very good house there for Elizabeth – especially useful during term-time as, from it, Matilda and Emily could walk to their school, the French Lycee round the corner. Robert farmed in Oxfordshire and, in 2002, they produced their daughter Alice Daisy.

HARRIET, after some ill health in 1994, became matron at Ludgrove School and, later, head matron of school house at the Dragon School in Oxford. She had her own flat and, from it, successfully completed her Montessori teacher training and took up a school appointment in London in early 1999.

She and I happily chased and caught the sun in Sri Lanka in 2000; apart from visiting Candy and elephant orphans, Harriet did water aerobics and me Jacuzzis, all very peacefully. Wonderfully for me, she did all my typing while she lived at home, though Susan and Anna sometimes helped out with the letters.

In 2001 and 2002 Harriet explored teaching jobs in the south of Spain, sensibly attracted, again, by the sun. This gave us all the chance to go and see her in order to get a tan and have a holiday. For Susan and me this, also, gave us car rides across Spain and the opportunity to see more than Malaga and the south-west tip of the country.

ADAM advanced up the hotel management ladder and in 1991 bought his own house in Northampton where he was working. After he moved to Stoke-on-Trent in 1994 he took lodgers to pay the mortgage and lived instead in the hotel. Then other jobs followed and he toyed with his dream of running a pub until, in 2000, he sold his house and took over the running of a conference centre in Godalming, Surrey. This was followed by a trial run into Information Technology and a flat in London, while organising a delivery food service from Croydon.

Meanwhile a very great and happy excitement, both for him and for us, during this decade had been that he was re-united with his mother. After 31 years they met and in September 1996 we all had a most happy reunion party at the Batch with her, Sue Russell, her husband

and thereby Adam's stepfather, Harry, and their family.

17. Family group at Batheaston Sept 1996. Back row from left: Piers Newton, Aubrey Newton, David, Matilda Kime, Ollie Newton, Elizabeth (with Emily Kime behind), Sam Newton, Susan, Garry Russell, Suzanne Ballantine (née Russell), Sue Russell. Front row from left: RC-G, Adam, Anna, Harry Russell, Ian Ballantine

DAVID, temporarily, lived first in London's Soho and did some acting in local pubs, then in his aunt, Jane Gibbs's house in Hampstead; he gave up being a porter at the auction house, Christies, to buy and sell antique furniture on his own. It was at this period of his life that he parodied the verse, which read:

> My name is George Nathaniel Curzon,
> I am a most superior person,
> My cheek is pink, my hair is sleek,
> I dine at Blenheim once a week.

with:

> My name is David Culling Carr-Gomm,
> By nature I'm completely aplomb, [which, he'd checked in a dictionary, means cool and self-possessed]

My cheek is pink, my hair's not sleek,
I dine in Chelsea twice a week.

When his Aunt Jane sold the house he got rooms in Chelsea until, in 1997, he married Rosalind Holness. They and I made up our own service for this and it followed the Registry Office legal formality in the middle of Battersea Park. The service and wedding reception were held in a lovely house on the Embankment and the "church" side was one of commitment and thanksgiving, containing all the spiritual strength that we, as lay people, could express. It was held in the drawing room and was followed by lunch in the garden with for the younger guests, a dance on a riverboat. A great and loving occasion.

They started a home of their own in Rosenau Road on the south side of Battersea Bridge and Ros, the daughter of Bob and Mary Holness, continued her role as personal assistant to her father who had become a household name as host of the television quiz show "Blockbusters" and whose career as a television presenter had already spanned more than 50 years.

Meanwhile David, having secured a literary agent, left the antiques business and got down to trying to write books, biographies and fiction. When these literary efforts didn't immediately take off he became involved, through a friend, in an invention which manufactured the printing of coloured designs on leather; this opened up a new world of opportunity and by the end of 2004 had his own business "White Hide", a machine, and was open for business. While all this was evolving, in 1998 their daughter, Lily Bea, was born.

Holidays with Susan

So, by the mid-Eighties, with the children all doing their own thing, Susan and I were free to do as we pleased . In 1987 we holidayed in Israel with my old friend Christopher Bulteel *(Ch. 20)* as our guide, and accompanied by his wife, Jennie; we had all been together at the start of Abbeyfield. Christopher, formerly a Franciscan friar and Coldstreamer, who knew the bible story intimately was an expert guide. We also delivered a box of prosthetic eyes to St John's Eye Hospital in Jerusalem; as a Knight of St John I was judged a trustworthy courier.

In 1988 Susan and I visited Morocco with James and Juliet Ramsden and Michael and Lavinia (Juliet's sister) Hamilton. We stayed at Christopher Gibbs's (Susan and Juliet's cousin) house in the foothills of the Atlas mountains and explored from the snowy mountain tops to the warm sea on the coast at Essaouira (once

Mogador) and the capital Marrakech.

We also enjoyed other holidays including Saint Ives, Cornwall (1991); skiing near Geneva, and to Maubec, a village near Gordes in Provence where – with all the family and often also with friends – we spent every August from 1984-1989 with Elizabeth and Jeffrey. Susan and her sister Mary visited Venice in 1985 and, with their brother William and his wife Sally, the Canaries in 1992, and once she went to Oberamamagau.

Then, in 1991 the Ministry of Defence asked if I was related to Field-Marshal William Gomm who had been Commander-in-Chief in Jamaica in 1831 (150 years ago); I was, and the Jamaica High Commission in London invited us to attend celebrations of his time in office. On his arrival in Jamaica in the 1800s the Field-Marshall had found soldiers dying from sea-borne diseases on the beaches; the War Office in London turned down his request for funds to build barracks in the clear air of the mountains behind Kingstown, but he ignored this, built the barracks and the soldiers, moving up, stopped dying and the War Office paid up. It was this act which was being celebrated and Susan and I were royally-treated when we flew by helicopter to the Gomm Barracks in the Blue Mountains.

My elder brothers should have represented the family but they were understanding and as I had been in the same regiment as the old man the Jamaican government accepted that. While the air tickets were muddled and important meetings missed, the reality of a free dream holiday in the Caribbean took hold and, indeed, we were looked after wonderfully and enjoyed a memorable tour and stay.

17

RETIREMENT 1992

As I settled into retirement my life gradually came to encompass a semi-public element. Each year in the early Nineties I found myself attending a happy number, for me, of house openings, formal church services and giving talks; there were birthday celebrations or cake cuttings too, and I thoroughly enjoyed them. Such events were for the Morpeth, Carr-Gomm and other affiliated societies such as St Matthew, and they were all a chance to pick up with old colleagues and to meet new generations of people helping in our work.

Public engagements

Then, in 1996 Abbeyfield realised that they were into their 40th year and asked me to join in various acknowledgements of that. This was great but increased still more the number of events I was attending. I soon became too emotional in my short addresses at these Abbeyfield appearances and Susan advised that I mixed into them some more down-to-earth anecdotes; it was good advice, though most of my appropriate memories were very old ones and had taken place in dim-forgotten days.

A good thing about retirement is that you can bring into it as much as you choose of what is on offer. This meant that while most of my life was spent in peace and quiet and occupied with family, friends and home, there was still the added zing of official duties and responsibilities to enjoy.

At one stage I realised that I was involved with eight of our different societies' houses in Bath alone – three Abbeyfield, one Carr-Gomm, one Morpeth, three Solo – and this (though I never saw as much of them as I would have liked), coupled with my enthusiasm for the Pimpernel Trust (about which I write more fully at the end of this chapter) and Abbeyfield's 40th birthday celebrations pushed along my mini public life.

I had since 1997 conducted Matins on the first Sunday of each month in Mells and the ten-minute sermon during it had become a forum for lively debate, even if the congregation comprised only two people. A most difficult but honoured task was giving addresses at friends' funerals. I also once conducted a cremation for an old soldier in Bath and occasionally read the marriage banns. Twice I christened (named) a baby: first, with the tacit agreement of the Bishop of Winchester, back in 1960 the child of a Society worker in Bermondsey; the second in 1996 for Anna and Piers' fourth son Punch without the agreement, sadly refused, of the Bishop of Bath and Wells. The namings were lovely, simple services held in gardens, and for Punch's, Piers produced very smart-looking order of service sheets – then he and Anna provided lunch in their garden for all the guests.

Susan, meanwhile, became "Best Man" to Tudor Edwards when he married Penny Brakes who helped us in Morpeth; Tudor had also been to Stowe school so we all had lots to talk about.

An old friend contacted me keen to start up a Carr-Gomm Society in Frankfurt and Lillian Baynes, a Mugandan living in London called about starting up a house in Uganda; such calls were not infrequent and I was to make an introduction for a possible house in Jamaica and, through Mary Pactus and an Archbishop in the Russian Orthodox Church out there, develop a ground interest in starting in Georgia.

Susan, siblings and home-life

When I reached my 70 years in 1992 the family all, at last, had jobs and Susan was caring for elderly friends and relations which involved annual visits to Argyll (usually with Mary Macdonald or, sometimes, Heather and Bobby Miles) to look after an old friend there. After a while I used to accompany her and we would break our journey at a Bed and Breakfast in Cumbria; that was a big plus.

My brothers came and went, and in 1996 we held a celebration party at the Batch to mark our combined ages reaching 300. I'm sure we maddened each other at times; one or other refusing to come to this or that, declining to pay for the upkeep of our parents' grave (atheism) or thinking someone had been cut dead. If I can't remember anything more serious than that, then indeed, we were harmonious. Most of our tense feelings and disagreements over financial settlements of inheritance were not too long-lasting and support was unstinting for Eardley in his concentrated determination to prove to the world that Francis Bacon (1561-1626) wrote all the works formally attributed to Shakespeare and Cervantes. He wrote copiously on it and regularly produced an admired news-sheet covering the subject in detail.

At home, I filled my time happily with the computer word-processor, which I had been given on retirement in 1992; after teaching myself to type I wrote 750 meditations in the first few years. Photograph and scrap books, stamps, coins and montages also kept me happy and I collected, not many, model Churchill tanks and elephants – the name of my tank *(Ch. 4)* – and tried to build a model of our first Abbeyfield house in Eugenia Road, Bermondsey.

When asked about my hobbies I used to say glibly, "golf, painting and backgammon"; I enjoy them all but do none enough for people to notice and I suspect they are really an insurance against retirement. But I cast these hobbies aside when I discovered the fun of building with bricks oddities such as family trees, giraffes and pyramids and now our garden is littered with these, not generally admired, creations.

I amused myself building a castle (with a bit of help from Bob Little) big enough to sleep in. I also made a papier-mâché crane to keep the birds from pinching the fish in Anna's pond (sadly it didn't have the desired effect) and a pyramid.

Susan hinted that these were all built for my own amusement but, while she was quite right, they might be fun, too, for our grandchildren – a right-way-up family tree and a bad-spelling board would also be instructive for them if they ever looked at them. Over the years I have added a sheep made from a broken Homebase trolley and a so-called Japanese waterfall with recycled trickling water.

I had fun, too, creating a family museum – this had started life in the sheltered car park at Mells; dividing the contending contents into "history" and "contemporary" was easy but listing and arranging them was more difficult. Some of my social work gatherings and papers may help the Societies with which I have been involved when compiling their biographies.

Susan and I attended countless local gatherings and I attended the Order of St John, Coldstream or church and churches-together meetings. We also visited many of the societies with which we have connections around the country. If I had to be in London, friends – John and Angela Stitt or James Macdonald –kindly put me up.

Susan, sometimes, spent a week at a naturopathic clinic, either Enton Hall or Tyringham.

Ruby Wedding Anniversary

In private, my retirement included many special parties, the biggest, perhaps, was Susan and my Ruby (40th) Wedding party, which all the children gave us in 1997. It was held at the house, Marston Bigot near Frome, in which I had been stationed in 1942 when I joined the 4th battalion. Now back in private hands the house was ideal for the 200 of us who gathered to celebrate. Adam made a speech and his real mother and half siblings were guests.

A wonderful mix of relations and friends from various fragments of our lives had gathered: Nanny Coombes, two of my Mowden prep school classmates and some from Stowe, friends from the Coldstream and all the societies, friends from Mells, Batheaston and our earlier homes, some of my few relations and many of Susan's – it was also her 70th birthday.

The children also once gave us a combined birthday present of three nights in the Centre Parcs camp at Longleat and they brought the grandchildren each day to explore.

Our first holiday at home since marrying was in 1997 and we seemed to have all the families' animals lodging with us while their respective owners gallivanted off. Another year it was grandchildren who filled the house to the point that our bedroom had a nine-year old and animals squeezed into it.

By 1998 there was some erroneous thought in the family that I had a problem and it was diagnosed as one of being bored. To stop giving that impression – for it was untrue – I purposely diminished my wandering around the house and making cups of coffee (though not my washing up in the kitchen at which I was quite good) and stayed in the study. In fact I really stayed in the study because I thoroughly enjoyed my newly-given computer and recording everything for this book.

Poverty and homelessness prevail

I was told, once, that in newspaper cuttings I was listed under "squash" because in 1953 I had played in an army squash match. Later I learnt that elsewhere my file had been moved to "philanthropist" and this description was repeated in an updated copy of the Doomsday Book made in the 1980s – I then owned 1/4 of an acre in Greenwich.

Meanwhile, the issues of poverty and homelessness remained all too visible. On my return from a Regimental dinner at the Savoy in 1995 I passed no less than ten people sleeping rough on the 100-yard walk to my car; two thanked me for winning the war for them – they were polite and did not seem to be begging. To another beggar I offered a home for life instead of money but he didn't take me up on it. Others appeared to be interested in accommodation only if they could bring a wife and/or a dog with them. Such beggars, mainly, seemed to be middle-aged men. It was the same in Bath where the homeless had moved from tents and shelters beside footpaths into old barges on the canal; I counted 12 such homes during a short walk in 2004, all looked cold and uninviting.

Knowing of this homelessness and hearing from our residents, when they told of their former lonely lives, how it was compounded across the ages with bad language from 10-year olds and rudeness from teenagers, made me all the more conscious of how little we were doing in trying to help combat a subsequent sense of resignation and bitterness in society.

It showed me, too, how my life cannot be divided into two distinct parts, as I have done in this book. For me, my life, work, army and Uganda are all together on the same road.

This was illustrated when, in 1998, I removed a covering from a stone in Africa near Kampala and read inscribed on it the name "Abbeyfield" – it was the master-stone for a house they were going to build there. And, in London, well past my sell-by date, I sit with friends, and take part in meetings of the Pimpernel Trust.

This is an imaginative initiative by the Intelligence Services and Foreign Office to help and advise their former staff and agents on retirement issues. These men and women, in the open or under cover, have given wonderful patriotic service to our country and, usually from serving abroad, they have stories to tell, which, in general, they can't share in nostalgic, hazy chat with most of us; they have, therefore, in addition to all the common worries, this added communication hurdle to overcome. The one time leader of some of them, Colin McColl, had the brainchild and I am enormously admiring of the Government and Civil Service in fully supporting him.

18

UGANDA REVISITED

It was in 1971, when I had accompanied the Kabaka's body back to his homeland for a great and dignified state burial, that I last wrote with knowledge of events in Uganda. For the intervening 20 years I was in touch with developments there only by newspaper reports, letters and occasional telephone calls from friends. I did not visit it again until 1993. When I was invited to attend Sarah Kissosonkole's funeral in 1974 I was unable to go because at that time I was undergoing hospital investigations for sarcoidosis. Sarah had been the Kabaka's favourite wife and was mother of their sons Ronnie Mutebi (the new Kabaka and Ronnie Owen's godson) and Richard Walugembe (my godson).

Throughout the late Seventies and Eighties Uganda was politically unstable and violent: the rule of Idi Amin became horrific and life was no more secure with the return to power of Milton Obote. He, too, was eventually overthrown and the rebel leader Museveni (born in Burundi) assumed power in 1986 and gradually restored order and peace.

For the royal family, too, came a period of political reconciliation: Freddie's Will was honoured, his children were allowed their inheritance and they were assured of security within the country.

When Richard finished his education at Achimoto College in Ghana he went to work in New York while Ronnie studied law at Trinity College, Cambridge. They occasionally came to stay with Susan and me at home, and for a while Ronnie lived in the Morpeth Society flat at 11 Morpeth Mansions. I became Ronnie's second guardian – Ronnie Owen and his wife (Ardyne) being his joint first guardians.

In the early Eighties, when the boys' stepmother, Damali's home burnt down – thought by some to have been the work of government men – she fled Uganda and, for a time, I got her a room in a Morpeth Society flat in Holland Park. I then helped her move to Little Giddings, the community in Rutland, but she soon returned to Uganda, where, in fact, she was safe and lived a quiet, long life in a small house in the shadow of the Cathedral.

Other Ugandan visitors came and went: the young (and new) Omukama of Toro worked for us for three months in Bermondsey; the

Toro daughters, Elizabeth and Mabel, stayed with us periodically at home or in Morpeth; President Lule, an older statesman judged too honourable to remain in command of warring factions in Uganda was another visitor, and we were also host to various Ugandan politicians, elders and to Freddie's relations.

In 1991, when Susan and I were settled in Bath, we cleared out and gave up the lease on the flat at Orchard House in London where Freddie had died. We brought the contents back to Batheaston and stored Freddie's memorabilia in the cellar – in 1993 to be joined by Ronnie Mutebi's belongings when he became Kabaka and ceased to see London as anything but an occasional place of retreat. The bulk of Freddie's possessions from his flat were returned to Uganda in the late Nineties and in 1991 Richard Walugembe took some pieces away for him and his brother to look through.

However their country was still not totally a quiet and happy land. In 1991, the Carr-Gomm Society in London housed a refugee from Uganda who told me, slowly, of the tribal persecution going on in the north and east of the country. He had fled and was now studying computer technology at a London polytechnic and being financed by DHSS benefits; he planned to complete his studies here then return to fight with the rebels if there was anything left to fight over. The warfare continues on through 2004 but I hope that this man, learning the true facts, found a more peaceful and positive role to play on his return

The Baganda invites ...

In April 1993 we heard from Mark Amory that Ronnie Mutebi's Coronation was to take place in Kampala on 24th July 1993. In 1971 I had seen Ronnie being taken through to Ssabataka or head of the family – all but the final 12th step of the ritual to Kabakahood *(Ch. 14)*. Now the Kingdom was to be restored and the 12th step, kingship, would be taken.

Susan and I held in storage two of his royal kanzus which we handed over for him to wear on the day. We couldn't afford to go to the Coronation but in mid June the Uganda liaison-team in London told us we were invited by the Lukiko (Buganda Government) and Bataka (Head of Clans) who would pay our expenses; we accepted joyfully and Susan began to worry about the heat, inoculations and what to wear. Sadly Ronnie Owen was unable to go, on medical grounds, and he particularly should have been there for he was both godfather and guardian to Mutebi.

On 13th July Susan and I drove to London for the flight next day then had a message that the Coronation was cancelled. The High Commission knew nothing but we heard that it had only been postponed. Susan decided to transfer her ticket to the later date. I, however went, Coronation or no Coronation. Parliament had passed the Resolution for the restoration passage for the Kabakaship and the postponement was, therefore, only for a week.

As the sun rose, I was driven the 20 miles from Entebbe to Kampala. The journey and the city were immensely depressing: the main roads were rutted, buildings were scarred with bullet holes or derelict; refuse was piled up on the streets and there were armed roadblocks against bandits. The sight of such ruin made me want to cry and brought home, at last, the truth of, and reason for, the title of Freddie's autobiography "Desecration of my Kingdom" (published 1967). Nevertheless, in the seven years since out-and-out dictatorship much had been done and it wasn't fair to criticise, neither was it right to be nostalgic about the "good old days". So I tried to congratulate on what had been done and join in the happiness for the forthcoming celebrations. I quickly got into the fun of it.

The Baganda put me up in the most luxurious hotel, all expenses paid. I told my hosts to forget me and concentrate on the Coronation plans and I, therefore, feeling lonely without a single plan or role to play, took time to adjust. For six days I kicked my heels.

Ronnie Mutebi's Coronation 1993

With the Coronation set for July 31st Susan arranged to fly out. By the time she arrived I had walked the dust-red roads and seemed to be the only white man doing so. I felt happy and at ease amid endless sightseers; people crowded round me in the town and when told, in Luganda, who I was they shook my hand – it was very moving and I felt totally inadequate. I wanted to be a "mukopi", an ordinary person, but wondered if I could be after experiencing the warmth of people who seemed generally to know my, and Ronnie Owen's, name and were so grateful for all they said we had done for Mutesa and Mutebi. People called in to the hotel to shake hands and a ceremonial staff officer came to consult me over the programme of Coronation events.

Then the week of ceremonies leading up to the Coronation began – dinners, church services, a regatta and more – during which me and Mark Amory, who had been Mutebi's tutor, enjoyed a long, relaxed lunch with him at his "hide-away" bungalow near his grandmother's home at Banda. Susan arrived and quickly met old friends and added new ones. In a whirl of activity we swam, walked, attended receptions and other events and sometimes supped with Mark and journalists working for UK newspapers.

The morning of July 30th was devoted to re-opening the Bulange (the returned, restored seat of Buganda administration), the first opening of which I had attended in 1956. In the afternoon we made a formal visit to the St John's Ambulance Brigade as I am a Knight of the Order; Susan didn't like playing the consort part but did it beautifully. One of the teenaged recruits wrote afterwards adopting Susan as her mother. St John's also let me sleep in their tent on Buddo Hill the night before the Coronation; seven of us including Mark spent a very comfortable night – on beds, not stretchers.

Coronation day, 31st July, following a glorious dawn, comprised seven hours of well-ordered ceremonial which included Ronnie being covered with four bark-cloths, one calf skin and a leopard skin and, atop his head, a crown. We had excellent seats for both the main parts of the ceremony and took lots of photographs. A little rain fell which was, we were told, an omen of good fortune and a blessing by the gods.

Mark made a symbolic presentation of a ring and there were presents from, and cheers for, the Owens. Princes, the Ugandan President and Ministers and other dignitaries numbered among the guests. We shook hands endlessly as I was the only one in Morning Suit and medals. That evening we attended a small cocktail party for the Swazis, and a big reception for the President and all the invited guests at the morning's ceremonies; the Coronation had been a great and wonderful success.

The following day Susan and I said our farewells to Ronnie Mutebi; he was in great form and had enjoyed his Coronation. At the great feast he gave to his people we sat with the Royal Family for the opening meal, but the party went on for a week.

On our last day in Kampala we went to the Kasubi Tombs to see the burial plots of Richard Walugembe (my godson) and Henry Kimera (Freddie's brother); both had died recently in England. Our visit ended in our usual flurry; we lost the hotel safe key and an air ticket was missing. But we had supper with Joyce Mpanga, her family and Mama Rose, and this was the happiest ending to our extraordinary and wonderful visit.

A dream comes true: Carr-Gomm family holiday 1998

For a number of years my thoughts of the whole family seeing Uganda had grown. It was selfish of me but Susan warmed to the idea and we managed to organise it. The first letter went on January 26th 1996 to a Travel agent in Kampala:

> I have a dream, which I have discussed with Ronnie Mutebi. It is of bringing Susan and our family out to Uganda for a holiday. I don't see it happening this year but, when it does come off, I suspect it will include friends.

Making contacts and plans continued, spasmodically and inconclusively. Ronnie Mutebi and I talked and so it went on. Eventually in March 1977, Jim and Barbara Kiwanuka, helped us enormously and kindly – much needed since many, including the British High Commissioner, hadn't answered my letters asking for guidance. Ronnie, however, asked for our dates and wrote very encouragingly. The following is an extract of the letter I wrote to the family on 12th May 1997 (big plans are best on paper):

> Dear all of you,
> ...we're still vaguely thinking about a three-week holiday in Uganda in the summer of 1998 (the rainy period is December to April). Any chance of you coming too?
> It will entail travelling over a large part of the country, including the main towns, Game Parks, jungle, the Nile, forests, lakes, the Mountains of the Moon (Ruwenzori) ...
> ...What do you think? I suggest grown-ups only? and the more of us i.e. friends, the cheaper it would be; we could be a party of about 20.
> Anyhow no plans are needed till Christmas so we could all discuss it then – i.e. whether a two-weeks holiday (safari!) isn't better (cheaper) than three, whether to stay put in one place longer, whether to take children, what, who to see etc. – so do think about it.

They all agreed that it was possible and we began to plan. They wanted the grandchildren to come too. The Kiwanukas came to the Batch for a couple of weekends and we to them and they did valuable spadework for us.

Ros fell pregnant and that, unhappily, meant she couldn't travel but David hoped that he could for a short while. With six weeks to go before take-off there was still, much to do. Air tickets, though, were paid for and Ronnie was ever hopeful of all being organised. We had our inoculations, but with no hotel confirmations, and so no swimming pool, Harriet bought a travelling paddling pool – just in case. Uncertainties were not dismissed by such replies as 'No worry', 'yes please' and 'Have a good stay'.

Piers and Anna took on house planning and Adam booked his flight. It looked like we were going to be about 15 including six grandchildren.

Political reports coming through from Uganda were gloomy: no one goes there, no tourists, turmoil all around, pictures of starvation on the border with Sudan and executions in the southern State of Burundi, Zaire in revolt. Only Ethiopia and Eritrea were worse: 80 students had been killed by rebels in Uganda, there was a move to confiscate tribal lands and there had been an attempted assassination on the President. We gathered for a despairing weekend but plans went ahead and so the journey started.

Full itinerary

On arrival in Uganda in 1998 we were swept past security to a warm welcome by the Baganda Government and court officials, and a cup of tea. Then a convoy of five cars, with security vans back and front, took Susan and me to our hotel, the Speke, and the rest of the party to private houses. I went for a walk before bed and was spoken to by six prostitutes. All the family settled into their households; our party comprised Adam, Piers, David and Finnian Fitzpatrick, Anna, Elizabeth Harriet, Matilda, Emily, Sam, Aubrey, Ollie and Punch. A strike made traffic more chaotic than ever and we saw desperate poverty all around.

The trees at Buddo and the ruins at Mengo were magical, the latter more so when a saxophonist played "God save the Queen" and the lovely Buganda national anthem for us. The days began to melt into each other and events – some most sad – stick out: the dead boy hit by a vehicle on a busy roadside with distressed silent crowds standing by him; the dignity of Sarah's grave (soon beautifully covered with marble) on her family estate and the lost quiet atmosphere of the neglected areas for other graves; the peaceful Gandhi statue where the Nile runs out of Lake Victoria and Punch being sick over patient Harriet in a Chinese restaurant.

In a shaking speed boat we went to Bukasa Isle in the Ssese Islands where we received a warm welcome from the owner. We bumped along in a jeep, past monkeys and deer, to his house and glorious sunset gave way to candles and a thunder-and-lightening storm which brought Matilda into bed with Susan. The return trip to the mainland took five hours instead of the one going out: the boat ran out of fuel as darkness fell, but a passing container carrying spare fuel hove to and lowered cans of petrol to us.

Everyone except me went on safari at Murchison Falls in the NW; some travelled in a bumpy little aeroplane. I seemed to spend the three clear days I had while they were away on the veranda/pavement – a bomb had destroyed the hotel lounge – receiving unexpected visitors. I read no more than two pages of a book at a time and did no painting; just talked with old friends and reminisced. A man who had come to us in Greenwich after 20 years in prison came to see me, and a courtier who had been a diplomat on the dais when President Sadat had been assassinated in Cairo in 1981.

I became an honorary Mugandan by being made a member of the Buttiko (Mushroom) Clan. I am the only white member and now have an African name "Wagaba" (a giver). At the model village of Bukalango I formally named an Abbeyfield Community Centre, due to be built about 40 miles north of Kampala, and laid the foundation stone. Ronnie Mutebi, Susan, me and the family members who had not yet had to go back to work, were met by cheering school children. There was a reception for the opening ceremony and welcoming and official speeches were made, then special songs, traditional rites and abeyances with tribal dancing for men and women.

18. Laying foundation stone for Abbeyfield Community Centre, Bukalango, 24 July 1998. With, from left: Emily, Sam, Ollie, Aubrey, Ronnie Mutebi

The model village is a brilliant Kabaka Foundation initiative since, because Ugandans think it disgraceful to put their old people into a home, this building will be non-residential although "things might change," said the Foundation at a meeting in London.

By the end of the second week we were running out of steam, so the children stayed at home all day and played in the garden while the grown-ups got a rest to feast and jaunt without them. With pressure gone, all ages eased into neutral and had an early bed.

We were later the guests at a Royal reception (Buganda and Toro) to say farewell and "Auld Lang Syne" was sung to us. With tribal and Western dancing and drumming beside the lake, it was an unreal, perfect evening. About 60 people attended and there were birthday presents for Sam and Aubrey. We gave a lunch party to all those who had given us hospitality, but we had had so much more in happiness and fun.

However, to keep us on our toes, we had one party with people we didn't know and we might easily have been kidnapped. It was in a village hall near a lake and with crowds of children and teenagers dancing, singing and beating drums. It was, almost, the best evening we had spent together; we danced traditional dances with skirts put on us, played musical instruments after Susan and I made speeches. When the lights blew all was pitch dark, but the party went on.

The return flight – Entebbe, Nairobi, Muscat, Doha, Heathrow – took nearly 24 hours but, exhausted, we staggered through the airports and were home by mid-morning. The whole family had been superb throughout and had much enjoyed the holiday; they'd made friends and contacts and took real interest in the country. The dream for the family to visit Uganda had become reality and was complete.

Mutebi's wedding 1999

The political situation in Uganda remained unstable and often violent, and with incursions in the south from Burundi and rebel involvement in the Congo, Uganda had a grim start to 1999. There were also reports of ambushes and deaths of white people in a gorilla camp in the west and civil war close to the Sudanese border.

In March of that year Ronnie Mutebi rang to tell us that he was going to announce his engagement to Sylvia Luswata, a Muganda and (necessarily) not of his (the Monkey), clan; she was resigning as a financial adviser to the UN in Washington and their wedding would probably be in August. It was joyful news and we were invited to the wedding.

Susan and I flew out on 23rd August. First, I passed out from exertion and didn't move from my Speke hotel bed for 24 hours. Then we sat for a week on the Pavement outside our hotel – years-old bomb damage to the lounge was yet to be repaired – and talked with Mark Amory, who had come with us, members of Ronnie's family and many other welcome visitors.

Next came visits to Ronnie's palaces: we saw him in his new, main, family one at Kireka; the wedding reception was held at Mengo, the traditional palace of his father and forebears, and we went to Buddo where the Coronation, traditionally takes place.

A selection of memories flood back reminiscent of the happily out-of-control, away-from-planning time we had spent there, including paperboys trying to sell us newspapers when our photographs appeared in them, autograph hunters, faces which brought back Mutesa memories, the new Equestrian Centre and Retreat at Munyonyo on Lake Victoria and changing restaurants between courses at lunch or supper parties.

We travelled to Ronnie's wedding on 7th August with Mama Rose; she was acting Queen-mother on the day and got us through the crowds before going off to her Royal duties. The service was lovely – traditional, with beautiful hymns and anthems and afterwards everyone joined Ronnie and Sylvia, now Nabagerika, or Queen, at a reception for more than 2,500 people; dancing, drumming and great goodwill and exuberance stretched into the early hours.

Friends and visits filled the days which followed, we met many new and young faces including Clement, First Prince of Zulus. So endless, natural, easy talk on subjects as wide-ranging as politics, philosophy, agriculture, Shakespeare, spies and life spans (theirs is 45, ours 82) then farewell and home to the Batch.

In 2001 Sylvia, the Nabagerika, brought their daughter, Sarah Katrina – who had just been born in London – down to Batheaston. Ollie and Punch came over for a party since it was close to both Punch and Katrina's birthdays. The following year Jjunju, Ronnie's eldest son, joined Monkton Combe School and, as we were his guardians, he often stayed with us at Batheaston whenever there were school breaks.

HOME AND DRY ...

In mid-1998 I had written to the Abbeyfield and Carr-Gomm directors saying that I felt need of a very part-time personal assistant; they, wisely, didn't reply. I was still hearing from various societies and that I much enjoyed.

In 2003, when I repeated my *cri de coeur* for secretarial help, the directors agreed to it and that encouraged me to begin sorting out memorabilia and think how best to dispose of it – to the societies or the places involved, to a university storehouse, the family or the dustbin? Susan, Anna and Harriet, being near to hear this *cri*, helped me hugely to sift through it all.

The television and the computer were, often, a distraction from strain. By 1997 my word-processor was replaced by a brand new computer with internet, fax and email, all of which entailed endless, usually futile, telephone calls to helplines. After three years I added a scanner – a sign of confidence – but when further updated that year my (and Harriet's) life was disrupted for weeks with all the machines going wrong. I suffered slight withdrawal symptoms and it was a salutary lesson on how technically dependent we had become; gentle friends, usually, restored technical peace.

As the Millennium turned we thought again about moving house – obviously to something smaller, but should it be with Anna and Piers who perhaps wanted something larger elsewhere, on our own and near Bath, or back in Bermondsey? We considered numerous options and looked around but eventually the idea was delayed. Instead, our builder, Bob Little, once again came and made some alterations to the Batch: new carpets, fresh paint and an update on the museum shed allowed us to stay put and put our search on hold.

Then on 1st March 2002, Susan and I embarked on a two-month tour for Abbeyfield in New Zealand, Australia, Canada and the USA *(Ch. 24)*.

In any reflective speech I, often, find myself starting: "The road on which you start your journey is the one along which you travel ..." It seems to have been like this for me several times outside and inside social work. In 2000, for example I took a party on a tour of Warminster Barracks – pure nostalgia for me since it was where part of my army road started in 1942 and here I was, 60 years later, further along the same road with our grandchildren.

On the subject of roads: I was driving my nearly-new car, alone, to St Albans for a friendly talk with Abbeyfield on January 14th 2003 when I hit a bollard at Brent Cross, overturned on the hard shoulder, and was suspended inside with my head in a pool of blood – luckily no-one else was involved. I managed to free my safety belt and passers-by pulled me clear and gave me a drink and chocolates. I was also able to give the police telephone numbers for Susan and the address I had been on my way to and was taken by ambulance to the Royal Free Hospital. I spent the next 18 hours undergoing various investigations in casualty and a little stitching on my head and a very stiff neck was the end result. David and Ros took me back to their Battersea home the following day then Susan, who had been in Wales drove me gently back to Batheaston. Shock and whiplash could sort themselves out there.

Home nursing, swimming, physiotherapy and time were the cure. While Harriet continued to help me with letters, Anna came over regularly from her busy home and shop life in Frome to deal with ongoing business matters and generally sort out my desk and files – long overdue.

Twice I failed a driving test and so my licence was withdrawn; they said I lacked adequate "perception", which meant I cut corners and drew up too sharply at traffic signals. The car was pulped and I became dependant on public transport and, mainly, Susan. She was wonderful about this but, in becoming the house chauffeur, she was taking on an awful lot. Harriet helped whenever she could while living at the Batch; the societies were generous when they heard about the problem and I did much more walking.

To cheer me up at the end of the year came the Beacon Society, a newly-formed charitable Trust, whose aim is to encourage individual contributions in charitable and social causes. They gave me a Highly Commended Certificate in the category of Lifetime Achievement and it came as a complete surprise. I was thrilled and, since it gave rise to some local publicity, I had occasionally to try and explain why on earth it had come about; people were kind and understanding.

2004 was heralded for me by a night in our local Bath hospital having a throat blockage cleared. Two months later I again suffered choking and became very breathless but this time it took eight days with an oxygen mask in our Royal United Hospital to sort out. However the hospital and our village surgery treated me brilliantly and kindly. To pass the time convalescing at home I was given some tree trunks and tried my hand (dismally) at carving and writing awful doggerel which included:

> In hospital I breathless lie
> But Susan, bless her, comes to try
> And make the nights and days less dry.
> She does it with a brilliant thought
> That what I'd like's a glass of port.
>
> A gift it'd been from Jennie B,
> Who, with a pancake, came to see
> What all this breathing fuss could be.
> A winking nurse just turned her back
> And let me drink a healthy whack.

PART II – THE SOCIETIES
First house for the lonely in Bermondsey; the societies: Abbeyfield, Carr-Gomm, Morpeth, St Matthew Housing, Byker Bridge Housing Association, Richard, Solo, Solon

Part I describes in detail what brought me to my decision to resign from the army and begin my work with the lonely in Bermondsey in September 1955.

20

WORK BEGINS IN BERMONDSEY 1955

Bermondsey is now part of the London Borough of Southwark. In September 1955, when as a bachelor I moved there from Chelsea Barracks, it was a Borough in its own right, with a resident population of 55,000. On the south bank of the Thames, between Lambeth and Deptford, and opposite Stepney and Limehouse, its north and south boundaries are the river and the Old Kent Road. It contains one end of London Bridge, Guy's Hospital, Southwark Cathedral and Surrey Commercial Docks (now closed) and, while having neither theatre, cinema nor bookshop, there were and are a lot of churches, chapels, pubs and betting shops.

The whole idea of living in Bermondsey was that I should get right away from the life I had known. For the first two months I didn't go out of the district and kept no diary of any sort; I merely had an empty calendar on the wall on which I noted down days when I went to the public baths or had to have my laundry ready for the bag wash to collect. There wasn't a single social engagement of any sort.

I felt I could not do anything unless I completely identified with the people I was trying to help – lonely people, including the elderly, within a residential street community. To achieve this is perhaps impossible but I believed I could come very near to it by living in the same conditions and circumstances as them.

Home-helping

I took a bed sitting room in Abbeyfield Road, and on my first evening bought a typical Bermondsey supper – peas pudding. Next morning, Miss Monk – Bermondsey's home help organiser to whom I had applied earlier for work – took me on my first home help job. With my newly-bought pail, scrubbing brush, apron and soap she demonstrated the art of scrubbing floors. She gave me a time-sheet, explained how to fill it in and left me with a list of people to visit during the coming week. I got down to work and to living.

On October 24th, a friend in the Coldstream, Quartermaster Arthur Ramsden, wrote from Chelsea Barracks:

Dear Richard,
 I thought it only right in these hard times to help you out in your present difficulties and so, could you come along and scrub a couple of floors in my Quarter, they are bloody filthy (I purposely made them so), and should tax you to the utmost.
 I will give you union rates of pay plus a break for Tea at approx 10.30 hrs, possibly you may get a glass of Red Wine, but only if the floors are spotless.
 Joking aside Richard you certainly shook the Officers of the Brigade. It's a certainty your story will never be published in the Battalion War Diary, but, nevertheless I still will have conversation with you.
 Bye for now, and remember Union Rates.

On the other hand, a Rotherhithe woman stopped me in the street and said, forcefully, that she and others were disappointed in me. They expected "leaders" from the better-educated classes and especially from the Brigade of Guards and seeing me scrubbing and home-helping was a letdown.

It was strange in those first two months to have no plans or engagements – nothing to do other than home-helping. It wasn't depressing and the outlook wasn't bleak; on the contrary, I felt that I had arrived and had come to peace and safety. From the time I first moved there I always felt happiest and healthiest in Bermondsey, that poor, residential area on the South Bank. I was there to stay. I was not excited so much as relieved. I didn't know the future, or mind.

On my second day in Bermondsey I bought a bicycle, for it seemed cycling would be the easiest way to get around. I bought a lady's one because it was much cheaper; this was important for, anticipating my inadequacy, I was not yet being paid to be a home help.

One of the first people I visited in my new unpaid employment, was a man of 89. The door of his room had been jammed shut that morning and his landlady, having failed to open it, had called the police. They found him on the floor where he had been all night. The windows didn't fit the frames and the draught in which he had been lying was considerable. A doctor diagnosed a stroke and put him back to bed. Despite his six sons and four daughters living in the neighbourhood, only one daughter came to help but, together, she and I looked after him.

He was a plucky old man but couldn't do anything for himself. He fell out of bed several times and had to have all his personal needs attended to. Later, his speech began to ramble and, with his family still declining to help, I persuaded the doctor to admit him to the local hospital, St Olave's, where he remained comfortable and well looked after for the few remaining months of his life.

I went to see an old woman when, by chance, it was raining. My job then was to spend the day with pail and mop, soaking up the water as is seeped through the cracks in the street door before it flooded the passage and her room. The old woman had given up; she said that life was too much of a struggle anyhow.

Another home help and I made a routine call on an old man who had been on a long holiday. We were expecting to do a tidy up. He welcomed us and gave permission to clean. My colleague took her scrubbing brush to the kitchen while I worked in the living room and bedroom. The dust had to be washed off it was so ingrained and, unlike normal dust, wouldn't brush away and shovels full of muck had to be swept up before the floor could be scrubbed. Our host was quite resigned about it, saying: "You must expect these things when you're as old as I am". He was 78. Eventually his home looked better and we left promising to come back the following week. His neighbours had done nothing and his family did not live close by.

A handicapped couple I home-helped for were unable to move beyond their bed and sitting-rooms. They had completely talked each other out but when I paid my weekly visit, they talked to me, incessantly and often at the same time.

Very few pensioners were ever grumpy and most were grateful to us home helps, for they depended on us to keep their homes clean; this was encouragement enough for me to keep going. Little things such as clean walls, a smart grate, a scrubbed floor or a tidy entrance made all the difference, and they were easy things to do. Despite their limited means, my hosts invariably offered me a cup of tea, a cigarette or a peppermint while I worked. My nastiest cup of tea was brewed with the tealeaves added to the cold water in the kettle and all boiled together.

I know now what I didn't know then; that far from being peculiar to Bermondsey, such struggle and loneliness was, and is, typical of abandoned or uncared for elderly, infirm and handicapped people all over the country. I soon realised that the state of resignation I so often encountered was brought about not by material worry, but by their acceptance of sheer and utter loneliness. So many people lived on their own, day after day, week after week, and the home help's visit was the only time they had the chance to meet and talk to anyone.

Just after the war about 80% of the houses in Bermondsey were owned and run by the Council. Though I hadn't thought much about it, conditions were worse than I had expected. When I had visited the area in my army days I must have been shown the better homes, prepared in advance for my visits and, anyhow, I never got far beyond the main parlour.

Cleaning houses, room by room, showed me how run down was the property and how dirty much of it had become. I enjoyed cleaning for I liked seeing the results of my labour – although a large, filthy, bare floor waiting to be scrubbed did make my heart sink.

I had been at my labours for only a few weeks when the press became interested in me. My name had come up at an open London City Council (later Greater London Council) committee meeting. Because I was working as an unpaid home help and this was unconventional, it had to be cleared – and it was – by County Hall. Because my case, among other business, was debated in public a reporter had picked up on it; the only male home help in the country was, it seemed, newsworthy and there was a flood of articles in newspapers and periodicals, not only in England but as far-afield as Australia, Germany, Austria, Canada and Switzerland.

Public reaction to these reports was sympathetic and I received many encouraging letters as a result. And, while there were some who wrote in a roundabout way suggesting marriage, only a few were wholly dotty, and none were rude. The only sad letter came from an elderly relative, who said she: "hoped I'd be feeling better soon and would return to London to do some decent work".

The press might have easily ridiculed my situation – I was certainly embarrassed at being photographed from all angles scrubbing floors. However, the journalists seemed to take their lead from the original article in the *South London Press*, which had been a kind one.

My family became concerned about this publicity – the family name and our estate in Bermondsey was in the spotlight and they didn't like it. A family conference was held in my little bed-sit. Roderick could see no harm in it, but there was much argument from the others. It was after all their name, too, which was being bandied about and it could affect their businesses and friends. My family, quite rightly, wanted to discuss the implications and, happily, our meeting ended amicably; perhaps they accepted that there was nothing they could do to dissuade me.

Some of my friends thought I was crazy to have become a home help. They thought there must be something wrong with me – that I had been jilted, or become a religious maniac, or that I was doing this work to redress some guilt about coming from a "landlord" family. They were mistaken. I was doing something quite ordinary that anybody could do if they felt as strongly about it as I did. So, I continued to home help and after a couple of months established myself as one of doubtful though improving efficiency. As a home help I saw, every day, the neglect and loneliness of those whose homes I cleaned.

After a year's hospital treatment for tuberculosis, a 65 year-old man had been driven back to his flat for a weekend by one of his sons. When I visited next day I found his bed wringing wet, unchanged since he had gone into hospital. Too weak to fix it, the man had spent the night in a chair. His other son, living in the next borough, did not visit his father at all during the weekend: "You can't expect more when you get old," the man said, "the young have their own lives to live."

A woman aged 85, living on her old-age pension in a Council flat, had given up any idea of seeing her married son and grandchildren. She told me she had seen them five years ago but: "they've got a car now and have gone all posh. They don't like to be seen around a place like this."

Identifying the lonely

By autumn of 1955, I had begun to get an inkling that something, and not something material or financial, was missing in the lives of those in my meagre care. I had faith that something would come out of quietly searching. Squalor and poverty were obvious enemies. In Bermondsey at that time 120 home helps were being shared among the 600 people who needed them; most homes were visited only once or twice a week. Clearly more home helps would be desirable.

But over and above the practical problems faced by those in need, and lurking behind even the most courageous and dignified facades, was a terrible paralysing apathy. An apathy which grew from and then, compounded loneliness. There were tales of children deserting elderly parents and parents persecuting children, but the vast majority of people alone and in need were simply victims of ordinary circumstances, the consequences of which they could not have anticipated.

Clubs, church groups, welfare clinics, medical aid centres, Council entertainment and legal and moral advice bureaux were available and free for people of all ages. Such services were much used, but there weren't enough of them and they did not necessarily offer the help needed.

None of the people I home-helped for felt that they could call on their neighbours for anything. It was this which saddened and worried me, for I felt that friendly neighbourliness could break the apathy and loneliness. Home helps couldn't do it; they were only occasional visitors and there to do a job of work.

Yet, I was sure that goodwill among men did exist and that it wanted to make itself felt. How it was going to do this I didn't know. If someone actually did something positive, such as put the lonely in the middle of a street and physically take the neighbour – perhaps as I as had done at Belsen *(Ch. 5)* – and explain that this person is lonely and you can get rid of that and make them happy by smiling/inviting them to coffee/passing on your newspaper/cutting their grass – but this was fantasising.

I began to think there should be an ordinary place, a house, where the lonely could live and be helped out of their isolation by their immediate neighbours, for no other reason than that they were their neighbours. Within the house, the residents might not like each other since I, not they, would have chosen them. It seemed more sensible that neighbours making mutual contacts of their own accord and without necessarily doing anything practical, were a better bet for goodwill and friendship.

An old couple who had lived in the same railway-owned block of flats for 30 years relied entirely on home helps for their shopping, cleaning and to carry their coal. Of neighbours they said: "Neighbours, they don't even ask how you are." It is easier to help those with whom we have work, games or thoughts in common, than next-door neighbours whom we may find unattractive or inconveniently needy.

There was an un-neighbourly atmosphere around in Bermondsey. A Church of England rector in the next-door parish advised his flock not to baby-sit for a Methodist minister's family because they were of a different denomination. A Jehovah's Witness thought poorly of an Anglican priest because he couldn't say where the water came from at the time of the Flood. An atheist in our street laughed at Christians because they put a lightning conductor on a statue of Christ though they knew lightning was an act of God. The Baptists living next door to me built a hall with a beautiful dance floor but didn't allow any of their congregation to dance. Many of the lonely people I met wouldn't have been so lonely if those round them had stopped such petty disagreements and got on instead with being neighbourly and kind. All that was needed to unleash the suppressed generosity and kindness, I felt simplistically, was the opportunity squarely presented.

Unlike the high- and low-born of the Victorian era who might move up and down the ladder, as it were, I could not help feeling that the different groups of people in society now moved along sideways; rich to poor, aristocrat to working class, religious to political.

Did religion come in to all this? I didn't think of this in any direct way but, as I became more informed and sensitive to what I was experiencing, I thought it probably did. Loneliness was a human problem, I reasoned, and humans have a soul. Religion, which is of the soul, must therefore be relevant, and for me religion meant Christianity. But many in Bermondsey did not agree and saw religion as a side issue. At a political meeting I attended Jesus was called the "first socialist", and at this the audience laughed. At another meeting they could only call him a "Nazarene" and referred to him as an "ordinary carpenter"; they stopped there, not acknowledging that he might also be divine and part of the Trinity

Faith re-affirmed

I had never questioned my faith, it had always been there, but realising that beliefs held by others differed widely from mine, I began to question the validity of my own beliefs. I therefore spent much of my first six months or so in Bermondsey trying to prove to myself that there wasn't a God.

I wrote down everything I could to show that he didn't exist – he didn't stop this or that happening, he could have prevented that – and then tried to find answers to disprove them. These answers I obtained from priests in correspondence, and even wrote to Pusey House at Oxford and discussed, inconclusively, with its Principal whether I could study a course to sort out the matter. All this questing got me nowhere. After about six months I had failed entirely to convince myself that God didn't exist so continued happily believing that He did.

One Sunday I was about to motor from Bermondsey to church in Stepney with a friend when several street boys asked if they could come along for the car-ride. When they heard that we were going to church they appeared all the more keen but when we arrived one boy asked: "Do we have to go in?" I said no and left them outside, but during the service I saw their small faces peering round the church door, twice; each time they were frightened away by sight of the verger. They asked questions about God all the way back.

Most people around me in Bermondsey seemed to believe in God but did not seem to make the link with Christianity, or with any particular denomination; and many, although they didn't go to either the church or to the clergy, wanted to know more. They wanted to be useful and helpful but didn't connect these feelings with religion. While I wondered about this I knew that for me the time was coming for action. I'd had enough of thinking and theorising.

The first house: 50 Eugenia Road, Bermondsey Nov 1955

I settled into the home helping and my thinking began to take shape. I'd buy a house. If I had a house I could bring into it a few of the lonely people I had met. Then I'd be able to invite the neighbours to come in and show their goodwill, to forget about differences and help the residents simply because they were neighbours; loneliness would be overcome.

I had been living in Bermondsey for five months when I made this decision in November, 1955. I went at once to a local estate agent and, by lucky chance, 50 Eugenia Road was for sale. It was in need of repair and the price was £450. I never doubted that it was the house I wanted.

I took the key, for that at least was proof of my claim, but the next day the agent asked for it back. He said they were going to sell the house to someone else. I spent a frantic hour while this report was queried, but at last it was resolved and I paid the deposit and kept the key. I could call the house my own.

I allowed a month to redecorate ready for a housekeeper and four residents, who would probably be elderly because most of the people I was meeting as a home help were old. Possible residents and the housekeeper had yet to be found.

Loneliness was the only qualification for residency, and neither age nor handicap would necessarily pose a bar. From those who know how people live – doctors, the clergy, milkmen, policemen, housing departments – I was given more than 80 names of the more destitute and unhappy people living in Bermondsey.

19. 50 Eugenia Road, Bermondsey, the first Abbeyfield House

When interviewed, only four of those 80 were willing to move and two backed out one week before they were due to come. That so many had turned down the offer was depressing, but nearly all did so in a friendly manner and some left it so open that I wasn't sure whether they might accept later. To move home, even with the chance of bringing some belongings to your own, new bed-sitting room was obviously a big step to take, and not one to be hurried.

An ordinary house in an ordinary street

All the more impressive, therefore, were the two who stuck by their decision to move in – with me as housekeeper – on 17th December, 1955. They were Miss Saunders, aged 81, who had been very unhappily housed for the past ten years by a surly landlady, and Mr Halnan, aged 79, who had been a widower for 29 years. His sight was very poor and he became totally blind within a month of his move to

Eugenia Road. Both our new residents had lived in Bermondsey all their lives, and steadfastly refused to leave it when offered homes in institutions outside the Borough.

With the help of army and civilian friends and from two neighbours met in the street, the house was painted inside and out by opening day. It had only six rooms: the four residents and me as housekeeper each had our own room; the kitchen, larder, washroom and sitting room were one; there was no bathroom, but an outdoor lavatory and two cold-water taps. It needed wiring (there was no public electricity available) and the gaps between windows and their frames needed filling. 50 Eugenia Road was an ordinary house in an ordinary street.

Baroness van Heemstra, mother of the film star Audrey Hepburn, had heard about me and at once became a fairy godmother to us. She would give money in anonymous brown envelopes which I left propped on the mantelpieces of the needy for whom I home-helped – one old lady was so thrilled she wouldn't open hers for weeks – and, over the years, the baroness continued to help the society both in kindness and with practical gifts.

Bermondsey had the advantage of being an almost completely working-class area. The red flag used to fly above the Town Hall, and there were meetings at which people referred to the Queen as the "young woman of Windsor" – teenagers in particular seemed completely uninterested in the Royal Family. There being no local class battle simplified things for us. Snobbery and condescension didn't exist.

Some of the neighbours came on opening day and helped the residents settle in. The Rural Dean blessed the house and the Mayor arrived with a bunch of flowers to wish us luck. From then on it was up to the people around the house to make it work, and somehow there was never any worry on that score.

The idea was that the residents would furnish their own rooms and their surplus pieces would either be pooled or sold. It never occurred to me to make rules such as having only men or women residents, or any special denominations. I didn't ask about religious beliefs and it was not until after our first Christmas that holding house prayers was suggested by a group of us, residents and friends, as we talked around the kitchen table.

The plan was that residents should have as much independence as possible, and that they should feel their room was their castle and very much their own. They had to pay their own way and the National Assistance Board, as it then was, made this possible with a

Supplementary Allowance for those who had no money of their own. We divided the estimated day-to-day expenses among the number of residents and each paid their share. It was arranged that they always had £1 pocket money each week.

I hoped the residents would be fit enough to look after their own rooms but realised they probably wouldn't be able to scrub the floors. I had doubted – although hoped – that this would be done by neighbours or relatives, but it was. After much encouragement, three housewives came to the first neighbours' committee meeting early in the New Year and two of them undertook to scrub and clean a resident's room weekly. This was tremendous, and though they didn't do it for long it was a good start.

20. RC-G and housekeeper

"Push" on the door

I put a sign on the front door saying "push", so that neighbours would find it easier to come in and get on with it without having to ring and wait on the doorstep to be let in; nobody seemed to mind nor worry that I had done this. Residents repaid neighbours, if they could, in little ways – a cup of tea, a cigarette, a story – and, as a result, friendships – the real means of overcoming loneliness – grew between the residents and their neighbours. When neighbours dropped out or moved away it would be the housekeeper's job to find new ones to replace them.

When the third resident, an old lady, moved in I asked her family if they would scrub her floor weekly: "You can always get a home help to do that," they replied. I explained that home helps were paid from the rates and were in any case in short supply. They argued but in the end agreed to keep the room clean themselves.

By March 1956 another man had joined our three residents, so the house was full. Of its four residents – two men and two women – two were adopted by neighbours, who cleaned their rooms; the third was looked after by her daughter, and the fourth was self-sufficient. The housekeeper co-ordinated the work, cooked, shopped and collected the pensions. There was a cooking ring in each resident's room but since three of them were virtually room-bound we planned to cook the main meal of the day centrally and take it to those confined in their own rooms. This arrangement worked well, providing that the housekeeper who did the cooking wasn't me.

At the beginning the residents had meals-on-wheels provided by the Borough at mid-day and, in the evenings, a meal cooked by me. But three weeks of my opening tins – though I remember trying a stew and once cooking some chops – was quite enough for the residents and they asked for a change. Barbara Bunton (nee Lodge-Patch), a girl from Bermondsey's Bede House Settlement offered and thereafter cooked their evening meal.

Friends and neighbours rally

My reign as housekeeper, however, continued into the New Year until to my, and the residents', great relief I was superseded by Arthur Sunderland. It was February 1956 and, having read about us in the newspapers, Arthur left his comfortable flat in South Kensington, and a good job as under-secretary at Brooke's Club in St James's Street, to move into the house at Eugenia Road and run it properly. Having seen my camp bed and orange boxes he brought his furniture with him.

This show of confidence was a great encouragement. Not only did it mean that I was no longer working on my own but also my hopes now for the work to grow could begin to take shape. Once relieved of my job as housekeeper I was able to return to the comparative comfort of my lodgings and was no longer "on call" for such emergencies as finding a doctor or a priest.

Various friends had come down and were helping – principally Jennie Previte and Susan Gibbs; both had brothers in the Coldstream and Susan, although I didn't know it then, would ultimately – and wonderfully for me – become my wife. Soon after I had moved to Bermondsey, Susan had come down from London with a mutual friend, Timmy Smythe-Osbourne, to see what was going on. Enthusiastic dreams to take on more houses in the future proved infectious and both Jennie and Susan offered to come and live in one of the houses and join in with the work.

A small community of volunteers grew up at 50 Eugenia Road, including Christopher Bulteel a former Coldstreamer, a Franciscan friar and schoolmaster; he later married Jennie and became headmaster of Ardingly College in Sussex. And the Handley family came as often as possible, from the first at Eugenia Road right through to the Sixties, to help in our singsongs and at Christmas parties. Marie always played the piano while Jimmy, her husband and their many children, led the singing.

The arrival of Susan's car gave us an introduction to a Bermondsey neighbour, Bert Strickett, who was aged about 15 at the time. Bert's remarks to our friend Mark Amory recall the event:

> There was a whole gang of us. We took [stole] Susan's car. Richard [Carr-Gomm] came down to the police station and got us off and we were very impressed. He seemed above the law, I mean we ought to have been had, at least for driving without permission.

A sort of collective guardian role developed for Bert, who was the son of a docker and sometimes he lived with us. He used to paint portraits and, with his gang, became part of our lives. They were always keen for knowledge and arguments would go on well into the night, over endless cups of coffee. On another occasion when he had been caught wrongdoing, Bert's view of my endeavours were thus recorded:

> Richard got out of bed and came over to bail me out. Some people were cynical and asked, "What's his game?" but mostly they were falling over themselves to help him. He was the son of a squire, well he wasn't but there was Gomm Road, it was a famous name. He never imposed himself; he had, well, charisma is the word they use now. I used to carry his case round at meetings and heard some

stories, one about a Buddha, must have been 15 times. I never think he gave up anything really, he enjoys it. He's a person who really has found his, you know a square peg in a square thing.

The Borough Council did all they could in supplying services to help run the house. Such services ranged from weekly car rides to the public baths, monthly appointments with the chiropodist and barber and a free, weekly bag-wash laundry, through to bringing books from the public library and providing meals-on-wheels, district nurses and home helps.

I continued to try and make 50 Eugenia Road the focal point for the goodwill of its neighbours. Whenever I read aloud – usually a murder or adventure story – to the residents, or we had a weekend tea-party, or our monthly singsong around the piano, we let it be known that any neighbour would be welcome. All they had to do was "push" on the door and come in. And this, in fact, they did.

Neighbours helped, too, in other ways. Some came and gave companionship to the residents, others gave things for the house, such as the water heater and the piano, and the children came at meal times and carried plates to and from the kitchen.

Only twice did we have arguments with the residents or their relations. Once, on a Sunday, I asked a resident's daughter whether she would sweep under her mother's bed and she refused, not on religious grounds but because she preferred to come back the following day, and be paid for doing it as a home help.

The only other time was when a resident refused to leave the room while we were sweeping the chimney and her grandson was extremely rude to us for continuing with the sweeping. He left muttering that if the old lady wasn't looked after better in future he would take her away – but he never did.

The winter of 1955 was bitterly cold; the streets were blocked with snow and the pipes froze. The house had no central heating but we kept warm with coal fires blazing and the residents stayed cheerful. They couldn't, however, venture out so visits from friends and relatives were more welcome than ever.

Mr Halnan rarely had any visitors and, knowing this upset him, the other residents would ask their visitors to call in on him, too; this made everybody happy. Shortly after coming to the house he had slipped in the public baths and broken two ribs. With that and bad eyesight he had to give up his monthly excursions to see his only daughter in a psychiatric hospital; visits that had meant much to both of them. At this, a neighbour who, although she didn't enjoy our singsongs or meeting people in groups, volunteered to drive him to visit his daughter, and to take laundry parcels to her.

There were others, too, who just turned up and got on with the job: cleaning windows, hanging curtains, sweeping the hall or making the fires. Their visits were particularly enjoyed, having the added pleasure of surprise.

Promises, promises

I was gradually learning the particular importance of doing what you say you will when trying to help someone on their own. Although the kept promises were in the majority, my teaching came from the unfulfilled promises by some of those who visited us at Eugenia Road.

Miss Saunders was always philosophical about such things, frequently reminding us "not to count our chickens before they hatched". But others weren't so capable of hiding their disappointment; especially Mr Halnan, after he'd been sitting – smartly dressed, hair specially brushed – for more than an hour for a visitor who never turned up.

Someone promised a canary and someone else a blanket – neither appeared. Some would visit regularly and then forget to come again, leaving a resident waiting, disappointed. The presence of a well-known person would be promised, or a journey by car, or the gift of a small piece of furniture for the residents' rooms, and none would materialise.

Although I used to get angry about these broken promises, I understood that it was all too easy in the atmosphere of the house and the residents' rooms to promise the earth and then back at home to forget, or let good intentions die away. Indeed, it was partly my own inability to reconcile two ways of living that had made me give up one and try the other. Being a West End soldier while helping in the East End just hadn't worked for me. I had tried full-time soldiering and it had seemed right to try next full-time social work.

However, during the summer of 1956, when I was feeling "settled in" at Bermondsey, MI5 contacted me. With possible strikes brewing in the docks and a good deal of local Communist activity going on, they wondered if I could help them with a few names – was I hearing of possible disturbances being plotted, and so on? I told them, truthfully, no, but anyhow didn't want to get to know people and later be embroiled in intrigue against them, even though it might be in my country's interests.

A similar dilemma arose the following year when the question of becoming a local councillor or magistrate cropped up. I did not want this type of responsibility or leadership; it was all very negative and cowardly but it meant that I could get on with my purpose of just working with the lonely in Bermondsey and being part of the agony and ecstasy going on there.

Having worked solidly throughout my first year in Bermondsey it seemed a good idea to have a complete break, so in October 1956 I accepted an invitation from Freddie, the Kabaka, to take a two-month holiday in Buganda *(Ch. 11)*. This proved a marvellous break, fascinating and enjoyable on so many levels, and I returned to Bermondsey in January 1957 refreshed and ready to get back down to the serious work in hand.

21

FOUNDING THE ABBEYFIELD SOCIETY

By March 1956 the household at 50 Eugenia Road had established a happy, working routine and impatient to do more I was already casting around for another house. Nevertheless, having crossed the river to make my new life in Bermondsey, the year that followed was, for me, a year for settling down. I received a letter addressed to "Herr Carr-Gomm, The Poor Quarters of London's East-End".

With the encouragement of neighbours, I rented the top floor of another small house in Eugenia Road, to accommodate two applicants from the street itself. Then the following month (April) I bought 36 Gomm Road, nearby in Southwark Park. It cost £750, freehold, and I was able to pay for it out of my army gratuity of £1,150; I had received this in lieu of a pension having served for 15 years instead of the normal engagement period of 22 years, and £450 had already gone on buying 50 Eugenia Road.

Over the next six months suitable houses in different parts of Bermondsey became available and they were rented and added to our number. Each house had a sign saying "push" nailed on its front door, encouraging people to drop in. By the autumn of 1957 we (Susan Gibbs, Jennie Previte, Arthur Sunderland, Barbara Lodge-Patch, Christopher Bulteel, and Anne Parry among others) were running Eugenia Road, Gomm Road and five rented houses, which together were home to 30 residents. A room at Gomm Rd had become an office and, occasionally, a helper slept in there.

It's official: the Abbeyfield Society founded, 19 Nov 1956

Thus we were up and running – a group of volunteers, mainly part-time and living elsewhere unless being a housekeeper; no committee but almost totally of a like mind about what we were doing. Somehow decisions happened without much discussion and plans were laid and carried out with minimal argument or debate; since everything just seemed to work we got on with it.

We were financed entirely by gifts and the residents' contributions from their pensions, heating benefits and food allowances; these three sources being public money, we were obliged for accountancy purposes to form ourselves into a legal company. We spent considerable time thinking up a name for the company. Reluctant to call it the "Eugenia Society", after the first house's street, what we really wanted was a gimmick, a name that people would remember, such as Oxfam, but we failed to agree on anything. Then we remembered that we were sitting and thinking at my lodgings in Abbeyfield Road; why not the Abbeyfield Society? It would give no clue as to what we were doing but it was inoffensive and sounded good.

Bermondsey Abbey on the south bank of the Thames was, in medieval days, as important as Westminster Abbey across the river on the north. Once bridges were built, people from the south crossed to Westminster, where the Court and Government were based, and so Bermondsey Abbey declined and died. The Borough, though, remembered its Abbey with pride – hence Abbeyfield Road running round what was once its boundary.

21. Abbeyfield Road, Bermondsey

Having checked that no other organisation was using the name, we laid claim to it and became the Abbeyfield Society. Although the first house had opened in 1955, the Abbeyfield Society was officially founded as a legal entity on 19th November, 1956 – in Bermondsey, London.

The inauguration went well. We had a large committee meeting followed by a service in a nearby church taken by the Reverend Leslie Timmins, our local Methodist minister who, with his wife, Audrey, helped considerably in our work. The Timmins had also taken me in when I was thrown out of my first lodgings, my landlady having objected to what she considered over-attentiveness by the press. A teetotaller, she had also objected to my going to the Gomm pub across the street in Abbeyfield Road, and when I went for help to the Manse, at the end of Abbeyfield Road, the Timmins gave me lodgings there.

The society was now official and legal; a proper seal was made, the constitution printed and a brass plate bearing our name was on the door of our honorary auditor in the City. The local public library asked for a copy of all our literature.

We started a newsletter and planned to produce it twice a year. It was sent to all those who, while not able to work with us nevertheless wanted to be linked in some way. Each had a commitment to pray for the work, and soon the number of people on our mailing list rose to more than 100. We printed a special Christmas card in 1956 and it sold some 500 copies.

At Christmas time on that and subsequent years the generosity of people both local and distant was enormous. This shouldn't have surprised us for they had shown throughout how helpful they could be: the baker gave us hot cross buns at Easter, the café hot turkey for a Sunday dinner, a publican free beer for the monthly sing-song, a docker painted a house and an importer gave a crate of tinned fruit, Harvest Festival presents came from local churches and schools and magazines from the hospital. From afar, people came to help in the office, stand in for a housekeeper or do odd jobs. Nevertheless, at Christmas they all excelled themselves and the residents were overwhelmed with presents.

The giving of gifts often led to further visits and friendships and the encouragement we derived from them fed the core of our work. The original aim continued: to prevent loneliness by involving people of all ages in an atmosphere of mutual kindness. We hoped, too, that by involving the young we could break the potential cycle of loneliness.

House prayers

Believing that each of us is made up of body, mind and spirit, I knew that each of these three entities must be considered when we were thinking of the whole person. Accepting this concept it seemed for us best that our houses should be run within the framework of a Christian way of life, while allowing the residents to make up their own minds whether to fit into that or not.

From the time I opened the first house at 50 Eugenia Road, I wanted to offer the houses to residents of all denominations as ecumenical "house churches", hoping they would become centres of worship for the street community. However, I was too timid and said too little about it to our neighbours, arguing with myself that we would be thought too holy and churchy and that that would put people off. So, instead, during the first few weeks when we were only a small number together, we instigated house prayers and, as attendance was voluntary, this posed no problem for those residents who preferred not to join in. To those who came, house prayers seemed acceptable and a reminder of the spiritual side of our work and of the presence of God.

For residents, neighbours and everyone else involved in Eugenia Road (and later in our other houses) reality and realism were the order of the day, but, almost without thinking about it, we hoped that the "spirit" was there too. In the summer of 1957, for example, Bobby Miles, chaplain to Bishop Bell of Chichester (later Provost of Mombassa) and Susan's cousin, had invited a coach-load of us for an afternoon's excursion to the Bishop's Palace in Sussex; we accepted and had a great tea-party while subconsciously knowing that spiritual initiative and pleasure somehow also came into it.

In 1957, the Reverend Tubby Clayton – who founded Toc H, a charity for homeless and/or out-of-work ex-servicemen after the Great War – invited me to lunch on Tower Hill. He talked about poverty and almshouses and recounted personal anecdotes. He knew about the work of the Abbeyfield Society and was glad we were encouraging young people to visit the elderly in our houses. He assumed automatically that house prayers were held daily and I didn't have the nerve to tell him that they were, in fact, held only monthly.

Ecumenical approach

House prayers were of an ecumenical nature since our residents were of different denominations or, more often, of none; the residents in one of our houses, for example, included a Quaker, a Roman Catholic, a Humanist and two non-believers and they were all happy taking part together in monthly house prayers.

Residents could always go to their own churches if they wished, or have communion brought to them, yet there still seemed a need to pray quietly and regularly together as a household. I always felt that I could see the difference between the houses where they said prayers together – which had a more settled, harmonious atmosphere – and those where they didn't.

Nevertheless there were onlookers and passers-by who said we should leave all that sort of thing to the clergy, that listening to the Sunday Service on the wireless or watching television's Songs of Praise would suffice, that residents were visited by their priests and that was enough. Others – unsure about or with only a casual interest in our work – persisted in thinking that we wanted to Bible-thump or convert and that we would embarrass or offend people. These were obvious risks, but we felt the wide and open ecumenical nature of our prayers guarded against such risks.

Being lonely is no bar against praying effectively for others. It is one way in which people with time on their hands – be they blind, old, bedridden, isolated, or just sleepless at night – can often help and be of service to the community; praying gives great support to, among others, the clergy and missionaries at home and abroad.

In medieval hospitals it was the sole function of the bedesmen to pray for the sick and those in need. In those days, people often withdrew to monasteries or convents to prepare themselves for death after the wear and tear of active life; followers of Hinduism still do. House prayers were a reminder that values such as simplicity, poverty, humility and prayer were still valid and they were, also, a way in which residents could positively help their neighbours. They were, too, a bridge between this life and the next; many of our residents were old or sick and close to death and to use this bridge seemed right.

Regularity in prayer needs self-discipline to maintain and – not surprisingly – many of the people in our care and working with us found this difficult. For if it is hard to pray consistently when healthy it is, perhaps, all the harder when weakened by loneliness, old age or infirmity. To make it easier for our housekeepers and neighbours to take part in house prayers we designed our own prayer book, which the Times Publishing Company helped print. Prepared by an Anglican friar, it was vetted by a Methodist and a Roman Catholic minister, it could be used as a collection of hymns, carols, poems, prayers, readings and meditations by people of any, or no, denomination. It was a book of devotional depth in which many found spiritual help.

I joined a Parliamentary commission set up, in February 1958, to consider whether any spiritual input could be included in legislation for social, welfare and housing work. Robin Turton (later Lord Tranmire) took the chair and other members included the Conservative politician Keith Joseph. The commission concluded that no spiritual input was possible from politicians and lawmakers – other than through their personal convictions and beliefs which, it was thought, were bound to influence their decisions; nothing formal or written down was possible and impartiality and clear, objective, thinking must carry the day.

House meetings

It had always been important for us to have meetings for prayer so, to them, we added music and included time for any necessary business or complaints. Frank Cope, a neighbour at Eugenia Road, played the piano regularly at these meetings from the very beginning in 1956 until by 1965 he had played at more than 300 sing-songs and meetings.

From around February 1956 we held these house gatherings, attended also by neighbours and friends, every month, and on different nights at each house so that residents could attend each other's if they chose. Music was the ideal entertainment side for it was a common denominator (like prayer) and appealed to everyone, regardless of age or nationality. Anyone who could play an instrument was welcome to join in, but the main focus was good, old-fashioned, communal singing of music hall and pub songs.

Solos or duets might be sung, and it was particularly rewarding to hear someone, perhaps after 20 years in a psychiatric hospital, singing songs from their childhood; their first creative step, perhaps, and in giving such pleasure to our community they derived self-confidence.

Even though my voice is awful, I have always enjoyed singing – both with my family and in the Army – especially the choruses and always looked forward to our musical house meetings. They were also good meetings for neighbours and friends from across the river, who could only attend in the evenings. Many of our friends who had volunteered to work for the Abbeyfield became firm friends to the residents as well.

Sometimes members of the staff – be they housekeepers, volunteers or friends – wondered how best they could collectively acknowledge the spiritual aspect of the Abbeyfield Society's work. They felt a need to do this, since they were becoming increasingly immersed in and distracted by the material, practical and financial problems of running the houses. Intercessionary prayers were begun and said once a week when all the staff gathered in a local chapel for a short service of rededication. Compline was sometimes held in the evenings but, when the original staff left to get married or move elsewhere, these things were discontinued gradually between 1957 and 1959.

However, with an ever-present awareness of the sanctity of life and the religious element both in general and in our work, from 1956 we began to hold Reflection Conferences. For these, all the Abbeyfield staff escaped from London to the country for a couple of days – away from residents and telephone calls – and reflected on what we had started, whether it was worthwhile and, if so, how we should best continue.

From 1957 we combined these conferences with a Quiet Day so that we could meditate as well as reflect. This led to some of the staff, residents and volunteers forming the "70 Group", named after the 70 people who were called, in the New Testament, to go out and spread the word. Our Group's purpose was not to preach directly but to pray for the work of the society so that it would reach out and helped as many people as possible, as well as to try to balance the material aspects and, we hoped, acknowledge and emphasise the "common good" contribution of our work with its spiritual motivation and ethos. Such considerations are part of social and humanitarian efforts worldwide, and we – the 70 Group – wanted to learn from others wherever we could.

Mixed reactions

But the Abbeyfield Society remained subject to disapproval; our insistence on spiritual existence was criticised by some of those who would otherwise have worked with, supported or funded us. We were taken to task by fanatical believers for accepting residents of no apparent faith or religious denomination: an Anglican couple withdrew their moral support because we took on a Roman Catholic housekeeper; An industrialist, having urged us to use the Sermon on the Mount as a basis for our work then asked us to exclude Roman Catholics from the houses; some Jews who told us they could not work with us if we continued to describe ourselves as a Christian community and a member of the public walked out of an open meeting at which I spoke saying, "This man talks about God; he must be a crank."

While there were clergy who worked happily with the society from the beginning, there were a few others who would have nothing to do with us. One vicar in nearby Southwark, for example, wrote in 1958:

Did it ever occur to you, my dear Major, that those who have broken away from the church into various sects are dividing the body of Christ, and sinning against that unity which our Lord desired? And that all who support them in this way are sharing the sin? The chapels not only broke from the church but also are now largely supported by present generation deserters of the church. I regret having to write so bluntly but I feel that it is my duty to administer this rebuke.

In 1957 we had started holding anniversary services as a form of thanksgiving and, acknowledging that our residents were of differing denominations, we held the services each year in a different church: Methodist, Church of England, Baptist, Roman Catholic, and so on. Some members of the clergy suspected that we were creating a new religion or, at the very least, that we were completely at variance with their own and refused to attend these services unless they were held in a church or chapel of their own denomination, many Abbeyfield residents, staff and friends, however, did attend.

The Society also met with a mixed reception from doctors. There was a group practice of dedicated Christian GPs, founded in the early 1900s, who were admired tremendously and the people of Bermondsey consulted them about problems of every sort. A number of other GPs, however looked upon their patients as numbers rather than as people.

One of our residents contracted a painful, infectious rash. The doctor gave her a prescription on early closing day and thus she couldn't get the ointment until the following day. Despite her pain, he made no arrangement for her to collect it from an emergency pharmacy saying that the problem was a social one and had nothing to do with him. When we asked him who would apply the ointment he told us that was up to us – infectious or not.

This doctor's view was typical of others who felt that as the Abbeyfield had taken on these problems we must see them through ourselves. When a doctor refused to admit one of residents to hospital because, although she was in pain, she had only a few months to live, we took matters into our own hands and a hospital bed was found for her.

Some GPs were afraid that hospital doctors would accuse them of referring patients to them rather than be bothered to treat them at home; others refused us help with alcoholics on the basis that such cases were social, not medical, problems.

Incidents such as these showed us how carelessly the powerless were treated; a far cry from treatment handed out to those in authority or with money. It emphasised the divisions in our class structure and the sometimes unfair use of influence and rule wielded by rank and riches.

Breaking down barriers

We became increasingly determined that the Abbeyfield's houses must be a means towards breaking down such a structure. If only we could have a house in every street to which everyone could come – the haves and the have-nots, the sick and the healthy, the rich and the poor, the grand and the humble, the victim and the bully – and in which everyone would be treated the same and share equally the care and kindness of the community around them.

As the Abbeyfield Society continued its work the houses became, in small ways, magnets for all kinds of people; they just dropped in and chatted. Two little children pushed into one house asking to see the residents, who, thinking they had nothing to say to them, asked the housekeeper to send them away. But the housekeeper let the children in and everyone met successfully.

Having overheard a young visitor say that he didn't believe in God, one of the residents, a man aged 80 who had spent half his life in prison, said: "Well, I know there is a God." "Come off it, you're one of us," said the boy. The man replied: "When I was in solitary I knew everyone was against me – the judge, the jury, the wardens, the police – but when the cell door shut I knew that God was in there with me." In such ways, the old and the young can learn from each other; if the old are given the chance to voice their wisdom and experience and the young are prepared to listen and, perhaps, learn.

Flying in the face of adversity

The general concept of the Abbeyfield's work – of putting service to others before self and security – didn't avoid criticism either. Officials on the Bermondsey Borough Council stressed the impenetrable unfriendliness of people in general and said that any social work based on their goodwill was doomed to failure. The Council thought that once the novelty and interest had worn off us, our plans would come to a sticky halt, however we persevered; they thought that we would never find good housekeepers, but we did, and that it was unwise to mix the sexes, yet we did not find this so.

And there were still more criticisms. Some visitors complained about the standard of the buildings we were housing people in. This was not an unreasonable complaint; Eugenia Road had no hot water and only an outdoor lavatory and some of our other houses had not been completely wired for electricity. In order to get our work started we had accepted that some properties were in a poor state of repair. Others, curious about our work in general, wondered if we were answering a need or creating a problem. What was the point of relying on unreliable neighbours? Were the houses too small to be economical? – we needed a minimum of four residents per house to make them viable. Was there too high, or too low, a proportion of staff to residents? – we had two office staff and one housekeeper in each house of four to seven residents. Were we too indiscriminate in our selection of residents, too rash in approaching all neighbours?

Some people, generally those aware of our work only at a distance, thought us no more than do-gooders amusing ourselves among the poor. We were told to get all this social sense out of our systems while we're young; that we would come to realise these people make their own beds, dig their own graves and are happiest like that and we should stop interfering.

But the Abbeyfield Society carried on. The housekeepers complained about the residents, and the staff worried about over-possessive volunteers who wouldn't let outsiders join in. Meanwhile our accountant said we were spending too much money on administration and that salaries, which we started paying in 1958 (we had paid our housekeepers since 1956), were too high.

Ill-informed criticism was tedious, but we took on board and tried to act upon any of an accurate and constructive nature. Though charges about houses in need of repair and renovation contained some truth there never seemed enough of them to close us down. Very probably the Welfare State should have be dealing with much of the work the society had undertaken, certainly the degree of need we were trying to meet was overwhelmingly large, and doubtless our motives were not always as pure as they should have been – meanwhile a new resident was arriving this afternoon and if no-one did anything about a mattress he or she wouldn't have one.

We used to discuss the morality and ethics of Abbeyfield's work at our Reflection Conferences in the country. However I, at least, never looked far ahead. I was not unambitious – sometimes I was fantastically so, I had a vision of the Albert Hall filled to the rooftop for an Abbeyfield sing-song – but I tried to cope with each situation as it arose, regardless of the future and without too many qualms about where the money might come from. Susan calls it lack of imagination.

It was certainly lack of imagination which kept me away from politics which were brought endlessly into most of our discussions and challenges. Though from a Liberal family, I have voted both Labour and Conservative, and Liberal only in the European elections. This waywardness was principally because I believed in only part of each Party's manifesto and rarely studied any political policy paper enough.

Happy miracles

Fortunately for our work, changes in Governmental social policy and any criticism directed at the Abbeyfield were, in the long run, counterbalanced by the miracles which happened.

These miracles were many and varied. For example, when we started the Abbeyfield Society in November 1956, we thought that to get £400 in the bank would be a sign that we had sound support behind us. After some publicity we quickly reached the £300s but then the flow of money stopped. The committee met and discussed, despondently, the society's future. Next morning an anonymous cheque arrived by post which took us well over our £400 target.

Most miracles, however, were connected not with finance but with the people who helped us and who came to live with us: a widow, who since her husband's death nine months previously had been unable to speak beyond a whisper, found she could speak normally and even sing within weeks of moving into one of our houses.

These happy miracles, or coincidences, were quite extraordinary. When we needed a car someone gave us one, and when it broke down a mechanic turned up and fixed it, just in time to transport the belongings of a new housekeeper who had arrived that very day. Whenever there was a spare room there was always someone to fill it, when someone needed a bed, one became vacant. Bricklayers turned up when we wanted to build a spare room, and goods appeared just when needed. On a day that neither the Women's Royal Voluntary Service (WRVS) nor the National Assistance Board could give us bed sheets, an American woman left four sheets on our doorstep.

The same sort of miracles seemed to happen with our staff; housekeepers had been paid from the start, and while food and general running expenses were covered by the residents' contributions, everyone worked on a voluntary basis until we began to pay salaries in 1958. Whenever the work became too much, someone would volunteer to help – as a housekeeper or cleaner, or making home visits to the lonely. Someone painted a mural on a garden wall, others helped in the office or built covered passages to the lavatories. Only a few volunteers thought we were doing everything wrong or badly, and they left quickly.

The lonely ones

I include the following examples to illustrate the variety and ordinariness of the roads which people follow and the sadness which surrounds them – and to show how it is possible to achieve a happier ending. However, the majority of our residents had no particular drama in their lives – alone through a natural progression of events they simply drifted into isolation.

Miss Townsend had been a nanny all her life, most of it abroad, and she remained friends with the families she had worked for. On retirement she went to live, quietly and cheaply, with a cousin in the country but her cousin became so unfriendly and difficult to live with that Miss Townsend began to show signs of nervous strain. She read about the Abbeyfield in a magazine and came to live with us until she died.

Mr Freemantle was a sailor who never saved much money and had to leave the Navy after he had a heart attack. A bachelor, he took a shore job but none of his sisters would offer him a home. When eventually he asked his favourite sister if he could park his caravan in her field to be near her and her family, she refused. Depressed, he was talking to a friend who suggested he should go and see us, which he did. He, like Miss Townsend, lived at one of the Abbeyfield's houses until he died.

Mr Bell had shared his bedroom with a teenage nephew, Mrs Round shared hers with a young granddaughter. In both cases this led to friction. It also created the loneliness of being forced back into their own private worlds, without those around appearing to understand. The relationships which each had within their families had become poisoned. Both Mr Bell and Mrs Round came to live with us after conversion had disappeared from their lives.

Mr Carter was brought by one of his daughters. She said unkind things about him to his face and used to come and see him only on pension day and took most of his pension away with her. She said she was buying him an overcoat with it but the coat never materialised; when we objected to her keeping his money her visits became less frequent.

An old man had cared for his wife who had had both her legs amputated. After she died, he was admitted to hospital for a rest during which time his brothers sold his home. Having nowhere else to go he came to us. But his hatred for his brothers had become so great that he bought a pistol and determined to kill them. It took the housekeeper months of gentle reasoning before he quietly went to Tower Bridge one afternoon and dropped the pistol into the river.

Mrs Jackson, unmarried, had lived a long time with a man. When she could no longer look after him he arranged privately for her to enter a home. Although he pretended to her that she was only going on convalescence, once there he refused to have her back. Heartbroken she was brought to us by a social worker.

When Mrs Barry left her husband to live with another man her large, young family was split up and put into care. Discarded at length by the man, Mrs Barry took to drink and her children, who hardly knew her, didn't want her to live with them. Thus, lonely and unhappy in old age she came to us and over the years she mellowed.

A murderer, his death penalty having been twice reprieved, had served a life sentence. With no family or friends to go on leaving prison he went first to the Franciscans and later came to us.

THE EARLY YEARS

As we got more houses going between 1957 and 1959 we needed to run a proper office, so we left the bedroom we had been using in the house of a dear neighbour, Mrs Lane, and set up our office on the top floor of our house at Gomm Road. We continued to involve neighbours as much as possible – they gave parties, mended clothes or stood in to allow the housekeepers a day off. When I remember those early days of the society, I reflect on them with real pleasure. We had great fun and there was much informality, as well as visits to my parents' home and occasional visits to old friends, cinemas, cafes or pubs away from the work. Many friends came and went, some staying to run houses. At various Christmases from 1958 we had three houses run by men – sometimes friends standing in, sometimes as full-time housekeepers – who vastly overspent the housekeeping allowance for food, to the delight of the residents.

From 1958 our houses were, on the whole, filling up with elderly people, perhaps because there were so many more of them in obvious need. We were submerged with applications. At the same time Arthur Sunderland, since 1957 the society's Treasurer as well as housekeeper at Eugenia Road, was now, in 1959, leaving but, fortunately, lawyers, borough councillors and other professionals volunteered their expertise and helped in the administration and with our ledgers.

We were lucky, too, with our housekeepers: two Bermondsey women, Mrs May Silk at our house at Marden Road and Mrs Doll Henderson at Gomm Road, were outstandingly good. However, we had some bad luck, too: four times in those early days housekeepers stole residents' money on pension day and disappeared. Some were convicted, including one spied by chance in the King's Road, Chelsea by Bert Strickett and a visiting school boy, both then living with us. She was on a bus, so they jumped aboard and held her until the police came and arrested her; she had stolen both residents' money and contents from the house and was ultimately imprisoned.

It wasn't easy to choose housekeepers by their references – the paragon of virtue often turned out to be extremely dirty, a bad cook or unkind and they would have to go; one refused to leave and had to be taken away by car and left at a railway station.

Open-door policy

Despite our stated aim to encourage them, not least with the "push" signs on the doors of our houses, visitors were not always helpful. A thief, dripping with blood, pushed through our house, the fourth at 3 Banyard Road, and jumped over the back fence. The police pounded through the house after him, pausing only to remark that if we'd locked the front door this wouldn't have happened. Our open-door policy also encouraged a local punter to pop in and place his bets using the telephone behind our front door and, before the days of betting shops, the bookie runners touting in the street would hide behind our doors when they saw the police coming.

Many of our visitors came from the local youth gangs. These youngsters sometimes made trouble but on the whole were useful, and they liked, too, to talk about all sorts of problems, often religious, which they didn't seem to have the chance to do elsewhere.

When the headmaster of the local boys' secondary school came to tea one day, some of his old boys chanced to visit. Most of them had been thought irredeemable at school but the headmaster found them matured and smartened up and was most surprised to find them in what was ostensibly an old people's home. The boys were no less surprised to find their old headmaster in the house and we all sat down to a surprisingly agreeable tea party.

Local teenagers, boys and girls, often needed a bed for the night, there were cheap hostels and doss houses for adults but these were not available for the under 18s. If they had a row with their parents or had been thrown out, sleeping at a friend's house or in the sleeper holes of a disused railway line on the nearby embankment were their only options. They took to asking to stay with us, and, if no bed was available they might sleep in an old car of ours in the street outside the door.

Having these youngsters to stay confirmed how right it was to mix the generations; everyone had much to contribute and young and old enjoyed each other's company. Sometimes, of course, they maddened each other but the older residents' grouses about too much noise made a change from their worries about pains in the back or letters which never came.

We were constantly learning more about loneliness among the young. Sometimes they wanted only shelter, advice, a meal or just to talk – they never asked for money. They were usually lonely because, whatever had gone wrong in their lives made them feel like outcasts, uneasy and no longer accepted by their friends or family.

It was the same for those in middle-age. They, too, had stepped, or dropped, out of the mainstream of life – sometimes only temporarily. They might simply feel unsure of themselves – nothing obvious – or have some kind of handicap be it spiritual, emotional, physical or psychiatric. Some were ex-offenders, refugees, or members of minority groups, single parents or, less commonly, strangers from another town.

Whatever their problem, they needed help to return to conventional life, and we could offer that life, for as long as they might need it, in an ordinary house among ordinary people. With the renewed confidence derived from this, they could either move on or stay; the choice was theirs.

A 16 year-old public school boy who was beyond his parent's control came to live with us as a last resort and stayed several months. Mixing with the local gang, he started well but when he began to boss them around one of them whipped out a knife and threatened to cut off his ear. He drifted into a separate life of jazz and films until he eventually disappeared into the London vortex and we never heard of him again.

Successes and surprises

But there were success stories, too. A disturbed young girl who would throw her shoes around, barge in and out of people's rooms, practise her music at all hours and take herself off without warning, settled in gradually, and over the years became popular and held down a proper job.

Sometimes men, unsettled in life, uncertain and lonely, would come and help us for a few months, hoping to find themselves a vocation. Such people came from all walks of life and those we encountered included an ex-scientist, a film-producer and a music teacher.

Life with our residents was full of surprises. One man shared his room with five cats and two dogs which stank so badly the other residents complained. We asked him either to leave or clean up but he refused to do either so the sanitary inspector came and cleared both him and his animals away. And there were three weddings in our households when three elderly residents married our housekeepers. This we felt was a little unfair, for good housekeepers were hard to find and, once married, they tended to go and live with their new husbands.

Sometimes the Abbeyfield Society was invited to help pet projects which varied from a group from North London who wanted to cut themselves off from the world and enjoy free love, to the opening of a Roman Catholic house for tramps in Westminster, and supporting the creation of a caravan town for old people. We declined.

Fundraising

For the first three or four years we didn't do much about raising money; we told people and it was obvious that we could use given cash. Sometimes we took a stall at a local fete and sold old clothes or bric-a-brac. Once or twice we asked in a pub and sometimes helpers took part in sponsored walks or runs. People passed hats around at meetings and occasionally we were given shares from church collections. Notes used to come in the post and, a few times, someone gave me a cheque. It was all very generous and unplanned and the money was spent on extras like outings, parties and residents. birthdays or celebrations.

But fundraising for the society was, of course, vital and, fortunately, the media were continually interested in our work. While we wanted and needed publicity about our work, I was concerned that much of it concentrated upon and about me. Journalists told me that articles about people were more interesting than articles about ideas and although during the Fifties the *Guardian* and *London Illustrated News* wrote about the society's work in terms of the social problem, the *Daily Mail*, *Sunday Dispatch*, *Daily Sketch* and *Men Only* magazine concentrated on the personal angle.

This flattered my ego and I rather enjoyed being recognised in shops, but I was always wary of being portrayed as a fool. And the journalists were right, their personal articles produced many more letters of encouragement than the ones written about our idea.

Most letters came from people who had suffered themselves and were therefore, sympathetic towards others in need. Although few of them sounded rich many, unasked, sent donations. Letters arrived addressed to "The Major" or "Richard", and would contain 10 shilling or £1 note, a book of stamps or a small postal order. An old lady from near Reading sent 50 crumpled £1 notes which she had kept under her bed, and two little girls together sent five shillings, asking that we buy some sweets for the residents.

I appeared on television, and both Radio Luxembourg and the BBC broadcast radio programmes about our work with Abbeyfield. The broadcasts said, quite clearly, that neighbours' friendships would make or mar our success, and that loneliness would be overcome largely by their interest; further that – apart from finance – it was on them, and not on visitors from different parts of London, that we depended.

I had wondered how our neighbours would react to the broadcasts and, fortunately, they reacted favourably – though there was no extra rush of help. Someone in Devon, however, had recorded of one of the programmes and after replaying it five years later, was inspired to start up a house there. In fact 14 years later someone who was inspired then to do something similar was reminded of our work by recalling one of those programmes.

Bermondsey locals were, however, annoyed when I was quoted in the press saying that the day of the Lady Bountiful was over and local people should look after their own neighbours and not expect others to come and do it for them. And on Radio Luxembourg I told how I'd found an old Bermondsey women in bed having had no food for 14 days. Both these were taken as a slight on the Borough and its residents criticised me for highlighting them.

A man stopped me in the street one day and told me that he was a socialist, a pacifist and an atheist – three things which he, then quite rightly, presumed I was not – and that I was only dealing on the surface and not getting down to real problems. And a woman told me I must be a Communist because I was backing the man in the street, then a Communist told me that I was his enemy because I was trying to make people satisfied with their lot within a capitalist system.

Anyhow, as a result of the media attention and the interest it generated, from 1957 people all over the country started to write asking whether I would start similar houses in their own towns or cities. I was thinking already of trying the idea of a small house in an ordinary street in some other town. Since loneliness is a universal problem, it seemed right to take the Bermondsey experiment – now a going concern and a reasonable if precarious success – and try it in a different part of England and broaden the geographical area across which Abbeyfield could help. My thinking was still largely theoretical, but it was guided by my experiences in Bermondsey.

April 1957: Abbeyfield in Macclesfield

Impatient to see the society expand, I decided in January 1957 to take a look at Macclesfield, a silk-producing town in Cheshire. I chose this town simply because I remembered Joe Barclay, an ex-Franciscan, who after working with us for a few months had returned to Macclesfield, his birthplace, to marry and settle down.

In order to establish the townspeople's needs I enlisted, in March, in my original role as a home-help, and keen to avoid publicity at this early stage I worked under a false name.

Conditions among Macclesfield's poor and lonely were not dissimilar to those we had encountered in Bermondsey: frail, isolated people consigned to dilapidated homes they had neither the strength nor the heart to keep clean. I came across hundreds of people who, for as many different reasons, were in need of care and affection. There was no place for pity but to find so many in need was depressing. Once again, I had a gut feeling that the situations I was finding were avoidable and that by repeating what we had done with our houses in Bermondsey, we could try to help prevent loneliness here, too.

In April that year I found a house, 34 Prestbury Road, for five residents. A man in Macclesfield who had promised to put up the money to pay for it backed out so I used my savings and bought the house for £1,150; I was soon, and wonderfully, reimbursed by Mr Wadsworth, a benefactor of real Christian standing who was head of one of the town's biggest silk factories and also head of Macclesfield's Council of Social Service. Within a month the house was opened with two residents and by July was home to five. Mr and Mrs Penal, whose house it had been, had to stay in it for several weeks before they could move into their new house in Blackpool and were very supportive of our work.

Contrary to what I had witnessed, a senior clergyman had told me there were no lonely people in Macclesfield thus my work was not needed. And there was a good deal more local opposition including a Council official who wrote telling me, although giving no reason why, not to go ahead with the house. The house came with one totally unhelpful neighbour and there were plenty of others, full of suspicion, telling me constantly how stupid I was.

However, there were supporters, too, our next-door neighbour at Prestbury Road, for example. Mrs Edwards, the almoner at the hospital was also the greatest help in finding and befriending residents, as was Mrs Alma Brown who, with her husband, took on the secretaryship of Abbeyfield in Macclesfield. I lived for four months with Mr and Mrs Postles who, although they did not normally take lodgers, let me have a room in their house and were most kind to me. These people, and others like them, more than made up for any opposition to our work.

With Prestbury Road full and applications from still more potential residents, that summer I tramped the Macclesfield streets looking unsuccessfully for a second house. Lack of local financial support had forced me to live on a tight budget in digs and, occasionally, hotels, and this gave me a better insight of the town and its people's needs. I tried to arrange free lifts between Bermondsey and Macclesfield, I saved on food and drink and sat in the cheapest seats if I went to the cinema. When I wasn't working I passed my time at the public library, in pubs with TV sets and in a café where the proprietor kindly lent me books. I used the public baths and attended religious services – Macclesfield is full of chapels – and in one of these sat next to a woman who had six toes on one foot; she took off her shoes during the sermon.

I came to know more and more lonely people and visited officials who could have helped, but within weeks I realised that the first house would have to prove itself before any real support would be forthcoming. They wouldn't have parties, prayers or visitors because they saw these as an invasion of privacy, but they did allow me to put a "push" sign on the door.

By July, with the house fully under way, local officials and church and chapel ministers became helpful and encouraging. More people began to be kind and cheerful and to give things for the house and its five residents. It became a happy house and a focal point for neighbourliness. By 1961, the Macclesfield branch of Abbeyfield had outgrown this first house and bought a larger one, 22 Crompton Road. Over the years these two houses became an example and a source of encouragement to other Abbeyfield Societies in the north which followed them.

July 1958: Abbeyfield in Brighton

After Macclesfield, the next town with which the society became involved was Brighton. Here, the instigator was the Reverend Peter Booth, vicar of Brighton, who having heard of our work in Bermondsey from Bobby Miles *(Ch. 21)*, had decided to try and repeat it in his own town.

In June 1958, just prior to the birth of our eldest daughter, Anna, Susan and I went for two months to this seaside resort to help get things started. We lived at the vicarage while I explored the town from its slums, alleyways and doss houses to its libraries, hospitals, museums and parks. Much new housing was already being built and there were many old people's homes and private nursing homes – good and bad. Over two or three weeks I began to identify with the town and felt that Abbeyfield could help there.

Early in 1958 Bobby Miles and Peter Booth had invited leading townspeople to the vicarage and asked me to come and talk to them. They were enthusiastic but very practical. Slowly a scheme was worked out and they even discussed having many houses in addition to the pilot one.

The town's ex-mayor and its town clerk encouraged us by suggesting that the Council should finance the first house and, perhaps, more later. They felt the less their help was known the greater our chance of success and suggested that while they would find, adapt and decorate the house, neighbours would co-operate more happily with a voluntary body than with them, the Council. Most of those who attended the meeting constituted themselves into a committee and never could a society have got off to a better start; it was an ideal tie-up between a statutory and a voluntary body.

The Brighton committee found the right house and with the help of the council opened it in July 1958. From the beginning, under the gentle and expert guidance of Mrs Joyce Wing, a local Justice of the Peace and housewife, it ran happily and successfully and many other houses in Brighton – by 1961 there were six – soon joined this one.

Aim and guiding principles

Largely because of the significant civic interest shown by Brighton an important question had arisen as a result of Abbeyfield's expansion there: what were the obligations arising from the use of the Abbeyfield name? I felt that these clearly included involving neighbours, putting "push" on the door and having regular parties and prayers, but the Brighton committee couldn't accept any of these conditions. They asked us to go away and think about what our real aims were then let them know; so, on the Brighton Belle to Victoria I worked out in words what were our aims and the principles behind them and, back in Bermondsey, put them to the others – Christopher Bulteel, Jennie Previte, Susan and the Timmins.

We knew, of course, what they were in practice but it proved difficult to transfer them to paper. And we had to choose words which would explain clearly our aim and principles to those people in other parts of the country who had never seen us or our houses. We decided to say simply that our aim was "to house the lonely, whether they were old or handicapped in any way, by providing a focal point for the goodwill and kindness of neighbours". Later, in 1959, having this aim proved a complication for the word "handicapped" needed explaining and we had meant it to include young people handicapped by loneliness.

The principles behind our aim were, also, simple:

to be lonely was normal and ordinary; good neighbourliness could prevent loneliness; loneliness had a spiritual element quite apart from the material, economic, social and cultural ones; it was everybody's job, either as a religious duty or a civic responsibility, to help those around them who might be alone and in need.

From 1958, outside London each town's Abbeyfield Society, being autonomous, reserved the right to apply, or not, our principles as they saw fit. If the London-based central committee didn't agree with what they were doing they could be asked to stop using the Abbeyfield name.

Brighton, for example, had adopted the spirit of the principles we had suggested but had applied and interpreted them in their own way. This became the pattern of acceptance for all the local societies, and seemed a sensible administrative approach to the growing, overall structure. This devolved approach was also less bureaucratic and allowed each locality to adapt for its specific needs rather than be dictated to by the society's centre in London. It certainly made it easier for us while Abbeyfield remained small, and we at its centre so few and still, in terms of management, inexperienced. It was many years later, during the Seventies to Nineties, when there were more than 600 local, autonomous Societies, that real difficulties of administration arose.

1959: Abbeyfield in Canvey Island and Oxford

Canvey Island (on the Thames estuary), for example, where a house opened in 1959, was another early one. Here, the moving spirit was a Russian émigré, Mrs Galperin, who having heard a BBC radio broadcast "This Day and Age" about Abbeyfield made her way, unannounced, to a singsong at Eugenia Road. Discovering there what the society was all about, she returned to Canvey and started an Abbeyfield house – which still runs today – among her neighbours. And in Oxford a similar start was made in 1959. Prior to going to live in Oxford, and to find out whether or not they might try our experiment there, Robert Darby and his wife, the author Mary Bosanquet, visited us in Bermondsey. Not only did they start a very successful Abbeyfield house in Walton Street but also Robert joined us at Abbeyfield's central office in London, and helped start other houses in central England.

23

ONWARDS AND OUTWARDS

By 1959 the society was established in Bermondsey, Macclesfield, Brighton, Canvey Island and Oxford, and had unlimited plans and hopes for expansion. The timing was, therefore, perfect to take up an offer to help us from Christian Teamwork, an organisation of businessmen pledged to the spreading of practical Christianity. After discussions with their chairman, Christopher Buxton, Christian Teamwork became involved, through committees, with our deliberations and by the end of that year (1959) one of them, Tommy Frankland, had become a full-time worker with the Abbeyfield Society.

Thus, while Abbeyfield was first established in 1955/6, it was in 1959 that – with Christian Teamwork helping to build up the administrative framework to carry a growing movement – a national organisation was properly created, still named the Abbeyfield Society, with an office in central London.

22. Abbeyfield committee group, Wokingham 1959, including Mr and Mrs Christopher Bulteel, Mr and Mrs Michael Bowers, Susan Carr-Gomm, Tommy Frankland, Kathleen Robertson and Heather Miles

New regime; rapid growth

Now, however, with a salaried staff, Frankland ran the Abbeyfield's central office from his flat in Manchester Square, London and, as development director responsible for finance and growth outside Bermondsey, he took the idea to Northern Ireland, Scotland and Wales. The building of a family of Abbeyfield Societies in which the material, human and spiritual aspects were given equal consideration, was thought through carefully at this stage, and it was in relation to this that later conflicts about things such as the close involvement of neighbours, monthly sing-song meetings, spending, and, by 1964, over things such as direction, control and management showed themselves.

Gillie Gunnis who had been an occasional volunteer, also in 1959, took over the full-time running of the society's Bermondsey-based operation which, under the umbrella of the Abbeyfield's national society, had, like all the others, become autonomous with a committee of its own and responsibility for itself in every way, including financial. This left me free to travel around and help start further regional Societies in other parts of the UK.

This growth was exciting and encouraging. Abbeyfield houses, based on our original ideas, were established in many parts of the country as people, both privately and in organisations and groups, picked up the idea and got their own houses going. The first step was always to establish good relationships between neighbours, local organisations and the society. And, by negotiating favourable borrowing and mortgage rates with building societies and banks, we were usually able to start new houses with minimal funds. House expenses, including mortgage and loan repayments, were met by the residents' weekly contributions with the help, where necessary, of their supplementary allowances from the National Assistance Board.

Financed in such a way, each house became economically sound from the moment it was full, so that once a local group decided to set up an Abbeyfield house, they could do so quickly, without much involvement in fund-raising; this also avoided financial competition with long-established local charities.

When, for example, in 1960 a group of people in Beckenham, in Kent, wanted to set up an Abbeyfield house, a building society gave them a 75 per cent mortgage and a bank loaned the remainder. Within two months the Victorian property had been converted by a local builder and five residents and a housekeeper had moved in. The Beckenham group formed a "Friends" of their society and soon bought four more houses.

The administrative simplicity and speed of development that the Abbeyfield's national organisation enabled was described succinctly in 1961 by the seamen's committee in Hull:

> An ordinary house was bought in an ordinary street. The minimum of alteration and decoration was completed, the house furnished and the housekeeper found. Four aged lonely seafaring folk, two men (one black) and two women, moved in. It was quickly done.

While in Leamington in 1962, members of the Rotary Club found a suitable house which the local Council bought and leased back to them at a reasonable rent. They installed central heating and the Round Table and Inner Wheel helped to furnish it. This approach had already been successful in Cheltenham, Gloucestershire 1960 where a headmaster, two doctors, two housewives, two civil servants and two councillors formed an Abbeyfield Society and persuaded the Council to buy a house and lease it back on reasonable terms; volunteers did all the necessary internal decoration, and within a few months the residents moved in.

Spurred on by Rupert Gunnis (Gillie Gunnis's uncle) and local GP Dr Raham-Williams's concern for some of his patients' loneliness and lack of care, an Abbeyfield house was started in 1961 the spa town of Tunbridge Wells, Kent. Here, the funds raised included £300 won on a local TV quiz programme, and, following this, an appeal brought in sufficient covenants to buy and make alterations to the house. The owner who had virtually given us the house – and left us a legacy – stayed on and became a wonderful housekeeper, organising coffee-parties and bring-and-buy sales and enthusing neighbours to such an extent that the house regularly attracted gifts from flowers, fruit and vegetables to a television set and a refrigerator.

Adapting to change

By 1963 there were 180 Abbeyfield houses in the UK; by 1979 there were 750. Inevitably, such rapid growth brought with it a change in atmosphere and this was felt most strongly by those who, since 1955/6, had been working and living voluntarily, and irregularly, at the Bermondsey houses. Over the years up until 1963 these volunteers had built up a distinctive pattern of existence made up of small, but important, things such as long talks, late meals, parties round a fire in the garden, excursions to Trafalgar Square on Guy Fawkes night or the *son et lumière* at Greenwich and endless discussions in the riverside pubs and cafes. This way of life had ceased with the advent of the Abbeyfield's salaried central organisation and the shift of importance to the new areas around the UK.

As a result, during the last few years up until 1963 these volunteers dispersed; some married, some found new jobs away from Bermondsey and Abbeyfield, others moved out of London. This did not affect the Bermondsey community too much and lives went on with no abrupt change in routine. But some of the spirit of the old days of Abbeyfield had gone and the few who were left missed it.

Financing development

Various trusts, foundations, businesses and industries gave financial backing to the Abbeyfield when the national society was established in 1959, so we were able both to pay our central staff and to cover our increasingly expensive administrative costs. While each area or town was responsible for its own financing, their contributions towards central funds were never realistic. Conversely, through funds donated to the society as a whole, we were sometimes able to help a little from the centre when there was a particular local need.

In terms of fund-raising – principally to cover administration costs but also to buy houses – we had both successes and failures. The failures came, on the whole, from our big attempts at appeals by post and on television and radio. Our successes often came about by chance when people decided spontaneously to help, but the impulsive generosity shown by so many individuals in our early days diminished as the society became more organised.

A theatrical fundraiser at a church hall in 1958 failed to raise much money but, the following year, a charity bridge tournament at London's Grosvenor House Hotel was a great success; Anne, the Princess Royal, gave away the prizes making her the first member of the Royal Family to attend any of Abbeyfield's gatherings.

From then on, at fashionable London venues such as Quaglino's, we held smart dances – named "Cobweb" balls after someone's pet budgerigar – run at first by volunteers then by paid organisers who raised in excess £1,000.

From around 1961 legacies began to bring in funds, but these were usually bequeathed to local areas and not, as we had hoped, to the central office in London. However, over some seven years we slowly built up our covenants to a realistic operating level.

Direct and indirect grants from urban, rural and district Councils as well as mandatory and discretionary rate reductions were helpful and the system in place in Northern Ireland was particularly accommodating for housing and benefit needs such as ours.

A few county councils were suspicious of us, or unconvinced they had lonely people in need or felt that they were already doing everything possible about housing applicants. Some were critical and difficult and got the facts wrong or were simply determined to keep everything to do with specialist and old people's housing firmly in their own hands.

In order to forge closer links and more direct contact with local helpers and Abbeyfield residents, we decentralised the office in 1960 so that some of the principal staff worked from their own homes in different parts of the country. This decentralisation also helped us to explain – more professionally and formally – the Society's guiding principles to those doing the work and to enlarge on the human and spiritual motives behind our thinking.

A visionary team

All this development stemmed from that time in 1959 when we gathered together a core of staff who were both wonderfully pioneering and creative: Tommy Frankland who ran the central office in London with our secretary, Mrs Freda Lincoln, and three great leaders in the regions – Robert Darby, who had started the Oxford house and then administered the Midlands and the South for us, Mark Tully (later the BBC's India correspondent) in the North and East, and Raymond Jolliffe (now Lord Hylton) in the West Country. Their coming – as with Mrs Muriel Dawn in Northern Ireland and Miss Alice Garrett in Scotland – and their vision to widen the society's horizon, made all our subsequent growth possible; all of them were involved in first starting, then continuing the growth and development of new houses in new areas.

Government departments were helpful, too. Dame Evelyn Sharpe of the Housing Department took great interest in our work and authorised Councils throughout the country to assist us whenever possible. Various Ministers and MPs on both sides of the House – the Conservative's Robin Turton, the Liberal's Lord Beveridge, and our Bermondsey MP, Labour's Bob Mellish, for example – supported us.

Abbeyfield continued its aim to involve people of all ages. In Wakefield, a group of teenagers created and ran an Abbeyfield house. They were advised to collect £300 as a token of real intention before they started; after 18 months they had collected it and were house-hunting with enthusiasm. At Guildford, two young boys on probation turned up at the local hospital asking if they could clean up the wards

– they had read about Abbeyfield and it had shown them that they, too, could be useful.

Those who made our ideal materialise continued to find that the help of neighbours eliminated loneliness and created friendship. Neighbours, after all, were always there and come celebration or crisis proved useful volunteers. Apart from the more obvious help they might offer – relieving a housekeeper, gardening, taking residents out for drives – one neighbour's daughter called at each resident's room, in her wedding dress; afterwards they all described her as "a vision".

Kind neighbours in Ipswich, even before the house opened, left gifts on the doorstep and the first singsongs at houses in Bradford, Cambridge, Witney and Hexham were swamped by neighbours of all ages who looked in to join in the fun and lend a hand.

Wealthy but lonely

Having begun with houses for the lonely living on low or middle incomes, we decided in 1960 to find out if Abbeyfield's efforts to combat loneliness could help people on high or very high incomes. (This idea was taken to fruition with the foundation in 1972 of the Morpeth Society, *(Ch. 27)*. Towards the end of 1960 we were looking for flats to rent in expensive areas such as central London, Camberley, Eastbourne, Gosport and Bournemouth in the south of England and Perth in Scotland.

Local reaction in these much more prosperous areas was often disappointing and well illustrated in the following extract from a letter written in about 1971:

We are all totally against you and none of us are interested in the work you do if it involves taking over a house in our area. It is a prestigious area and all of us have put hard-earned money into our properties and are not going to sit back and see all this hard work go down the drain.

Maybe we don't know everybody living in our street but we don't want your type of people living on our doorstep adding to the dangers we already have ... all measures will be taken to ensure that we put up a fight.

I had spent six months during 1959 visiting smart hotels in central London, penthouses, service flats, nursing homes and so on in order to find out if there really were "lonely rich" – people with a lot of money who were, nevertheless, lonely. They had been hard to find, often protected by hotel managers keen to hold on to their wealthy residents. Twice I was thrown out of grand hotels for being too inquisitive about these layers of golden eggs, while I was welcomed by those wanted to rid of long-term guests who cluttered up the sitting rooms and didn't tip as generously as tourists would.

The rich people I met and who wanted our help could afford colour television, chauffeurs and paid companions – pretty much anything they wanted – but they were missing the kind of friendship that is given freely, unprompted by any expectation of reward, cash or otherwise.

There was an assumption by the general public that as a charity we would help only the poor, but now we had identified lonely people among the rich, too. As they had no financial worries, society in general assumed the rich had no other problems. There were plenty of appropriately-converted country houses and luxurious service flats into which they could move should their needs dictate. But if the wealthy wanted to live as part of a community with an actively neighbourly spirit, why shouldn't they?

With its fundamental aim to prevent loneliness, as opposed to poverty, Abbeyfield's constitution allowed us to try and help anyone who was lonely, including the rich. Because we were targeting smarter, more expensive locations for this venture we could not possibly afford to buy property, so I began trying to rent flats and was met immediately with opposition from landlords. They objected to us sub-letting and thought either that the society might try to make a profit or could create a dangerous precedent which other "undesirables" might follow and become, they reasoned, a canker in the landlord's bosom.

So, no help from such landlords and my chance to rent more than a dozen flats was lost as a result. One owner demanded a higher rent due, he said, for extra wear and tear on carpets and the additional hot water which our proposed four residents would use; we refused. Five flats – with a committee keyed up and housekeeper already engaged – were withdrawn shortly before the legal arrangements had been concluded when the landlords suddenly realised what we were actually doing.

Rutland House, South Kensington (1960); Wyndham House, Chelsea (1962)

In 1960 we managed to rent our first flat (for four residents) – in Rutland House, Marloes Road, South Kensington – but only with a little calculated deception; we told the lessee of our purpose, and he agreed not to tell the landlord when he passed us the lease. This made it easier thereafter as landlords could to come and see exactly what we were trying to do; most, though, still turned us down. The flat in Rutland House was disbanded after a few years because the rent became to high, but not before it had been joined in 1962 by one in Wyndham House on Sloane Square, Chelsea – taken over in 1965 by the Carr-Gomm Society *(Ch. 25)* and ten years later by the Morpeth Society *(Ch. 27)*.

Our more expensive properties were funded in exactly the same way as our other Abbeyfield houses: the residents made equal contributions to weekly outgoings which included rent, the housekeeper's wages and reserve maintenance – costs over and above this were still found from donations.

Believing the rich wouldn't want to be "labelled" as Abbeyfield residents, critics claimed no-one would want to live with us and, certainly, potential residents were slow to come forward; it was more than a month after renting Rutland House before its first resident moved in. This slow start may have been due to the novelty of our idea making people understandably cautious about throwing up their homes and former ways of life. Running these places for the wealthy gave us difficulty in finding staff to fill the role of cook/housekeeper/befriender – Wyndham House, for example, went through nine housekeepers in its first four months –but, in these flats, at least we were able pay staff well and did eventually find good people.

Upmarket uptown

Our West End neighbours responded much as had our East End neighbours – many were kind and helpful but the interest overall was not as great as we had hoped. Prayers were said and the "push" sign was on our doors. East End singsongs became West End sherry parties and dinner was called luncheon but the ethos was the same. Our landlords – concerned that such actions would lower the tone – asked us not to circulate leaflets or visit neighbours to explain our aims nor to issue a general party invitation, but we did meet our neighbours in the lifts and passages and several visited us.

Renting such costly flats (there were three) meant a large financial commitment from the Abbeyfield Society and even brief vacancies in them created problems for our treasurer. In London's East End where property was cheap we had not had this scale of financial problem, but our London West End committee was patient and, by the mid-Sixties we even had a waiting list.

The backgrounds from which our lonely, albeit wealthy, residents came was richly varied: one woman's brother had been executed by the English in the Irish Rebellion of 1916, another had been captured by a sheikh in Tangier; one was the widow of a Tibetan missionary, another a prison reformer. There was an ex-headmaster, a retired writer, a philosopher, several clergymen, artists and various relations of Members of Parliament, ambassadors and peers. While we tried in the flats to keep a balance between the sexes, we tended to attract more women and the average age of our residents rose to more than 80 years.

Extra care and specialist houses

Since the early Sixties National Abbeyfield had wanted to experiment with extra-care houses where our residents could go when they needed skilled nursing care as well as specialist housing for identifiable groups and secure housing – for those suffering from dementia, for example. Such houses, we thought, would be regional and each would cater for several local Abbeyfield societies. By 1962 specialist houses had been provided for groups such as women-only, Muslims, the blind and Huguenots, and by the early Eighties specialist and/or secure houses had been established, specifically staffed and adapted for those suffering from dementia, Alzheimer's and Parkinson's disease. We continued to wonder if we should try to achieve a greater mix up of age, races and income groups and always continued to experiment in order to find the full extent of need which the Abbeyfield pattern of living could reach and help.

Abbeyfield in the early Sixties

Meanwhile, the society's general knowledge of how to apply our principles in different circumstances grew. Some residents were living on fixed incomes and some in reduced circumstances; some had little or nothing at all put by; occasionally they had far too many belongings, more usually they had none. They may have lived abroad for most of their lives or never moved from their home town; sometimes they were well provided for and sometimes they were still working. The result was that by the early Sixties under the umbrella of the Abbeyfield Society we gradually gathered a diversity of flats and houses suitable for an equally diverse range of incomes and people.

Within each house the residents were of a similar background, with each area committee free to decide which type of resident would like the place most; Northern Ireland, especially Belfast where we had good mixed denominational committees, was the most progressive and successfully helped people from all backgrounds. Morecambe in Lancashire and the Scottish capital, Edinburgh ran them a close second, and Brighton, Oxford and Canvey Island all expanded quickly with a diversity of houses. Radlett in Hertfordshire was the first to start a house for people on upper-middle incomes, followed by Colwyn Bay in North Wales; Rutland House in Kensington was the first for the very rich, while Bermondsey remained a relatively deprived area. As a charity we could not by law make a profit so each house balanced its own books against the contributions of its residents.

DIVISION, DISMISSAL, RECONCILIATION

As the society grew during its first decade its work remained a drop in the ocean compared to all the other work being done for the lonely and for the elderly throughout the UK. Since the mid-Fifties, despite improvements in housing, education, health care and financial provision for the unemployed, problems in all these areas remained. And for many life was far from easy – a tiredness and apathy prevailed among the large numbers facing long-term unemployment – thus, with the advent of the Abbeyfield Society at this time we were able to try and translate some of these concerns into action.

The Welfare State, which came into being in 1948, tended to centralise social welfare and that in turn tended to take independence and responsibility away from the individual. This helped to create loneliness and we hoped that we could help counteract this tendency by giving our residents power to run their own lives within a supportive neighbourhood.

Conflict

However, while the society continued to help the lonely, we were facing difficulties within our own organisation. By the summer of 1962 a clear division had arisen within the central Society between those concentrating on the overall operation of its administrative, financial and practical aspects, and those dealing with the sensitive, emotional human aspects of the Society's work. Neither was exclusive, but co-ordination and co-operation between the two "sides" was weakening the whole.

At first, we thought these divisions merely mirrored similar, perhaps inevitable, problems faced from time to time by most voluntary organisations and committees. It is, after all, quite common to have a division of interests or priorities between the financial and the human, and usually a healthy, democratic compromise can be reached. Within Abbeyfield's central executive committee, however, we failed to reach such a compromise. Our arguments started peacefully enough but became more antagonistic – principles became involved, then personalities; opinions became fixed and opposing positions became firmly entrenched.

I saw the issue as a simple one; that in Abbeyfield, the

financial/administrative and the human elements should continue be considered equally and run together as one and that neither should take precedence; this was the principle on which we had successfully created our team of staff and built up the society. I saw myself continuing to lead and co-ordinate these two elements and asked for the administrative structure to be so defined.

However, most members on the committee wanted Abbeyfield to operate with a clear separation between its administrative/financial and its human elements. They were of the opinion that, because of the personality differences between me and Tommy Frankland – of which I had been unaware – the society would function more smoothly if its administrative/financial and its human elements were run in parallel by Tommy and me respectively, and with Tommy in ultimate charge over both; necessary liaison and co-ordination between the two would take place at committee meetings. The majority of the staff in our houses objected on the basis that the committee met only every few months and the type of problems which arose had to be dealt with daily. They were over-ruled.

A strong argument against the central committee's case was that concentrating on the material aspects without adequate regard for the human needs had led already to the formation of, by 1963, about one third of the Abbeyfield's 120 local societies who didn't understand the full vision of Abbeyfield. These 40 or so societies had certainly housed people in need but had not taken in the importance of involving neighbours. They had set up houses more akin to conventional boarding- or guest- houses, locked the front doors, discouraged neighbours, never had a party and wouldn't acknowledge the spiritual aspect. They brought together groups of staff and residents, sometimes happy and at ease, but always to some extent insular and detached from the local community and therefore not fulfilling the ethos around which Abbeyfield had been designed. Several staff and committee members had discussed and made known our views against this tendency in the hope that it would stop. But to no avail.

Dismissal from Abbeyfield, 1964

Neither Tommy Frankland nor I could accept that we should run Abbeyfield in tandem. For my part, the sticking point was the move away from the original ethos of Abbeyfield which the society's present situation was already causing; for Tommy's part I don't know for, regrettably, he and I never discussed sharing enough and unhappily he died of a coronary in 1975, our differences still unresolved. Thus, in

1964 it became apparent that one of us must go. Neither of us wanted to and I believe it was at this point that the committee saw it as a direct choice between Tommy, the practical and brilliant administrator, and me, the dreamy idealist. We never all, committee and staff, talked about it together.

I was accused of power complexes and egotism and banned from the central office, except on a pre-arranged morning once a week. I was not allowed to see the files without requesting permission in advance and was told that I was now on the fringe of the society and was to make appearances only when requested. Committee members, becoming angry with me, said that I acted as if I had invented lonely old age and, eventually, in 1964, the secretary wrote to me: "I have discussed with the others and we all feel that it would be in the best interests of the Society, if we accept your resignation."

After two or three weeks, as I hadn't resigned and didn't intend to, the 35 members of the Society (which included the committee of 11) met in March 1964 to vote on whether Tommy or I should go. The vote went 18 to 17 in his favour. It was a complete shock to me; I had not taken in that it could happen. As I was leaving someone, unnecessarily, advised me not to speak to the press and I became angry though, as usual, speechless.

Robert Darby, Mark Tully and Raymond Hylton, our regional directors in the Midlands, North and West Country respectively, soon left, too. My supporters had been overruled, some were dropped from their posts within the society, and a leaflet was produced emphasising the practical housing aspects of the Abbeyfield Society's work. Local societies in London and the rest of the country had not been involved in the dismissal decisions taken by the Abbeyfield Society Members, and while some of these broke away as a result, most, fortunately, ignored the storm at our centre and continued as before.

I remember well all those with me in the first nine years of the work we did and all the fun we had. All the helpers and the "livers in", all those on the ground; wherever we were, whatever town we were in, we had a great time together – residents, housekeepers, neighbours, the local gangs, officials and staff, regional representatives and committee officers, presidents, patrons and members.

The vision to spread across all geographical boundaries and social brackets and to be spiritual focal points for the lonely of all ages in their neighbourhoods and communities would I hoped, and hope, continue to be both the dream and the reality.

A founder must learn to cut loose, a parent to let go of its child.

This doesn't mean that affection disappears or that ties are broken, it just means what it says – let go. I had been forced to do just that, but there were no plus points for disappearing. I found that being an absentee founder for Abbeyfield was a strange role and best forgotten about. It was not easy, though, to forget and I found it difficult to come to terms with it; perhaps it's easier to understand from the outside.

In 1971, the year before he died, the novelist and journalist Sir Compton Mackenzie came to Bermondsey to see what I was up to and went off to write a foreword for a book which never came out. I wish his executors had been able to find the piece he wrote. In the late Fifties he had written about me in "Moral Courage" but he died before this book about the Society's work was finalised.

My memories of our houses in those days are mainly of the people who lived in them: Joe Gladwell, our third resident in London, saying, "I have no one in this world"; Tommy Sharr, explaining his loneliness in lodgings where he'd lived for 23 years without realising his next door neighbour had a son until they met at his neighbour's funeral; the 16 year-old charged with violence who when asked why he wore a crucifix replied "Don't know, all the fellows wear them, don't know what it means"; blind George Seymour who married another resident; three women residents, Nellie Griffiths, Mrs Worthy and Mrs Roust, and other early pioneers who lived with us; when she died in 2004, one resident of 45 years; standing left me a note saying how much she had enjoyed living in one of the houses

I remember, too, appreciative gestures by residents such as this extract from a verse written to cheer me up:

> Richard had a calling,
> To help the lonely hearts,
> It's where his social work began
> In London's Southeast parts.
>
> There he met his Susan,
> Who came to lend a hand,
> And at this time his heart for her
> Did into love expand.
>
> Now they have children,
> And open home for all.

Or this verse from another who parodied JH Leigh Hunt's poem:

> Abou ben Carr-Gomm (may his tribe increase)

> Awoke one night from a sweet dream of peace
> And beheld an angel in his room
> Writing in a book of gold

I never saw what I was doing in the light described by these kind verses, and neither did Susan; what we were doing always seemed perfectly obvious ordinary and it all fitted into the general pattern of our lives. It was also fun, and I never regretted it.

I also recall with pleasure the times I spent reading aloud to our residents – usually fiction or the classics. Storytelling enriches mind and spirit and neighbours, too, would come to listen and always wanted to hear more. A Dean of Winchester, Michael Stancliffe, wrote:

> ...stories form an almost essential part of the diet of the human mind. ...And from the earliest times and in every age stories in some form have played so great a part in feeding the human spirit.

Are these the snippets of memory which make up the "old" Abbeyfield and are not part of the "new"? I hoped it was not like that – the old, forgotten society created in 1955/6, now set against the new, dynamic one pushing into the new Millennium. Such disparaging sentiments were put to me in a letter from an Abbeyfield committee member in 1981:

> Speak and write on the early days whenever and wherever you please but it is 18 years since you left Abbeyfield ... and it was a different affair from what Abbeyfield has now become.

And in 1986 an Abbeyfield executive wrote:

> While we freely credit you with the start of the Abbeyfield idea in 1956 the foundation of the Abbeyfield movement proper, under the co-ordination of the National Society, should be dated to start from 1959.

Abbeyfield expansion abroad

That Abbeyfield should spread to other countries had always been an obvious next step. In 1958 I had talked to Billy Graham about starting a house in the USA and one of our first helpers, the Baroness van Heemstra *(Ch. 20)*, who was Dutch, offered support in her country.

In 1988, Abbeyfield International took its first steps when it started in English-speaking Australia, New Zealand, Canada and South Africa but by 1994 Belgium, Holland, Jersey, Eire and Italy had swelled the numbers. By 2004, outside the UK, there were almost 100 Abbeyfield houses around the world with more to come perhaps in Japan,

Cyprus, Germany and the USA; Richard Biddlecombe and his successors as Executive Director, Peter Newbery and Richard Seaman, supported by Peter Unwin and John Turnbull, were giving them inspired and lively leadership. As, also, was Allan Snowie, Air Canada's chief Pilot, who was and is a great pioneer and herald for us.

23. Abbeyfield House, Masterton, New Zealand

In 1997 I was invited by Bob McMullan to visit the Abbeyfield houses in British Columbia and Vancouver, and in 2002, Susan and I attended an Abbeyfield International Convention in New Zealand following which we visited most of the Abbeyfield houses on both the North and South Islands as well as houses in Sydney, Melbourne and Mortlake in Australia, both Canadian coasts and the sole USA house in Chicago. On Vancouver Island Susan visited the house and people to whom she, her siblings and a cousin had been evacuated during the war *(Ch. 16)*. The Convention was a great success and the atmosphere and feel of the three "Ps" –push (on the door), parties and prayers, i.e. involvement with people – on which Abbeyfield had been born were tangible.

During this tour, a New Zealander asked what motivated me to begin Abbeyfield and he, then, told how he felt destined to start such homes for the elderly in China where he worked. He was interested and receptive to Abbeyfield and I wondered if this is how things grow and what possibilities lay ahead.

The imperative remains that we should continue to make whatever small contribution we can towards world unity: by 2003 13 United Nations countries were part of Abbeyfield and Germany looked like being the 14th with Uganda, China, the Russian Federation and

Poland all possible.

Olive branch

So time passed and in 1978, thanks entirely to the valiant and kind initiative of Abbeyfield's newly appointed chairman, Noel Burdett, an act of reconciliation between Abbeyfield and me took place. I was, thereby, able to write to those friends who had been closely connected in the break-up days and an extract from my letter reads:

> It is now about 16 years since the parting of the ways with Abbeyfield. During that time there has been no contact with me on their part, while on mine there has only been the odd message with a local society.
>
> Early last year, however, the then new Chairman of Abbeyfield, Noel Burdett, whom you will remember and who lives near Cambridge, rang me. He had been a founder member of the Carr-Gomm Society and he and I had kept in touch through his consistent support and encouragement for our work.
>
> From that telephone call, meetings and visits gradually developed which, over the period, have led towards a sort of coming together of the two Societies. Committee members and office staffs, as well as residents, have met and mixed; finding that our aims were common has made these interchanges all the happier.
>
> I don't know where they will lead but I want you to know about them ...

They all replied positively and since then the Abbeyfield and the Carr-Gomm Societies *(Ch. 25)* have co-operated in general ways. When Frome Abbeyfield wound up they gave their spare money (about £13,000) to the newly formed Frome Carr-Gomm Society, and when Harrogate Abbeyfield closed down they made it possible for Harrogate Carr-Gomm (then looking for a house) to buy theirs.

Various residents, staff and housekeepers moved between the Abbeyfield and Carr-Gomm Societies, and occasionally, from 1978, I talked at Abbeyfield conferences or opened one of their houses. And in 1990, when my sister-in-law, Jane Gibbs, wanted somewhere to live Abbeyfield took her in happily.

The overture made towards reconciliation between the Abbeyfield and myself in 1978 had an element of distance in it, but it was genuine. I felt Abbeyfield wasn't too sure that I was still around but, as I was, they'd put aside their concerns and accept it. Beyond my real friendship with Noel Burdett, I was never invited to meet any committee members nor – apart from the opening of their 1000th house about 1992 – was I invited to any of the society's regular and frequent big national events,.

But I was cheered when I read about two speeches given at their annual conferences. The first, in 1987, was by Robert Runcie, then Archbishop of Canterbury, who emphasised the importance of neighbours and the community in overcoming loneliness and the second, in 1990, by the Prince of Wales – who had become the Royal Patron to Abbeyfield some years earlier – praised the society's volunteers and its initiatives to help ethnic minorities. Prince Charles's patronage was enormously valued by the society, and in the course of carrying out various major engagements he managed to fit in visits, highly welcomed by the elderly residents, to our houses. He also entertained some of the Abbeyfield's committee at Highgrove and I met him, too, at Clarence House.

These strong blasts for neighbours and minorities were reminders of the thinking on which the society had originally been formed, and they were mirrored elsewhere, such as in the lead being given to the society by Keith Arnold, Bishop of Warwick, when he urged it not to forget prayer underlined by "the tradition of prayerful support for our endeavours" which follow from "the Christian basis on which our Society was founded". He also welcomed the opening of a house for people of other than Christian faiths.

Abbeyfield is a great and good society; it is growing and it is healthy and there is invariably a strong and lovely religious feeling in its houses. As a result of Abbeyfield's longevity, funding in more recent years has been helped enormously by legacies and bequests. In retrospect, we probably made a mistake when, in the late Fifties, we gave local societies complete autonomy; they owned their own freeholds and therefore didn't need to have much contact with the central organisation – they may also have been less willing to contribute towards national funds. This situation was changed last year (2004) when the national Abbeyfield UK was formed. And Abbeyfield's original aim to offer help to the lonely – body, mind and spirit – across all creeds, cultures and classes, is what this newly-named society wants to achieve.

Back in harness

After our 1978 reconciliation I still felt a stranger to Abbeyfield as a whole. Then, suddenly, in 1996 a member of the Abbeyfield staff wrote telling of its 40th birthday coming up and asking if I would participate. I replied that I would. At the society's request I wrote a letter for general distribution noting the birthday and suggesting each local society might like to organise some celebration for it. An immediate response from Kent read, "Your letter cuts no ice with me – don't waste paper", but others were more receptive, and to me very welcoming.

Although I had been involved in three Abbeyfield events during the previous six years – opening a house in Thirsk, talking to some housekeepers in Colchester and attending the official opening of the new head office in St Albans – I was unprepared for the reception I was given at a party hosted in 1996 by the Chief Executive, Foster Murphy: I was greeted by two Cabinet Ministers, I met distinguished people whose parents were living in Abbeyfield houses and everyone was enthusiastic and kind. I felt like Rip van Winkle, though in my case returning after just 33 years absence.

Emboldened, I made chance visits to two Abbeyfield houses and that put me back in my place. I did not tell them who I was because I wanted to see how strangers were received. On the first occasion I rang the front door bell and asked if, while Susan was shopping in the town, I could come in and wait with them. They were friendly and gave me a chair to sit on in the porch outside the locked front door until Susan turned up; we were not invited in.

At the other I asked for a cup of tea and was told to go away because they didn't know who I was. I gave my name, explained that I was founder of the society and suggested they telephone to check this with Abbeyfield headquarters. Instead, they rang their chairman instead who told them to keep me out and that I could return in an hour and meet a member of their committee. When I did this the housekeeper sent the window-cleaner to tell me to go away or they'd call the police. The chairman later, on the telephone, supported them. I was staying a few doors away, and by 10.30am had retreated there and was deep into whisky.

But in March that year (1996) Susan came with me to the AGM and there I was overcome by a standing ovation from nearly 400 members – among them representatives from around 150 UK towns and cities including 50 houses in Scotland. Since then, to my wonder, I have been warmly and generously embraced.

In the excellent "Vision of Abbeyfield" written in 1984, Philip James reminds readers that the guiding principles were prepared as a simple statement of beliefs and had stood the test of time. Their philosophy is based, James points out, on the caring structure of Abbeyfield and is the whole raison d'être for the existence of the society; he states:

> I wrote a book on loneliness in 1927 and my researches for it showed me that for all new works it is the written word (usually called the 'Charter'), which goes on and lives forever. People and the spoken word die and are forgotten, monuments and buildings get knocked down and overgrown. The written word, even though it may be altered wrongly or torn up, has a habit of returning in its original form and being re-discovered; copies are unearthed and old cupboards hide first editions – it is, often, decades and centuries later, that they are found.

24. Abbeyfield International, Canada 2003. From left: David Ogilvie (Abbyefield, Motueka, NZ), Allan Snowie (President, Abbeyfield International, Canada), RC-G, Bruce Kaye (President, Abbeyfield NZ)

Reflections on Abbeyfield

So it is the Society's written aim "to help the lonely" and its guiding principles (that loneliness is a natural and normal presence in society, that it can be overcome by the friendliness and care of neighbours – often called volunteers – and that there is a spiritual content to it, which needs to be attended to) which are important and which I was aware of during the years of separation from Abbeyfield.

That separation in no way changed the original guiding principles. Nor did separation from Abbeyfield influence my work and time with the Carr-Gomm Society *(Ch. 25)*, the Morpeth Society *(Ch. 27)* and other allied societies (including St Matthew, Solo, and Richard *(Ch. 26 & 28)*; these societies share the same guiding principles as those of the original Abbeyfield.

25

A FRESH START, A NEW SOCIETY

When my dismissal from Abbeyfield in 1964 stopped me from doing all that I had worked for over the preceding nine years, I was neither consciously depressed nor did I continue to be angry; I just retreated from thoughts and feelings. But I did need to pause, and to think about something else. To help take my mind right off Abbeyfield I thought about happy things, and one of these was my 1956 holiday in Uganda *(Ch. 11)* with Freddie, the Kabaka. So where better now to go again? I wrote and asked Freddie if I might visit, and he replied, "Come". This was bad timing for Susan since, with Harriet our third daughter due in three months (May), she couldn't travel. But if my holiday was to have any benefit at all I had to go there and then, so, in March 1964, I went alone *(Ch. 13)*.

I returned from my three week break in Africa and, with – as far as I knew then –Abbeyfield over for me, I decided to work again as a home help. I thought that if I went back to the beginning – to the scrubbing – I could relive those early days and, in remembering what I had been trying to do with Abbeyfield, I would perhaps see the best way forward.

I cleaned for an old man who had resisted all previous attempts to clean his flat, but after just one week of my daily visits he barred his door and got rid of me. He said his coal fire was his only friend and he would light it come winter or summer, it was active and lively and didn't answer back. His wife had been dead for 20 years, his children never came to see him and neighbours said he had become increasingly introverted and resentful of people. If only there were a house in every street where people such as him could be helped and steered away from loneliness – but there wasn't.

It was time, I decided, to get away on a family holiday and in the spring/summer of 1964 we spent three glorious months in a rented villa in Corfu *(Ch. 13)*. Back in England, Susan, the children and I spent a few months touring around visiting some of Susan's many relatives, mainly in the West Country *(Ch. 13)*.

In the summer of 1964 I began to think once more about social work and the home-helping I had done earlier in the year. Sadly, I had torn up and never sent my farewell letter to the 150 local Society chairmen and now it was too late to bring up the whole affair again and write another. At the same time there was some tidying up of my own affairs to be done and no paid work in view.

In reshaping my life, two things had become obvious: I couldn't stop doing and thinking about the work in which I had been so recently and so intensely involved; and I had to earn some money. I hoped to combine both in any future work. Abbeyfield had ceased to pay me from the day they told me to go and, while we had survived the past year on proceeds from the auctioned tea-set and our savings, this state of affairs couldn't continue.

The librarian's lot

Making an income was a priority. We returned to London in autumn 1964 and I went to the Labour Exchange. I offered my services as a park gardener but none were needed at that time of year and a postman's hours were, I discovered, rather awkward. I was sent to see a local firm about a job as an office-boy but on my way there I rang the employment officer to ask if there might be a job in the local public libraries – I was attracted by the idea of working with books. I was given the names and addresses of chief librarians and set about approaching them.

Two libraries were already fully staffed and another wouldn't employ me because of my age (42) – they wanted young blood offering more years of service than they could expect out of me and, anyhow, school leavers were cheaper. However, the chief librarian at Bermondsey was kind and helpful and, once rubber-stamped by the library committee, in October 1964 he took me on. Because I had passed my School Certificate (with five credits Stowe reminded me) I was paid a slightly higher salary (£850 per annum) than most temporary library assistants. I joined a Trade Union, NALGO, (thereby accepting the "closed shop") and ticked the box indicating that no part of my subscription should go to the Labour party.

Although everyone made them as easy as possible, my first few days as a library assistant were strange and tiring. I had to rewrite constantly book tickets which I had completed incorrectly, tear up catalogue sheets where I'd made mistakes and correct my incorrect letter entries. I put the wrong cards in books, looked them up on the wrong dates and put them on the wrong shelves. I never seemed to have enough time and became angry with the borrowers when they seemed deliberately to put, for example, the "A" books among the "Ms" or the "Ts" with the "Ws", or who plonked their books on the counter and walked past without a greeting. But borrowers who, despite my beard, called me young man, boy or son were good for my morale.

Patience and perseverance

I began to get the hang of things and after three months was employed as a permanent member of staff. I worked the customary 37 ¼ hours per week of a local government officer and received the statutory pay rises due to my rather lowly grade. I continued to make mistakes and remained slow to find tickets when books were returned. I became interested in the "illustrations and pictures" section, which was extensive and rare, and wanted to reorganise it but, as a junior assistant, this wasn't permitted.

I was checked for reading when I should have been working. There was no time to read newspapers properly, let alone the books, and, even away from the library, I developed the bad habit of flicking through them and reading only the "blurbs". I found my name in at least four library books – by Godfrey Winn, Compton Mackenzie, Billy Graham and Leslie Timmins – and in several reference books; no-one at the library was aware, or anyhow mentioned this, and while I worked there my name appeared in newspapers at least six times and none of the library staff, perhaps tactfully, remarked on it. But, owning a miniscule bit of England – one fifth of an acre in Greenwich – I was listed in "Burke's Landed Gentry", and that was enough for one borrower to tell me he'd read about me in Burke's.

It was the children's library which really stretched my patience and I viewed my tours of duty there with apprehension. We got off to a bad start when some children threw a firework into the post-box outside the library after I had posted letters in it and I was not therefore well disposed towards them when they came into the library. Children always seemed to be noisy, rude and pushing, with no respect for books and no idea of orderliness or tidiness – they seemed to delight in putting the books out of order, upside down or back to front. They stole tickets behind my back and often had to be ejected, forcefully. I took our parrot, Ezekiel, to work one day and he caused great surprise. Fortunately he ate neither the books – which he did at home – nor the children, though perhaps that I would have allowed.

Over the period I worked at the central and branch libraries up until 1966 I became increasingly irritable, unresponsive and humourless – as a child approached me at the counter I heard his mother tell him, "don't be frightened, don't be frightened".

Some 400 books passed in and out of the adult library every day, and each year some 200 gramophone records; £35 a year was collected in fines and about 35 books a year were stolen. There were more copies (20) of "Grimm's Fairy Tales" than any other book and, while there were 50 books about the Bible, there were only five copies of it. Of the books borrowed, one quarter were reference (mainly cars and sport) and half the novels were from the cowboy, thriller, science-fiction or romance shelves – one woman read eight romances a week. The library's popularity surprised me, as no commercial bookshop had ever survived in Bermondsey.

I always enjoyed coming back to the Central Library after occasional afternoons at the branches or sitting it out in a caravan with the mobile Library. The staff was always welcoming, and when anyone left their last day was marked by sticky buns with our mid-morning coffee. And there were some curious incidents, such as when a man who believed he had been libelled and wanted the author's address so that he might kill him, and occasional requests for "sexy books". The library was also used as a refuge by those who under the guise of reading newspapers came simply to get warm and, of this, most of the staff were kind and tolerant.

Advent of the Carr-Gomm Society 1965

As the months went by my position as a library assistant began to feel more akin to that of worker-priest – unruly children, the poor and lonely taking sanctuary from the cold and my, albeit fringe, involvement with occasional incidents on the street outside the library involving ambulances or police.

Since returning from Corfu I had, in my spare time, continued some involvement with social work – visiting previous contacts and so on – and hoped, after a breathing space, to return to it full time. I had kept up an interest in Bermondsey's Abbeyfield houses and retained contact with the local Council's social services.

The Abbeyfield's drift into housing only the elderly had never been intended. We had, always, meant to help the lonely of all ages and it was only because most of the lonely people we originally encountered in Bermondsey were elderly that those Abbeyfield houses had ministered to them. Next time, I thought – if there were to be a next time – we must try and keep to the original intention to help the lonely of all ages.

In October 1964 I wrote to nearly 40 friends who had helped and stayed with me throughout and after my dismissal from Abbeyfield:

I am now back and have had time to think and formulate a few ideas. There is nothing definite and anyhow there is plenty of time, but nevertheless I would like very much to see you again and talk about them all.

If you were willing and could make the journey to Bermondsey, would you come down on THURSDAY NOVEMBER 26th 1964, and come to our flat – 28 Orchard House, Lower Road, SE16, We will have a meeting and discuss the future in general. Come about 7.00 p.m. and there will be some food as well as drink.

If you can't come, I will let you know what develops, but, nevertheless, I do hope you will be able to make it.'

About 20 of these friends met at Orchard House and it was then that we decided to start again. We elected a small committee comprising Edward Palmer as Chairman and Treasurer, John Stitt as Secretary, Juliet Bingley and me. (Eight years after we founded the society officially in February 1965 this original committee remained in post; their help with general administration was superb and, because we were unable to fund a qualified social worker, their advice on resident selection was particularly invaluable.)

Drawing on our experience with the Abbeyfield we planned to provide houses for lonely people of all ages with a special emphasis on involving neighbours. The wider, educational side of our aim was that by working with people from teenagers to the elderly we could deal with the problems of loneliness not only in the present but also, with luck, try and lessen the problem for the future.

Having considered other possible names – Orchard House Society (where we met), Society for the Lonely, Old Road Society (the office road), New Road Society (Bermondsey's Abbeyfield Road runs into Rotherhithe New Road) – we agreed to register as the Carr-Gomm Society; although I was initially against the name I accepted it, though I still find it embarrassing and wonder what people think of such supposed vanity and conceit.

First Carr-Gomm houses: Major Road and Storks Road, Bermondsey

In February 1965 I wrote again to the same 40 or so friends that I had contacted earlier telling what had transpired from our November meeting, and that while the legal machinery to set up the Society was going ahead we had bought our first house: 13 Major Road, Bermondsey. I explained that further funds (not from them) would be needed for alterations, improvements and for running expenses. The aims of the new society will be, I wrote:

(a) to help good neighbourliness and (b) to help the lonely. I have put them in that order because obviously if (a) was achieved then (b) wouldn't be necessary; until it is, however, both will be needed (probably in reverse order).

Perhaps from it might grow the reality of multi-aged houses, with some residents being elderly and static and others younger and changing.

Reactions were mixed: some – concerned for me should the Society fail – were against naming it the Carr-Gomm Society, others thought it unnecessary to start another Society and, out of kind consideration for me, a few felt that in the aftermath of Abbeyfield I should forget about the past and distance myself from social work; the Abbeyfield's Bermondsey Society had refused us use of their office at 36 Gomm Road for our original meeting. Bermondsey's Director of Social Services told me in 1964 to stop fooling around with small charities, that they were usually useless and that the State did 85 per cent of the country's necessary welfare work. I was reminded of this discouragement when the Morpeth Society *(Ch. 27)* started later. When their earlier offers of help were needed, nine out of any ten people "couldn't see me now", were "away" or suddenly "too busy".

Gifts and interest-free loans had raised about half the £2,250 needed to buy 13 Major Road, then a further £750 for decoration. With my father's will recently promulgated I found the balance which, following the success of the house, was repaid to me. Around the corner from the library, it was a small, ordinary house, towards the end of an ordinary terrace, with three rooms on each of its two floors and three more in the basement. It had neither bath nor hot water but, unlike 50 Eugenia Road, it had an indoor lavatory and electric light – though no power points.

With the Mayor and lots of neighbours in attendance we opened Major Road in March 1965. Bobby Walker, aged 26, was our first resident and he made himself useful, not least by allowing press photographers to picture him in each room of the house to show the variety of décor. Then, around September that year we bought a house in the next street, Storks Road; sadly, in the process of renovation and decoration, thieves stole all our lead and zinc piping.

Return to full-time social work

Carr-Gomm Society commitments were by 1966 intruding on my work at the library and I was beginning to think I must leave. I was holding up queues of borrowers while I added up our housekeepers' weekly accounts and receiving telephone calls concerning Society business at work – all of which I accepted was quite wrong and wasteful of borrowers' time and ratepayers' money. And sorting out problems, such as one resident charged with indecency or another inciting his fellows to join him on a thieving expedition, out of library working hours was proving difficult.

In 1965, along with some friends, Susan and I had taken the children on holiday to Inch Kenneth, a small outlier off the larger Isle of Mull. We stayed in the remote islet's only house – where Unity Mitford, a Nazi sympathiser, committed suicide when war was declared on Germany – and enjoyed a carefree holiday. We went to the Highland Games on Mull where we also visited Chips (later Lord) Maclean, with whom I had soldiered, at Duart Castle.

When I returned to work at the library Billy Graham, out of the blue, sent a year's salary intended to enable me to leave the library; not realising his intention I, instead, paid off some Bermondsey Carr-Gomm Society debts – I later confessed my misunderstanding to the Society and to Billy, both of whom forgave me. However, after an application by the Carr-Gomm committee City Parochial Charities gave me a three-year salary (later extended) as manager of the Society and I gave the library one month's notice.

On my last day I was presented with a blotter and pens and, in return, produced sticky buns for the traditional farewell coffee break. Although hardly a dedicated librarian I had written a history of the three adjoining London boroughs – Bermondsey, Deptford and Greenwich – which, while never published, generated some local interest.

On New Year's Day 1967 I began work full time for the Carr-Gomm Society. During the Abbeyfield's first eight years only about a dozen people under the age of 60 had stayed with us – some for a few weeks, others for several years. I wondered whether with the Carr-Gomm Society we would succeed in helping them – the lonely of all ages.

Abbeyfield Bermondsey split: Bermondsey/Carr-Gomm amalgamation

In 1967 Abbeyfield's Bermondsey committee decided to break away from the national Abbeyfield Society for the new Carr-Gomm Society and Bermondsey Abbeyfield had been working on top of each other; we were operating in the same streets, working with the same Borough social services and we all knew each other. Though strengthened by this – both psychologically and with the prospect of shared resources – I was frightened for them; nationally, the Abbeyfield was a large, well-run organisation and there was obvious comfort and security in belonging to it.

Then the Abbeyfield Bermondsey committee suggested amalgamation with Carr-Gomm but not all their members were in favour of the Carr-Gomm Society. Some members were against our aim to mix age groups, believing it would upset their elderly residents and feeling that the committee had enough on its plate without the addition of under-60s. Although they stayed with us, some committee members voiced their disappointment at our new approach believing it would complicate matters and create new problems, others simply left until, gradually, the remaining seven came in with us and brought with them their eight ex-Abbeyfield houses. The new Carr-Gomm Society could now go forward with ten houses.

At the same time as getting the Carr-Gomm houses going we had to reactivate and reorganise the office at 36 Gomm Road after Bermondsey's break from Abbeyfield. We had some money with which to do this but after two years of low spirits and now only a few helpers there was much to be done. Helpers were invariably short-term, voluntary and untrained therefore all procedures, needed to be simple to understand and as foolproof as possible.

We wrote to all the Bermondsey Abbeyfield Society's old "Friends" offering those who didn't wish to remain with us as the Carr-Gomm Society the option to drop out; our Friends fell from more than 500 to just 80. Thanks to City Parochial Charities we were able to employ a secretary, Betty Winter, for about a year until the money ran out and we had to let her go. Into the breach stepped a consistent and invaluable help from Community Service Volunteers (CSV) and various young people with time to spare.

We were short of residential housekeepers up until 1971 so we had employed friends – including Jane Whitteridge and Susannah Edmunds – and several CSV helpers who, despite their youth, coped superbly with problems from alcoholics to hysterics and threats to murder. As decades passed, their children sometimes helped us too.

As our two houses in Major Road and Storks Road were experiments to determine any demand amongst the under-60s, we were taking almost anyone who claimed to be lonely.

Housing the young
We set out first to discover the needs of society's younger lonely

people, then establish whether what our houses were providing was meeting those needs and, if not, make the necessary changes in our approach. To begin with the houses were run in the same way as the original Bermondsey ones: single rooms, a housekeeper who cooked the main meals, "push" signs on street doors, regular meetings which included sing-songs and prayers, and the involvement of neighbours.

By the end of 1966 our houses in Major Road and Storks Road were full with nine residents overall all of whom were under 60 years of age. As vacancies arose in the eight former Abbeyfield houses we filled them with people of different ages so that by the end of 1967, just under two years since the advent of the Carr-Gomm Society, we had ten houses with a good balance in each of male and female residents whose ages ranged from fifteen to ninety-one years – an average age of 45 years. Some had specific problems such as physical or mental illness, dysfunctional family backgrounds or poverty which led to loneliness, others were lonely for no apparent reason.

Ultimately, assuming that integrating the lonely across a wide age-range proved successful, we hoped to persuade other people or organisations to follow our example. Carr-Gomm's committee acted as a watchdog and was particularly exercised that we shouldn't expand too quickly and risk overstretching our ability to administrate the Society effectively.

Nevertheless, ultimately we would aim in the UK, and then worldwide, for a house on every street and a flat in every block where the lonely could live for as long as they liked. Ideally we wanted, and want, to establish our houses as accepted, ordinary, places familiar to all; people will know where their nearest house is and recognise it not with suspicion but with affection.

We hoped, and continue to hope, that if we can give a lonely person a home, even if only for a short time, it will be better and happier than the one they've left. We hoped that living in our houses would help dispel loneliness and that, with luck, residents – and those lonely who lived around and visited – might find affection in them; home, after all, is where all goodness starts, and from here well-being and happiness can spread to immediate neighbours and to nations throughout the world. This is living the life of love, which is the love of God.

Communication

Thinking about the first Carr-Gomm houses, I was intrigued to read in "Life of Robert Louis Stevenson" that in 1876 aged 25, he had lived in a small artist's commune in Provence of which he wrote:

> Theoretically the house was open to all comers. Practically it was a kind of club. The residents protected themselves. Formal manners being laid aside essential courtesy was the more rigidly exacted. The new arrival had to feel the pulse of the society and any breach of its undefined observances was promptly punished.
>
> A man might be as plain, as dull, and as slovenly, as free of speech, as he desired – but to a glance, a presumption or a word of hectoring, the household were as sensitive as a tea party of maiden ladies.
>
> I have seen people driven forth from the house. It would be difficult to say in words what they had done, but they deserved their fate. They had shown themselves unworthy to enjoy their corporate freedoms. They had pushed themselves; they wanted tact to appreciate the fine shades of the house's etiquette.

These residents, Stevenson's friends, were part of a group and his account describes accurately the realities of residential community life. Living under one roof isn't always enough to overcome loneliness; it's the inter-action and communication between people and the quality of communal life which does that – being together in an atmosphere of good-will and friendship. And this concept of community shows the importance of the spiritual; when the Spirit and its influence are left out a community, like a person, becomes lopsided and words such as "punished" and "driven forth" are used – a state of grace cannot grow without the Christian virtues of love and hope and the cardinal ones of justice and tolerance.

Over the years, together with friends, residents and staff, I would mull over such aspects of our work, and I would talk about it with the Carr-Gomm Society directors (Ian Robinson, Robbie Mathers, Tim Osborn Jones, Dennis Walker and Paul Wilson) and chairmen (Edward Palmer, Christopher Diggle, Richard Stanley and John Thomson). Such searches never end.

26

ALONG THE ROAD

When we established the Carr-Gomm Society in February 1965 the first thing to discover was which people we could help. We knew we couldn't provide for anyone needing specialist, professional help, such as alcoholics, drug addicts, recidivists and gamblers; and the Society did not meet the needs of anyone simply wanting bed and breakfast or lodging house accommodation. We could, we found, help ordinary lonely people, but we learned this the hard way – the Society's first seven years were marred by a succession of inappropriate residents, broken promises and bad debts.

Learning curve

Jimmy Skinner, for example, was an extremely lonely 34 year-old ex-soldier with a long history of delinquency who had been brought up in a home for unwanted children. Like many others he had acceptable references but, unable to keep his promises to quit his excessive drinking, he fell behind in his rent and ran away – twice he asked to return but the other residents wouldn't allow him back.

Then came Brian Taylor, lonely and recommended to us. A recidivist and father to at least one illegitimate child, he soon married the housekeeper – an unmarried mother with two young (and a third elsewhere) children. Brian's new wife ceased housekeeping and the couple began looking for lodgings elsewhere, during which time they rarely paid their rent, the children angered the neighbours and the house became filthy. Eventually I obtained an eviction order and a Housing Trust helped them move to a new house and job in the Midlands. In bad debts alone the Society had lost more than £100.

A particularly likeable person, but another we could not help, was John Duncan who by the age of 35 had served 24 years in prison for a range of crimes. He had been brought up in institutions and while he liked freedom he preferred prison. When he first lived with us he purposely committed a petty crime in order to return to prison and complete the sentence which had been suspended while he was placed with us – a pattern he continued to repeat.

After a three-year sentence he came back to us, but it wasn't long before he was up before the magistrate again having stolen and run away with £50, some from the Society and some from fellow residents. A week later he wrote from prison in need of much sympathy. During the times he was with us we got to like him immensely. At one stage he even took over the running of a house and did it well. He made friends easily with neighbours and fellow residents and had begun to re-involve himself with the Roman Catholic Church.

Alan Bean – an alcoholic, a meths drinker and separated from his wife – was another former resident who returned to his old life. He held a small position of responsibility with us and was much liked by everyone, but whenever he saw someone living a happy life he became melancholic and would spend his own and other residents' money on drink. When eventually he was arrested for drunkenness we found in his room empty bottles of surgical spirit which he would mix with the sweet, fizzy drink Tizer to make it palatable. However, unless their behaviour posed a physical threat to fellow residents, we rarely forbade anyone from returning to our houses.

There was much humour, too, such as when two residents in their 70s got married and the bride – who had been a barmaid in a riverside pub – expected the vicar to issue them with a baby. Mispronunciations like Westminister, Buddyism and arthuritis produced know-alls, as did stories such as how a resident's father had committed suicide twice because he had failed the second time, or that "I can't hear without my glasses" and the promise of a tune in Latin on the piano.

Good neighbours: the key to success

We continued, as was our aim, to rely on the help and friendship of neighbours. After problems with a housekeeper at Major Road a neighbour took on the role and, with her bus-driver husband as a much needed father figure and sergeant-major, the couple began to pull the house back together until six months later it was once more a happy place to live.

This coincided with a sympathetic and helpful newspaper article about the Society, but one in which our neighbours felt that they should have featured more and we had to throw a party, with a bottle of port, to bring them back onside; while a house could survive for a short while without a housekeeper, its neighbours' continuous friendship and involvement was crucial to its success.

By 1970 the problem of loneliness was increasingly accepted and better understood by the public at large, and the media – as it had with Abbeyfield – began to take an interest in the Carr-Gomm

Society's work. Sympathetic media support – especially television – was the quickest and most effective way of communicating our experiences and we willingly accepted publicity. This publicity encouraged not only potential applicants to contact us direct, but also social services, the police and the clergy to refer cases beyond the most pressing ones and this enabled us to find those who were lonely for more ordinary reasons.

In the same way as they had at the original Bermondsey house at Eugenia Road, neighbours helped in a multitude of different ways from posting letters and baking cakes to sitting with the sick and inviting residents into their homes – all of which drew the residents into the local community. Thus, ideally, we helped to build up a two-way relationship with our residents proving useful to their neighbours in return. Our younger residents sometimes visited the nearby housebound or helped to decorate neighbours' houses, while elderly residents might animal or baby-sit. And, of course, our house telephones – coin boxes by the open street door – proved an asset for the entire street.

Neighbours reluctant to become too involved avoided us while others were too shy to offer help and some suspected our unlocked street doors were a publicity stunt. But others found that helping others had helped them, too, and several felt moved to return to church worship or a prayer life. There were occasions when potential troublemakers said they were aware of so much enthusiasm surrounding our houses that they felt compelled to put all they had into helping, not destroying, them. Most importantly, our neighbours knew about their local houses and this was partly as a result of our evening meetings and prayers; even if neighbours chose not to come, they knew when they were held and that they were always welcome.

Criticism and complaint

There were not always enough good neighbours and several only got in touch to complain or tell us what we could or couldn't do, and some husbands refused to let their wives help us lest it interfered with their own family routine. Occasionally a neighbour wrote, unbeknown to us, to his MP or the Town Hall complaining about some incident or that a room was dirty or a meal uncooked. Day to day, we tried to avoid upsetting people or to give grounds for gossip and all we could do was deal with complaints as they arose. Despite all efforts things sometimes went wrong and residents would feel the atmosphere of the street against them, sometimes for weeks on end – neighbours would turn away, wouldn't smile, wouldn't say good morning – and invariably the residents, even in the face of their own problems, saw us through these difficult periods. Official investigations by statutory officials were sometimes carried out in secret which was disappointing for we hoped they would have taken us into their confidence.

Residents, too, sometimes lodged official complaints against us, writing to their MP's or local authorities about anything from supposed financial mismanagement and strangers looking in the windows to – and sometimes justifiably – administrative bungles or delays in making adequate repairs to properties. The majority, however, were wonderfully uncomplaining about the difficulties our inexperience sometimes inflicted on them.

Solace

To counteract the sadder aspects of our work, I found particular pleasure in carrying out my duties as an officer with the Venerable Order of St John of Jerusalem. This is an order of chivalry whose practical work is carried out by the St John Ambulance Brigade and to which I was privileged to have been elected in 1965, and in 1970 made a member of Chapter-General, its governing body.

My involvement included helping at the Order's traditional ceremonies, being dressed in a cloak and mantle and carrying a wand and driving people, including Douglas Fairbanks, to and from official functions. On top of the pleasure I derived from this, the dignified drill and pageantry counter-balanced my work with the Carr-Gomm Society. The beauty of the language and the intricate drill of Freemasons I found similarly helpful and often moving.

In the Carr-Gomm Society, the idea of our houses becoming house churches found no more favour than it had with Abbeyfield; my hope that they would become centres of street worship open to all denominations remained unfulfilled. Occasionally ministers or priests from different denominations – Roman Catholic, Methodist, Anglican – would take a service at house meetings, and Lenten courses would gather in several, but there was no enthusiasm or continuity. However, in the Carr-Gomm Bermondsey houses monthly house prayers and our annual thanksgiving service continued. So, in Bermondsey at least, we ploughed a satisfactory, albeit solitary, furrow with our devotions and the residents were tolerant in their acceptance of our ecumenical approach.

I found it particularly moving when one of our residents read the Bible at house meetings; many were illiterate or had poor eyesight and some found the language difficult, but read aloud by those who were able, its stories and teachings seemed especially significant.

Realising the dream

An astonishing mix of people came to live in our houses: a 45 year-old civil servant childless and separated from his wife; a young husband and wife – she, afraid to be alone while he was at work, soon regained confidence to return to their own home; middle-aged widows and elderly spinsters; strangers to London – the African refugee and the Mohammedan student from Nigeria; transvestites and trans-sexuals; the parson's son who had turned from religion to witchcraft and wanted to revert to religion; victims of torture; and the girl who had drifted from modelling to pornographic photography.

And we were surprised by the high number of lonely people in their late teens. They nearly all came from broken homes – often rejected by both parents who following divorce saw them as reminders of their former partner. These young people needed a period of peace, security and, ideally, work – as inactivity tended to lead to temptation and trouble. The society understood the machinery and knew the employment agencies to contact, and in 1978 we organised our own workforce to undertake maintenance work on our – and sometimes neighbours' – properties. In the same year we instigated a Residents' Association, run by the residents with a brief to help administer the houses and organise outings and events.

Government organisations providing children's officers, probation officers or social and mental welfare workers were invaluable in helping to provide the firm base and job that would give our young residents a chance to recover. The interplay of ages within our houses was helpful here, too, older residents sometimes "adopted" younger ones and this level of give and take proved helpful to all.

It was also important for our residents to have paid employment not only for the sake of their own independence but also in order to pay their way with us. The Carr-Gomm Society had no funds to subsidise residents and needed their financial contributions to meet its running costs. We were financially sound only when the houses were full and no-one's rent was in arrears, and this allowed us to direct all donations towards starting new houses, paying staff and developing the Society.

Funding: charity shops 1968-1974

To help the Carr-Gomm Society's finances we decided to open a charity shop in the hope that this would provide a regular income to meet all our work and running expenses. In October 1968 Bidda Mellor, a cousin of Susan's, gave us three months of her time to help us get started. She searched hard for a suitable property and, on the last day of her three months, produced 223 Greenwich High Road. Owned and unused by Greenwich Borough Council for the preceding three years it was very dirty, but Bidda had persuaded them to rent it to us for just £3 a week.

The first cleaning party had to take the floorboards from the windows and replace the floor before they could sweep and scrub, and a friend of a friend fell through the skylight as she cleaned it, but only the skylight was damaged. Supporters planned the layout and the décor and a group of student volunteers from Lewisham did the bulk of the work over several weekends. The Electricity Board quoted £215 to get the electricity going again but Douglas Noel, an army friend, did it all for free in his spare time from the War Office. Susan named the shop "What Next"; a friend of a friend who worked at the Victoria & Albert Museum painted the name on the door in psychedelic colours, and an artist friend, Diana MacFadyen, painted an enormous, eye-catching mural on the outside wall.

Six weeks later, in May 1968, we opened. We benefited from some local newspaper coverage and the shop found early success. Volunteers – and for a short while a full-time employee – managed the shop and we sold a mixed bag of items donated to the Society alongside those given by local people.

I would collect donated items in our family van or with a pram and people would leave items for sale outside the door; we had to put up a notice asking people not to leave anything of value for things sometimes disappeared before we got them. We gradually pushed the jumble of clothes to the back of the shop and concentrated on "things", such as silver, glass, tin boxes, travelling trunks, ration cards, toys and furniture, which sold better and looked more attractive in the window. When it rained the water came in and some thought our shop gloomy, but still people came to buy. A volunteer mistakenly sold our doormat and an old woman getting married at the Registry office across the road bought a pair of boots to wear for the ceremony.

One day a short, breathless, man brought in a new suitcase full of, he assured us, "good stuff". While we were explaining that we were only allowed by law to sell items we were given, a police car drew up and two policemen removed the man, his incompetent look-out outside and the suitcase. An arrest on the premises, all smoothly done.

The shop was broken into and money stolen out of the cash box on several occasions, nevertheless, our takings for the first month exceeded £300. As holidays came and our helpers left to look after their families, our takings dropped and it became a struggle to remain open for five days a week until, quite out of the blue, two wonderful women named Evelyn and Eileen volunteered to run the shop for us. At the end of our first year we had made £1000 profit and were sufficiently confident to continue.

In 1971, with Carr-Gomm's expansion in and outside London, the Society's financial commitments had increased so, encouraged by sales at our Greenwich charity shop, we decided to open a second one – this time north of the river. My brother Antony's daughter, Sarah, found us a boutique in the old Ponting's building on Kensington High Street; the store had been closed prior to modernisation, and on her way home from school Sarah noticed concessions were being offered to small shops.

Fortunately, the concessionaire's daughter was fond of someone who was working for a charity and we were given a site position at no charge. After scrubbing and decorating it looked as good as any other boutique in the store when we opened in March 1971. But it had a short life because the site attracted young people and hippies and the residents objected; drug use was suspected, fire precautions were deemed inadequate and the site was closed down.

In the same year, together with another charity, we accepted responsibility for another charity shop in Bayswater but this was not particularly successful and lasted only a few months. Then in 1972 the artist and diplomat Henry Jenkins, an old friend, managed by persistent, gentle enquiry to secure on our behalf a rent-free space at 121 Walton Street in Knightsbridge. It was a small, well-decorated shop and once we cleaned it up it looked welcoming and friendly.

The committee worked hard and we opened and ran the shop for a year until the building was pulled down. People were kind – we managed to staff it entirely with volunteers – and sales high and the shop became not only a valuable source of income but also a good centre from which to publicise our work.

In 1974, again thanks to Henry, 9 Eccleston Street in Victoria – formerly an undertaker's – was leased to us by Grosvenor Estates. Despite the fact that the whole area was due for demolition it looked as if we might be there for about five years, so we settled in. The Grosvenor Estates allowed us to sub-let a part of the building which we couldn't use to the "Point", a music publishing company; the rest we made into a flat for the Society's Director and shop manager Robbie Mathers and his new wife, Lal Gibbs – a cousin of Susan's. The "Point" and the Mathers were highly imaginative in the arrangement and décor of their allocated spaces and it was always fun to see the latest alterations they had made.

Grosvenor Estates claimed no rent but sub-letting meant that most of the rates and other expenses were covered and thus we could keep most of the profit made from the shop. This was not much to begin with and for a number of reasons: the site was poor for passing trade; we had its old reputation to live down and we rarely had enough volunteer helpers to keep it regularly open. In addition, several times thieves broke in and occasionally volunteers, frightened by a customer, would close up early. Nevertheless, in the long run, it was worthwhile and made enough money, and when we lost it four years later to a commercial enterprise we missed it.

Funding: State and residents' contributions

In 1974 each resident's contribution in a Bermondsey property housing four people and a housekeeper was £10 per week; in 1967, at the newly-opened Sloane Square house in Chelsea (formerly a Bermondsey Abbeyfield house) each resident's contribution was £57 per week and few but the elderly could afford it – the same applied to the Morpeth Society's *(Ch. 27)* properties (Morpeth Mansions, 1972, Oakwood Court and Holland Park 1973), all prohibitively expensive for younger residents. Sloane Square had been first taken over from Bermondsey Abbeyfield in 1967 by Carr-Gomm and subsequently by the Morpeth Society.

As a charity we didn't aim to make a profit and in each borough charges covered all day-to-day household expenses including the housekeeper's wages, board and lodging but not laundry bills and some electricity costs. If a resident had no money they registered with the Department of Health and Social Security (DHSS) which paid their rent – even at Chelsea rates if, by rare chance, the resident was penniless and part subsidised by a relative – and gave each resident about £3 weekly pocket-money.

Nearly all the difficulties we had about residents not paying their rent came from the young. The old defaulted occasionally, but in the first two years of accepting younger people we amassed more than £400 of bad debts. Some had defaulted on payments for a few weeks then disappeared; some, usually men, began by paying regularly then fell behind having spent the money on drink and gambling – it often took them a long while to repay, or we would recoup the money, slowly, through the courts.

It was difficult to know how to avoid this kind of action. All residents signed a rent agreement prior to moving in and rent was payable weekly in advance. Perhaps we should have been more careful in our selection of residents and reacted more quickly to recoup arrears, however small. One resident took us to a Rent Tribunal and, although as a charity we were not subject to rent control, we were keen to know if the tribunal would consider his rent a fair one; the case was dismissed and the resident told he was lucky to be getting away with so little.

St Matthew Housing

In 1967 Oliver Fiennes, Rector of Lambeth (later Dean of Lincoln and an inspired leader for our work in St Matthew Housing in East Anglia) *(Ch. 28)* asked me to advise on turning a house in his Lambeth parish into an Abbeyfield-type home for the elderly. During our discussion he, too, became enthusiastic to welcome people across the age range and, eventually, we agreed a tie-up between the Carr-Gomm Society's mixed-age Bermondsey houses and the Lambeth one. The mixed-age Lambeth house was run under Oliver's great leadership and with its own sub-committee. Carr-Gomm was, as with subsequent local societies, seen as the overall organiser. The late Diana, Princess of Wales was the first president of St Matthew Housing, and under its Director, John Miller, and successive chairmen – Peter Strutt and, in 2004, David Pownall – it succeeded magnificently.

Carr-Gomm's expansion to Thamesmead 1970

Since the late Fifties I had wanted to try setting up houses for the lonely in new rather than established communities and was keen to see what might happen if we got there first – before the neighbours – or if we and the neighbours moved in at the same time.

When in 1969 I read of the Thamesmead development just starting, I asked for a meeting with their social worker. I had hoped she would be sufficiently interested in our work in Bermondsey to help us start in neighbouring Thamesmead; she was and she would – working through the Thamesmead Christian Community, to which she was attached.

Thamesmead, built on the Erith and Woolwich marshes and extending onto the old Woolwich Arsenal site, was planned as a space-age city to house more than 40,000 people. In 1969 only the first 1,000 residents had moved in and the early infrastructure was brand new – the roads, walkovers and underpasses, the parks, the lake, the shopping areas and the bird sanctuary; scenes from Stanley Kubrick's 1971 film "A Clockwork Orange" were shot around Thamesmead.

With the Carr-Gomm committee's support I applied in 1970 to the Greater London Council (GLC), the landlords, for a house on the estate. Having received three negative replies, apparently from different sources but all in fact sent by the same person, I traced and rang him up suggesting we meet. He was friendly but thought there was no need to meet and said he'd contact me two months later, then added another month since he was going on holiday.

Then, just a few weeks later he offered a house entirely suitable for our work. Its rent was nearly three times the amount we paid on our Council properties in Bermondsey but, encouraged by Edward Palmer, our Chairman, and prepared to risk a financial loss in the first nine months or so, we accepted 78 Lensbury Road.

The GLC then offered us a second house, identical to the first, Wolvercote Road which we also accepted. Both were four-bedroomed houses on three floors and the paint was hardly dry; they were set on stilts in case of flooding. They had plenty of electric power points, central heating, TV, a bathroom, two lavatories, a garden and a garage (£1 a week extra). We were happy.

Opposition

With a month in hand before the first rents were due we began our preparations. However, neighbours – not immediate ones because as we had intended we were the first in our short rows – had begun to object to our plans. They had been disturbed by stories from someone on the estate who had previously lived in Bermondsey and remembered some of our earlier escapades there.

I invited those in opposition to come to Bermondsey one evening and see what we were really proposing; this some of them did and most agreed that they would now support us. But the Thamesmead tenants had been told by the GLC that good families would be selected to live on their estate and some remained concerned about the society's potential residents and still wanted to stop us moving in. It was depressing.

We hoped, nevertheless, that the general effect of the visit to Bermondsey would ultimately win over the remaining objectors but two days later we heard that a petition asking for signatures against us was going around the estate.

When one of our supporters refused to sign her neighbours started ignoring her and complained to the authorities about her dog. Then a group of seven angry mothers caught me in an empty room and talked loudly against our work. Out of all this emerged the fact that the existing tenants considered people in the following categories to be unacceptable neighbours:

1. The divorced: there's got to be a guilty party, hasn't there?
2. The old: the children will upset them and the old will shout back
3. Diabetics: they have spasms
4. The blind: they will trip over the children's bicycles
5. Ex-offenders: they'll assault our children

We tried to reassure and promised to consider their objections. We suggested they select two representatives to act as advisers on the suitability of possible residents and invited the still-angry ones to tea and further explanations. Of the 20 or so objectors invited only six came but that was enough to air the problems. Between them they had a mass of children towards whom they envisaged complaints from our residents which could lead to them being thrown off the estate. However, by the end of the meeting we did decide that in our Thamesmead houses we would not accept as residents anyone who had been convicted of sexual or violent crimes. Good as Thamesmead's existing tenants thought our work was, they still felt we should not operate in houses near them, although they did agree to come to our opening party a short while later.

Having been set in motion, the wheels of protest couldn't be stopped overnight. Letters and telephone calls had led to local newspaper articles reporting that our neighbours were preparing placards and planning to obstruct us on opening day. Fortunately some reporters were on our side and the neighbours, to their surprise, were branded wrong and inconsiderate. Approaches by objectors to the national media, as well as their MP, were ignored. In a public statement the GLC strongly supported our work but didn't confirm our tenancy for three weeks and delayed cashing our rent cheque for a month. The local policeman, however, was very helpful and promised his support. So we started.

Doors open at Lensbury Road and Wolvercote Road

Bobby Walker, our first young resident in Bermondsey, now aged 28, had camped alone at Lensbury Road until he was joined by the housekeeper on the day before our official opening in September 1970. Sadly, from the moment she arrived our new housekeeper complained that we had treated her badly and made inadequate preparations for her until, within the week, she asked to be removed. Susan Bark, a young CSV worker, took over successfully. Meanwhile one of our elderly Bermondsey residents, Bernard Hancock, keen to move to a smart new property, joined Bobby and the nucleus of a household was formed.

We were particularly fortunate in discovering kind neighbours in the park superintendent and his family who had moved in two doors along; they also fed us on the evening of our first party. And our immediate neighbours at Wolvercote Road, the local doctor and his wife, who had come to Thamesmead after 25 years in peaceful Northumberland, started off our party particularly well with a bottle of expensive sherry.

So things settled and even the principal objector asked if I would persuade one of our residents to baby-sit so that his wife could go out to work. Other neighbours were generous with gifts such as flowers, curtains and furniture, and a local church gave £25 – because the clergyman was dismayed that our house was open yet incomplete; that we should present an empty house to the neighbours and ask their help to furnish it was quite new to him.

Reaching terra firma

The build up of residents was slow because for many Thamesmead was too far from the centre of London. Nevertheless, by February 1971, within nine months of our first proposal, we had established eight residents aged between 22 and 75 in the two houses. The GLC had been bold in allowing our independent voluntary society to experiment in social group living and soon offered a further two houses. By 1974 we had six houses in Thamesmead, the last two being next door to each other and which we ran jointly and successfully with a shared housekeeper. Having rented us six houses up to 1974 the GLC wrote, "we'll give you no more houses in Thamesmead"; perhaps they felt enough was enough and didn't want to appear to be giving us preferential treatment. Nine years later additional houses were provided in Thamesmead, and I wish that those who had supported us against the opposition at the beginning had still been with us to see how it had grown.

In the first two years at Thamesmead we had problems. We lost five housekeepers: one was admitted to a psychiatric home, two took the rent money with them, one got drunk on duty and one became bored. Luckily, throughout it all we had Nell Condie who was a superb housekeeper, often looking after two houses at once. After the death of her husband – a man of whom we were deeply fond – Nell stayed on as leader and trainer of our housekeepers at Thamesmead.

There were also problems with residents: five had to be taken by ambulance to psychiatric hospitals; one a woman left the house, hopelessly drunk, and was found dead in a warehouse three weeks later and one was beaten up by a gang because he had no money to give them. Our residents were a mixed bag who, over the years, included a colonel, a priest, a hotel receptionist, a tube train driver, a Barnado's boy, two civil servants, an insurance collector, a doll maker, a Mauritian soldier, an ex-offender from Holloway Prison and a gipsy.

As our number of houses increased our neighbours showed both tolerance and understanding. Despite being subjected to abuse from psychologically disturbed residents and endless rebuffs our neighbours' generosity in giving everything from gifts to their labour and friendship was undaunted. They even forgave us when, not having received his records, we accepted as a resident a repeat offender who fitted most of the categories we had promised our neighbours not to have living with us on Thamesmead.

Our houses settled and established our routine which, as always, included a monthly meeting, or singsong, and the saying of prayers. Perhaps due to a greater need for security in this totally new environment, our meetings on Thamesmead were better received there than in Bermondsey where, in 1973/4 meetings were at rather a low ebb. On Thamesmead someone would sometimes play an electric or mouth organ for us, poetry readings were quite popular and, as we had found in Bermondsey's early days, making that contribution to the group helped some people's confidence.

But at Thamesmead and Bermondsey house prayers were in need of a re-think. They had been going for many years during which enthusiasm had variously waxed and waned. In order to rejuvenate the spiritual aspect of the Society's work, in the early Seventies we sought even more help from the ministers and clergy of local churches and while our requests in the early days had sometimes fallen on unready ears, this time we found a quicker and kinder response.

Roman Catholics, Anglicans and Methodists were particularly helpful and only some of the fraternal or Free Churches refused to support anything encouraging ecumenicism. The outcome was that churches of a variety of denominations agreed to take over the pastoral care of those living in our houses. This was not well received by all our residents, some of whom feared they would have to pray when they might rather do something else, or that they would have to tell the minister their secrets; some had as much fear of a priest as of a policeman and were equally suspicious of both coming into their houses.

25. Contrast in the Society's places: a flat in this block in Bermondsey; a wing of the convent in Bartestree, near Hereford; a house on Thamesmead

But a few of the clergy were of a tough breed and not only persevered with their visits to our houses but also brought members of their congregations. Thus when a priest moved on the relationships between residents and members of congregations would be maintained, although sadly many of these contacts later faltered and mostly died.

During the early Seventies there was some trouble afoot between the Society and the Thamesmead Housing Committee one of whose members, at a GLC public meeting, had demanded that we improve our image before we could expect further help from the housing committee; that same committee appeared to be making it difficult for us to obtain eviction orders against three residents who owed more than £900 in rent. We did, eventually, through the courts succeed in evicting these residents and from 1976 the Carr-Gomm Society and the GLC recovered a happy working relationship; our six houses were full with a total of 24 residents and there were at least ten on the waiting list.

NEITHER POOR NOR RICH

To our charity shop north of the Thames at Walton Street in Knightsbridge came those who were lonely and in 1972 this encouraged me to make fresh efforts to increase the Society's work on their behalf in Chelsea and London's smart West End. The flat in Wyndham House, Sloane Square (once Abbeyfield and now run by Carr-Gomm), was going well but the residents were all ladies aged over 80, and one was 99. However, inquiries at the Knightsbridge shop – and from 1974 at Eccleston Street in Victoria – were mainly from the middle-aged, thus the aim for new houses would be to help this age group as well as the elderly. But would they be able to afford central London rents, and were there even enough middle-aged or younger people who wanted our sort of help?

I discussed the idea with the Sloane Square committee and, while they were generally in approval, they felt that, before expansion, more help should be sought to investigate the financial viability of such a project. With this in mind, I invited a retired stockbroker on board and began to look for, and found, a good and suitable flat.

We had sufficient money guaranteed with which to rent it and, at the original enquiry, the estate agent was prepared to let us do so. However, when I explained the nature of our work, which meant that the house would be in multiple occupancy, the agent found this unacceptable and withdrew the agency's original offer; they thought it would lower the tone of the neighbourhood and create a precedent for sub-letting properties. I tried several more agents and landlords but received the same reaction. I found myself up against the same arguments I had encountered during my Abbeyfield days when, in the early Sixties we had first tried to house the lonely on high incomes *(Ch. 23)*: "They've got their own money", "they can look after themselves", "let them get on with it".

Morpeth Mansions

But in the spring of 1972 we struck lucky with the agents, Freshwaters, who even found a flat for us – in Morpeth Terrace, beside Westminster Cathedral, on the top floor at 11 Morpeth Mansions. It had been home to Sir Winston and Lady Churchill and included a study where he had written some of his books. Churchill

Famous: Morpeth Mansions

Be at home in the flat that Winnie owned

IF ONLY homes could speak, the tales told by a Westminster maisonette would have biographers flocking to bid for 11 Morpeth Mansions at Allsop and Co's auction next Thursday at the Intercontinental Hotel in Mayfair, London.

Sir Winston Churchill once lived in this seven-bedroom penthouse. He took over the lease in 1930 from Frances Stevenson, then secretary and mistress to David Lloyd George, whom she eventually married.

A decade later, after he became prime minister in a frantic move to save Britain from seemingly virtual destruction by the Third Reich, Churchill and his family left for 10 Downing Street.

Today, the flat is in need of total modernisation, but there is an 85-year lease and fine views of Westminster Cathedral. Gary Murphy, of Allsop and Co, is optimistically hoping for bids of around £300,000.

had taken the flat in 1930 from Miss Frances Stevenson, secretary to and mistress (later wife) of David Lloyd-George, and had left it in 1940 to go to the Admiralty and then to Downing Street. The flat, therefore, had connections with the Prime Ministers of two world wars and, for interest, we made a collection of references about their times in the flat. It comprised 11 rooms over two floors and reminders of Churchill included – the bell system, the rope banister-rail and the oval window through which Lady Churchill had so enjoyed the view of the campanile of Westminster Cathedral. The flat held resonance for me personally, too; in the early 1910s my uncle (Hubert) had been Churchill's PPS, and I had helped guard him occasionally at Chequers during 1943 *(Ch. 9).*

While the flat was suitable for our experiment, the rent was high and would bring Morpeth's total weekly outgoings to £206 divided between seven people compared to Bermondsey's £32 divided between four; the financial risk was considerable. After a series of meetings, Carr-Gomm's Sloane Square committee decided they couldn't take it on as it was too great a responsibility and would need more time and work from them than they had available to give. And, feeling that the financial risk to great, our stockbroker adviser withdrew.

The Carr-Gomm Society committee also declined to take on the flat on the basis that time could be better used helping those with less money and that it was too far away from our base in Bermondsey for easy administration. No less than three banks refused to allow a guarantee to be used, none would provide a bridging loan, and the Charity Commissioners stated they would be unlikely to consider it within our charitable status to support and run such a flat: according to their Elizabethan Charter of 1601 charity meant helping those without adequate financial support and we weren't going to be doing that. Our residents, although lonely, were going to be financially secure –wealthy, even – so if this venture was to go ahead it must be without the Carr-Gomm Society and not seek charitable status. I would have to do it alone.

Against all odds ...

In order to pursue the experiment I resigned one fifth of my salary and my time (one day a week) with the Carr-Gomm Society. The landlord of 11 Morpeth Mansions let me take on the flat in my own name – he even reduced the rent to make it easier – and I went ahead and registered a company name for the venture, the Morpeth Company; it was three years before we could, properly, call ourselves a charity.

27. Morpeth: an evening meeting in the Morpeth Society, including Mary Harrison and Anthea Osborn Jones

Susan thought I was mad but didn't try to stop me, she is usually critical of my ideas and solutions to problems and this, maybe, has prevented our marriage from becoming stale. Knowing Susan won't necessarily think my ideas good ones, I never take anything for granted. The principle of the devil's advocate is useful – but maddening (but not for long) when it's one's wife. Anyhow, the flat was mine. Friends rallied and we formed an informal committee comprising myself (chairman), Jane Strutt (secretary), Philip King (treasurer – he ran the estate agency, Omnium), Juliet Ramsden, Mary Harrison, James Macdonald and Ian Fleming (not the author); Mary, James, Ian and I then got on with preparing the flat.

Some of our Westminster neighbours and some members of Westminster City Council claimed the rich were not lonely and even if they were they wouldn't know we existed to help them; they, also, claimed the high rent would be prohibitive for the young and middle-aged, and that the flat didn't contain enough wash-basins, bathrooms and lavatories to be practical. The Lord Mayor of Westminster told me that he wouldn't have "strangers" in his Borough and he didn't want us encouraging them to live in our flat, nor should we house the sick who would put extra strain on local doctors; a halfway house for local ex-addicts would be fine, as they would move on, but the lonely might settle and must therefore be discouraged. Two bishops suggested the lonely we proposed to help had no particular needs, and a social worker wrote of her concerns that we would overlap with and discourage other voluntary societies, and stated her personal view that:

> ...too many people create their own loneliness because in their prime years they do not go out to help others, and unless they are housebound or bedridden the under-sixties have no business to be lonely at all.

By Christmas 1972 the flat had been furnished with second-hand goods picked up in the King's Road and was – after a fashion– ready to open: the hot water and the lift were cut off by electricity cuts beyond our control; the curtains weren't hung and the gas piping had been stolen so the central heating didn't work. And there were no applicants. I slept the first night in the flat and then a helper from earlier days, Betty Carpenter, came as housekeeper. The first 40 people to whom I had offered rooms had, politely, declined but our first resident moved in on 7th December 1972, a middle-aged, former Customs and Excise employee who had suffered a breakdown during the introduction of VAT.

While the staff and community of Westminster Cathedral supported our work, the chairman of the Morpeth residents' association visited the flat on spec and wrote that while near-by residents were in favour of our work they intended to move us out of Morpeth Mansions. He worked up a petition against us and when I went to put our case to County Hall's planning department I was told that my application for the flat's change of use would be turned down. But County Hall failed to formalise its decision and as the months passed we breathed again and continued our work.

Winning through

By May 1973 interest in residency was beginning to grow: a one-time millionaire now penniless, an African Princess, a baronet with four ex-wives, an antique dealer, a lawyer, a dentist, MP's dependants, ex-Judges, the "monarch" of the cloud-cuckoo Kingdom of Redonda (an unpopulated island in the Caribbean) and a divorcee afraid to live alone. We had our disturbances, and once the police had to remove a millionaire who drew a knife on Susan's nephew, James Macdonald.

Twice a week, we had lunch parties to raise interest from organisations and individuals concerned in housing – volunteers and our families and friends came, too, and sometimes Carr-Gomm staff from Bermondsey. A kind neighbour, Judie Pigot, served more than 100 of these lunches in our first year; when she asked originally how she might help she couldn't have imagined she'd become cook and fairy godmother to so many people.

By the end of 1973 the flat had only four out of a possible seven settled residents and three of those were in hospital and many applicants had withdrawn anticipating that their expectations would be unfulfilled. With such low occupancy, coupled with the Charity Commissioners continued unwillingness to accept Morpeth as a non-profit making charity, there was not enough income to help me pay the rent – which was in my name – and I was running out of money. At the same time, towards the end of 1973 the landlords offered an additional flat in Oakwood Court, Holland Park. The Morpeth Company committee agreed to take it on, and – despite spending £1,000 on recarpeting – a timely rent freeze helped to keep the society's overdraft within its limit – just.

Finally, by July 1973 the Morpeth flat had six residents and became a proper household. The housekeeper, John Phipps, had only recently left public school but he settled everyone down and kept up morale when one of our residents set fire to Churchill's study – six months later the same resident left the basin tap running and flooded the flat below. The Victorian mansion blocks in which our flats were housed were used occasionally as television or film sets, and seeing the stars and directors in action brought a little excitement into our lives.

Memorable residents

As a result of their wealth, our Morpeth Company residents were rather different from our Carr-Gomm ones: one said she had never emptied a wastepaper basket in her life, another wanted the housekeeper and cleaner kept busy because "idle servants complain". A resident gave Susan a cheque for £10,000 for playing Scrabble with him; she tore it up but a trustee told her later that she should have cashed it – the giver could easily afford it. But the recognition that riches cannot dispel loneliness was ever present; a Persian resident, for example, who – like other Iranian aristocrats who fled after the Shah was shot – had escaped from Iran; his wife and baby had died in a drowning accident and he told me, as others had, that I had everything which he had lost – home, job, wife, children. He was neither bitter nor resentful and he reminded me how lucky I was and what an immense amount I had to be grateful for.

Conversely, a resident, who soon became a friend, initially took against me because I had both spouse and house while she had neither; she was Mary Pactus – daughter of Joseph Stalin, the Russian dictator. An only daughter and brought up in the Kremlin with the KGB as nursemaids it was not surprising that she found it difficult to maintain relationships and show tolerance to others.

I read her autobiographical books, which I found fascinating, and we enjoyed long, interesting talks about her life. She, for a while, referred to herself as my "carpet" (car-pet – a driving companion to stop me falling asleep at the wheel). She returned a ticket I had given her for the dress-rehearsal of the Queen's Birthday Parade on Horse Guards because the Queen would not be there for her to see.

She showed me once a photograph of her parents, two brothers and grandparents; the only one she had of them together it was therefore closely protected by her. She loved her father despite knowing that more than 40 million Russians, and thousands of Poles and other nationalities, had been killed in his name; she knew he was evil and felt that his slide into degeneracy started with her mother's suicide.

She – once widowed, twice divorced and mother to one daughter – had become a devout Christian after her first marriage and, after she came to England, an Anglican. After her second divorce she tried living in a convent – indeed, during her third marriage she converted to Roman Catholicism. Marie, as she liked to be called, stayed happily awhile in a London Council flat before moving – incognito – through several Abbeyfield, Carr-Gomm and Morpeth Society houses, during which time she obtained British nationality. According to Mary, her father had not thought much of Churchill or Roosevelt. She had met Churchill once on friendly terms and I always thought it strange that I should be the instrument through which Stalin's daughter should find her bedroom next to what had once been Churchill's study.

Distinguished visitors

11 Morpeth Mansions attracted a number of distinguished visitors including Lady Spencer-Churchill and, in May 1975, Mother Teresa of Calcutta; she talked of her work in England and Northern Ireland – she said she didn't know why she had come to see us, but she felt that the Holy Spirit did. The Conservative MP Robin Turton (later Lord Tranmire), Father of the House of Commons came to discuss our work and revive Churchillian political memories, as did the Conservative MPs Alan Lennox-Boyd (Lord Boyd) and James Ramsden (one-time Minister of State for War) whose wife, Juliet (a cousin of Susan's), later joined the Morpeth Society committee; James and I first met in our respective prams at Mancetter *(Ch. 2)*. Cardinal Basil Hume was a neighbour and, over a cup of tea, we gained his much-valued support and the further confidence and blessing of the cathedral staff.

During the IRA's London bombing campaigns in the late Seventies and early Eighties, security police stationed outside the homes of local politicians occasionally came to us for tea. When we heard an explosion, people would gather at the block entrances to speculate where the bomb might have gone off then hurry away to find news of it on the television or wireless. In this atmosphere of uncertainty, frustrated by bomb-scares and traffic diversions, central London seemed at times beleaguered – then on top of it all came petrol rationing and increased parking fines.

Administration formalised, the society grows

By the middle of 1975 our two flats were fully-occupied – seven residents in Morpeth Mansions, six in Holland Park – and proving economic to run; we were also planning another house, suitable for five residents, at Gunter Grove in Earls Court. The Morpeth Company also absorbed 6 Wyndham House in Sloane Square which since 1962 had been an Abbeyfield house and since 1965 had been run by Carr-Gomm.

The time had come to formalise the Morpeth Company and its administration.

James Macdonald and then Ian Robinson had been overseeing Morpeth's day-to-day administration; James and Ian were friends of friends employed by the Carr-Gomm Society and Carr-Gomm's committee had given approval for them to undertake this work for Morpeth. They, with voluntary help from our treasurer, Philip King, had been dealing with Morpeth's books, maintenance and interviewing potential residents; Robbie Mathers (another friend of a friend) and others – mainly from Carr-Gomm in Bermondsey, and with its committee's full approval – had also helped enormously.

While further expansion would require us to remain involved with these things, we employed Philip King's estate agency, Omnium, as managing agents to take on the general administration and bookkeeping, and Philip organised us into both a company and a charity. After a year of negotiation the London Borough of Kensington and Chelsea had accepted us as a community home for (in loose terms) unsettled young adults, and described as such the Morpeth Company was able to claim charitable status and, thereafter, could and would be rightly called the Morpeth Society.

The Society – despite various efforts by the landlords to oust us – ran the flat in Morpeth Mansions for a further 17 years and, for me, staying regularly there throughout our tenancy was an added bonus; to have an off ice and bed in central London always available with a well-ordered meeting-place and car park was very convenient, and the hospitality of the housekeepers and residents gave me a secure London base, particularly after Susan and I moved to Mells in 1975 *(Ch. 15)*. Because the Morpeth Society's excellent manager, Gordon Wolsey, did his office work at home I benefited from his un-needed office space and often worked into the early hours.

In connection with the Morpeth flat, though, in 1974, I did experience a "down" in my life. I was beaten up by a former resident – a middle-aged ex-miner who had been evicted from one of our houses outside London more than a year before after refusing to pay his rent, breaking furniture and daubing graffiti on the walls. He forced his way, drunk, into 11 Morpeth Mansions where he frightened the residents and demanded from me, with a kick, £250,000 or he'd kill me. I refused and he left. For several weeks he tried to find me alone and finally did, in the office at Gomm Road. As he was a trained boxer I was no equal in swapping punches and when I was helpless on the ground he left saying: "I can't even bloody well kill you".

I managed to get to hospital for cleaning and at Guy's I was X-rayed and stitched up; there was some bruising, nothing serious but I was a nasty sight and didn't like being seen by the children. He was given three months' for assault, suspended for two years.

In 1984 the Society contemplated starting up a flat in Maidenhead and when this didn't come off we, instead, rented a big flat for eight residents at Richmond Mansions in the Old Brompton Road. Our failure to fill it quickly enough cost the society about £100,000 for we had borrowed from the bank to buy at the top of the market and had to sell it two years later at the bottom; the debt was paid by interest-free loans from well-wishers and repaid to them by the society over the ensuing two years.

28. Abbeyfield House, in the centre of Malmesbury

With luck, the Morpeth Society will spread to wherever the lonely without money worries might be, perhaps abroad, rather than wait for them to come to central London. To try this working outside London we opened a Morpeth house in Bath in 1991. The usual miracles had fallen into place: we heard of the house, available at an affordable rent, via Bob Little (the builder who had converted our home at Batheaston); we found a good housekeeper and some funds were donated. Possible residents surfaced and willing helpers materialised. The Morpeth Society's new director, Robert Cazenove, was on hand to help along with the perfect chair-couple (James and Pippa Diggle) and a dedicated and enthusiastic committee, which included Susan. The house is still going strong in 2004, and early dreams have long since become realities.

ALL THINGS CONSIDERED ...

With the Carr-Gomm Society's expansion, first with the Lambeth tie-in in 1967 *(Ch. 26)* then at Thamesmead in 1971, our next step outside Bermondsey was in January 1972 when we took over the Quadrant Housing Association's property in nearby Plumstead. Meantime, Ealing's Director of Social Services, the Reverend Nick Stacey – looking for a solution to his borough's homeless mentally disturbed, ex-offenders and social misfits – had suggested our pattern of house might work for them and, in March, we opened a house there, too.

In Ealing we, once again, hit problems. While this time our neighbours were friendly and helpful, the committee of local people we had randomly selected wanted to house only those suffering from severe mental illness. In their effort to turn the house into a mental home they refused entry to neighbours and removed the "push" sign from the door. In revolt against the Society's wish to house the lonely suffering, or not, from mental illness, the Ealing committee lodged a complaint with the Council that we had obtained the house under false pretences; they then took over an office at the Town Hall and produced their own agenda.

Their complaint against Carr-Gomm Society was over-ruled and with a new committee and local support we re-established the house on our usual terms. But over the first two years the house fell into greater and greater debt and we had problems with a housekeeper who ran off with the money. There were problems, too, with residents – one set about another with a chopper, another used the house to store stolen property – but thanks to the work of Robbie Mathers, Ian Robinson and some Scandinavian volunteers by 1975 the house was fully occupied and become a well-run and a happy place.

The Carr-Gomm Society's expansion continued. In Newcastle-Upon-Tyne a group of voluntary social workers took an interest in us and, after reciprocal visits a management committee was formed. After various unsuccessful attempts to find a suitable property they elected to form themselves into a separate company, while maintaining their connection with Carr-Gomm, and in 1973 opened their first house – financed by Alison Greenlees, a friend of ours from Abbeyfield days – in Newcastle's Sydney Grove. A friend of Alison's,

Anna Knox (nee Micklethwait), returned from the USA to take charge of the house and her imagination and tenacity kept everyone going. Anna also started a workshop where residents and anyone else around could work and sell their products; in 1991, under this regime, the Newcastle operation became the Byker Bridge Housing Association.

In 1971, after preaching (as a lay preacher) at a Remembrance Day service in Norwich Cathedral, the Lord Mayor and the Director of Social Services asked whether we could start our work in Norwich – the Dean (Alan Webster) and others also took an interest. In London, at White's Club in Pall Mall, I met John Wright, a merchant banker who took over responsibility for fundraising and legal formalities, and with inspired help and enthusiasm from a friend of a friend, Clare Anley, and Hugh Frazer (who had been in the army with me), a house was found, bought, opened and residents ensconced – all with remarkable speed.

A separate society, the Carr-Gomm Norwich Society, was formed, affiliated loosely to the National Carr-Gomm headquarters in London and our ideas, and further houses were soon set up on the same basis by independent committees in other Norfolk towns: King's Lynn, Dereham, Wymondham and Thetford with the help of Horace Wilkinson, a local businessman who worked indefatigably for us. In 1990 they were reformed as St Matthew Housing. The Carr-Gomm Society continued this pattern of expansion throughout England with autonomous local societies, each with its own committee, working to our original principals, under the Carr-Gomm or their own name.

With Carr-Gomm I saw, not for the first time, how a seed can grow then perish. An example of this was a lovely Queen Anne house – sadly lost to the Society – in the village of Batheaston, very close to our family's home there *(Ch. 16)*.

Peter Goodwin, having recently retired from Rolls Royce was now chairman of the fledgling Carr-Gomm Batheaston Society, having taken over from Kate Grixoni – Jessie Matthews's adopted daughter. Peter and I called on the owner of the house to ask if we might rent it for our work and she agreed, then said that she would rather give it to us; we excitedly and gratefully accepted and began to raise money for its conversion for our use. The house would have needed a great deal of work done on it and deer, badgers and foxes roamed its garden; the sort of wild garden Susan had always dreamed of and I had never provided – as a volunteer on the committee she had been immediately intrigued and, had it come to us, would have enjoyed being involved in its development for our work.

But the realists took over and delayed legal acceptance because of issues such as charitable ownership and financing repairs until, after a year, the owner withdrew the offer. Fortunately the monies already raised were able to be transferred to a substantial house in Weston, on the other side of Bath, which remains to this day a very happy household for about ten people and a wonderful housekeeper who has been with the Society for more than 30 years. (In 1993 three other Bath houses became independent from the National Carr-Gomm Society to form the Solo Society.)

29. Carr-Gomm Society house, Frome

By 1979, in addition to London, Newcastle, Norfolk and Bath (through a local newspaper article by Edward Goring and his persuading Naomi Buchanan to gather a local committee), we had houses in: Suffolk (with Peter and Gay Strutt at the helm); Frome; Cambridgeshire; East Grinstead (through Anne Bywater – boldly challenging one of her relatives who had petitioned against us at Morpeth Mansions – lent her house there and persuaded the local Council to give £5,000 towards a mortgage); Hove (through the drive of Susie Sainsbury, wife of the local MP); Launceston (through June Barbour, of the county's Social Services department and secretary to a group which had produced a pamphlet on loneliness for the National Council of Social Service); Hereford (here the trustees of Bartestree Convent made contact after reading an article about us in *The Times* – from this grew a wonderful partnership between us and its team who first came together working for Mother Teresa in Calcutta. A wing of the convent was converted by platoons of officer-cadets from Sandhurst; it became our "house" supported by the nuns and the local community).

Carr-Gomm consolidation from 1970

Following its absorption into the Carr-Gomm Society in 1967 the Bermondsey branch of the society, with its houses fully occupied and therefore with increased funds, was in 1970 able to employ David Hill to run its affairs at the office it shared with the national Carr-Gomm Society at Gomm Road. When he left in 1972, unhappily so soon to die, Robbie Mathers took over the Bermondsey branch's administration with Ian Robinson as his chief assistant. In 1973 Christopher Diggle became chairman of Carr-Gomm's national committee and Mary Harrison, Peter McNeal, Juliet Ramsden, Simon Cresswell and Michael Graham Jones joined me and John Stitt on the national committee (though as paid members of the Carr-Gomm Society and therefore not entitled to sit on its ruling committee, John Stitt (its solicitor) and me soon had to resign); Dick Jones worked part-time to organise our finances, then Anne Anson took over in 1972 as treasurer and general secretary. In 1975 Anne became my secretary, Lois Bowman became treasurer and Gloria Hughes general secretary.

In 1977, Tim Osborn Jones joined as the national society's director, bringing with him the professional expertise of which we were beginning to feel the need – he was a pleasure to work with and under his directorship the Society's work continued to prosper; assisting Tim were Julian Terry and a flow of helpers including Roger Harrison (then chief executive of the *Observer*) and a dynamic American, Dee Lind, a descendant of Jennie the "human nightingale" who lived on Blackheath in about 1830 and popularised the song "Home, Sweet Home".

In 1986 Jane Strutt took charge of Bermondsey and Carr-Gomm's other London houses, while Paul Wilson (who had become Chief Executive) oversaw the national Carr-Gomm Society with, later, George Ramsden and Kate Gibbs to help; so the national team built up. I continued to hold overall responsibility for the National Society (which obviously included Bermondsey) and concentrated on travelling the country promoting our work, trying to create interest and helping the director and his staff to start new committees and houses. With our administrative team and committee in place alongside reliable senior housekeepers in Doll Haydon (followed by Ellen Carr) for Bermondsey and Nell Condie for Thamesmead, the Carr-Gomm Society was shaping up. From 1986 we had the valuable support of Angus Ogilvy and, later, Sarah, Duchess of York; I had known both Angus and Sarah's father through the army and was always grateful for the enthusiasm and encouragement which we had from them all.

30. Carr-Gomm Society reflection conference, Mells 1982. Back row from left: Julian Terry, Anne Anson, James Macdonald, Angela Stitt, Michael Graham Jones, John Stitt, Christopher Diggle. Middle row from left: Juliet Ramsden, Tim Osborn Jones, Susan Carr-Gomm, Mary Harrison. Front row from left: Robbie Mathers, Jennifer Graham-Jones, Anna, RC-G

Whenever offered any sort of rank or role in any branch of our work

I accept, but always think that the role of being a "stranger" would be a nice one – "I was a stranger and you took me in". But "frustrating to work with"; "doesn't accept other people's feelings" and "doesn't bother to lobby people and get them on his side" were some of the criticisms levelled by colleagues at me – I hoped they were not all too true, but if they were this team had all the more with which to cope, and cope they did, exceeding well.

The Society successfully ran national conferences in London at which all the local societies (35 towns by 1984) were represented, we organised annual thanksgiving and rededication services – for the first four years at Southwark Cathedral then at churches throughout the country, we planned country-wide public relations events and sent staff on training courses. Crises with angry people and residents were overcome where possible; including one with a resident who, prior to being admitted to a psychiatric hospital, spent his six months with us writing libellous letters about me and the Society to the Queen, the Prime Minister, the Chief Whip and so on. There were several other such periods when we felt the presence of the devil among us – gossip, rumours, discontent and a lack of harmony in our work. These periods occurred every few years and just had to be corrected if possible and lived through.

The forces of good and evil, right and wrong, God and Satan are always around and I, by being too black and white, often exasperated those trying to sort them out. However, these often dramatic periods emphasised the need to recognise the fallibility of man and the importance of not relying too heavily on anyone. I didn't have to look far to be taught this, only to myself; I forget, I tell white lies and can behave badly. I am frequently impatient and thoughtless but I do trust and rely upon people – I believe them and expect them to keep their word and am, therefore, often disillusioned. Despite and because of relying on people while knowing the futility of doing so, I am certain that if I didn't have a religious faith, belief and trust in God, and if I didn't know that He is the only consistent factor for good in everything, I would have given up and retreated from all our work.

Pet Projects: schools, cathedrals and expansion abroad

My work with the Carr-Gomm Society included three personal pet projects: schools, cathedral closes and abroad. First schools – state and private (public) – but we began with public. In the early 20th century many public schools, and also university colleges, had set up settlements in the poor areas of London and other large cities to bring public-school and working class children together for the spiritual and material betterment of both. This had tended to take the form of patronage in that pupils from schools, often nowhere near the areas they chose to try and help, would visit poorer areas for inter-school games and sport or to organise events for those less fortunate than themselves. But over the years cities and towns accepted responsibility and did what was needed for their own citizens.

In an article for the *Headmaster* magazine in 1975 I suggested that, with wars, travel, education, the "gap year" and the passage of time changing everything so much, each school – state and public – might start a house for the lonely in their local towns. Pupils could then take an active interest in the house on their doorstep and to this would be added the consistent friendship and involvement of the local committees and bands of neighbours. This, I proposed might also help to inculcate in the pupils the concept of, and need for, service as part of ordinary human living and community.

It would perhaps be easiest for urban-based schools but we started with Stowe, which lies a few miles outside the county town of Buckingham. I chose Stowe not because I was an old boy but because I had preached at the school's Armistice Day service in 1976, and when I talked afterwards about the Society some senior boys took up the idea enthusiastically. With the support of Stowe's headmaster, the boys involved the town, the local newspaper and social services in order to get a house going; the Aylesbury local authority made a house available. We hoped that if this pilot scheme was successful other schools would follow Stowe's example; the school did start a house and it ran well. Seeds, though, are often slow to grow, but there was a stir of interest in one of the Bermondsey comprehensive schools.

Cathedrals

The "cathedral" idea came from a talk I gave to the annual conference of cathedral Deans in 1976. Accommodation in the Cathedral closes had, conventionally, been let on a grace-and-favour basis and often such houses and flats, perhaps originally occupied by a family ended up being lived in by just one remaining family member; he or she might be lonely and the building had become under-occupied.

The Chapters of two cathedral cities, Norwich and Lincoln each proposed the Society take over one house in their respective closes and offer it to those living alone and nearby; this would provide companionship in the area with which they were familiar and their former residences would be released for full occupation or conversion.

Norwich in 2002 was the front runner here.

Finally, my pet project that the Society should expand to other countries. This would show, first, that we were available to go wherever openings showed themselves and, secondly, that loneliness was not just a British problem with a British solution. Loneliness is, of course, a global issue although, I believe, more prevalent – as a general rule – in Western than in Eastern countries with family ties, for both religious and economic reasons, being more observed in the East.

Expansion abroad

First, in 1973, I went to Paris at the suggestion of John Vanier of L'Arche, a marvellous man, son of General Vanier (then Governor General of Canada), who has a deep spiritual understanding and who founded in France about 1958 an excellent organisation called L'Arche which houses those handicapped by psychiatric problems. Christopher Diggle (Carr-Gomm's Chairman) was working in Paris for one week every month and Stephen Ford, who occasionally helped us in England, lived mainly in Paris and had promised to help there. Jean-Jacques Vitrac, Count Antoine de Clermont and Madame Genevieve Willcox, French friends of friends, helped by trying to raise local and government interest in France and by offering to help if we got houses going. Friends in England, Charles Milbank and Martin Spurge in particular, also gave strong support in terms of trying to raise interest.

After several visits to the French capital a committee was formed and the machinery set in motion. The legalities were taken care of and we took the name "*Jamais Seul*". (never alone), but it was not until the early Eighties, when I gathered a committee of mainly Avignon locals, that the Society acquired its first, and only, French flat, and this from the Statutory Authority in Avignon.

One of France's few medieval sanctuary towns (where, protected till judged by a court, any victim of revenge could claim sanctuary from pursuit by an avenger), Avignon was therefore an appropriate place in which to start. Our flat there ran smoothly and successfully for some two years until the French Government placed a general moratorium on all social benefits which meant we ceased to be economically viable. Closure was sad for all our local enthusiasts but, while we had been thwarted by politics, we had shown we could cross geographical boundaries.

In my quest to expand abroad, I was motivated continually by two thoughts: first, how short life is and therefore how pressing the need to get on with things; second, the wider the areas in which we pioneered – be that geographical or across different age groups and degrees of poverty or wealth – the easier it would be for others to follow.

In 1975 I went to Brussels and the administrative centre for what would become the European Community (EC); even before the 1975 referendum in Britain this seemed to offer the best network for the Society's expansion into Europe. Michael Palliser, who had been in the Coldstream with me and was British Ambassador in Brussels, and his wife put me up and were exceedingly helpful and encouraging; he introduced me to officials dealing with social issues, gained me platforms from which I could speak to groups involved with community living and gave me a chance to find out what charities in Brussels and other countries were doing. Barney Milligan, Chaplain to the European Parliament in Strasbourg and another long-standing ally was also very supportive. When I returned to England I submitted a paper on loneliness to the appropriate directorate but, though received, there was no follow up to it by them.

But, while the Carr-Gomm Society has yet to find a foothold outside England and Scotland, a friend, William Barnes, asked me in the early Eighties to write about our work for a magazine published throughout the Continent; so things work slowly and may take years – tradition says 20 – to reach fruition – Abbeyfield took almost as many before spreading properly abroad through Abbeyfield International *(Ch. 24)*.

I made overtures in the USA through correspondence with unknown enquirers, Germany through Anne von Gleichen (sister of an ex-Grenadier), in Romania through Indrei Ratou (a Romanian ex-Prime Minister's son), and in India. In 1992 I met a Russian Archbishop to talk about his country's social and welfare predicament after the fall of the Berlin Wall – the Russian Orthodox Church having been given the task of tackling social affairs; they had property everywhere and anywhere for us to run but, for ten years, with no Government financial support, and as we, neither, had any spare cash, the project had to be shelved. Research continues and there are, still, hopes.

I longed, too, to go to Africa, not only because of my friendship with the Baganda tribe *(Ch. 11)* but because here was a continent which hadn't yet met Western Europe's issues of great longevity, intense technology and the domination of time. I wanted to see if Carr-Gomm's principles couldn't help them ahead of these issues arising.

When I accompanied the Kabaka's body back to Uganda in 1971 *(Ch. 14)* I had spoken to President Idi Amin about it and he had been interested. He had asked me to write, but despite me doing so on several occasions he had never replied. So in 1975 an African who offered himself as a go-between suggested a new approach but, meanwhile, our main committee had stepped in and ordered a pause – although they did allow me to make a few unsuccessful enquiries in Kenya.

Our aim remains the same

I think the Societies survive because they stick to trying to help the lonely and will not be distracted from that. This is because with Abbeyfield they had recognised from the very beginning that there are lonely people everywhere; that they are in need of help remains all too apparent. Whether they are Abbeyfield, Carr-Gomm, Morpeth or any of their allied societies; their aim – to help the lonely – is the same. The method of small units, with a degree of unobtrusive care and the principle of looking on everyone as whole individuals – body, mind and spirit – is identical. All non-profit making, there are really only minor variations in constitution and administration. The only major

31. Family group, Templeton Award 1984. From left: Harriet, Susan, David, RC-G, Anna, Adam, Elizabeth

difference is one of age: in 2004 the average age of entry into Abbeyfield's 950 houses was about 81 years, for Carr-Gomm, Morpeth and affiliated societies it was about 36. The Societies are not in competition; there is room and need in the world for each of them to be themselves.

It was lovely, for example, for this vision to be given public recognition when the Templeton UK Project Trust awarded me, in 1986, a prize for making a "signal contribution to the field of spiritual values". Sir John Templeton wrote about "introducing more spirituality into helping lonely people". I valued his backing enormously and also that of St George's House at Windsor Castle who promoted and administered the award.

Office ditty

As the national Carr-Gomm Society (superbly led by Richard Stanley, a brother Coldstreamer) grew, in 1989 it needed to move from our office in Gomm Road to a larger one at New Cross. (The Morpeth Society used its own office in Morpeth Mansions.) Carr-Gomm staff made up this ditty incorporating names of colleagues, residents, our houses and their street names; they sang it to the tune of "In the Quartermaster's Stores":

>   There was Alma, Alma,
>   Never having drama,
>   in Carr-Gomm, in Carr-Gomm,
>   and there was Mary, Mary just got wed to John,
>   in the Society of Carr-Gomm.
>
>   CHORUS: My eyes are dim I cannot see,
>   I have not brought my specs with me ...
>
>   There was Setchell, Setchell,
>   Always smashing fed well,
>   in Carr-Gomm, in Carr-Gomm,
>   Just look at us -- it shows,
>   in the Society of Carr-Gomm.
>
>   There was Gomm Road, Gomm Road,
>   With lawns so beautifully mowed,
>   in Carr-Gomm, in Carr-Gomm,
>   and there was Maggie, Maggie,
>   who loves her whiskey haggie,
>   in the Society of Carr-Gomm.
>
>   There was Abbeyfield, 'field,

Whose true colours are now revealed,
in Carr-Gomm, in Carr-Gomm,
and there was Jen, Jen,
Och! she loves the men,
in the Society of Carr-Gomm.

There was Reverdy, Reverdy,
Where everyone's so cleverly,
in Carr-Gomm, in Carr-Gomm,
and there was Eth, Eth,
Bermondsey's top chef,
in the Society of Carr-Gomm.

There was Tyers, Tyers,
Still muddled up with wires,
in Carr-Gomm, in Carr-Gomm,
and there was Eileen, 'lean,
who tries to keep it clean,
in the Society of Carr-Gomm.

There was Moland, Moland,
Which just keeps right on rolling,
in Carr-Gomm, in Carr-Gomm,
and there Ellen Carr, Carr,
who deserves a loud hoorah,
in the Society of Carr-Gomm.

There was Thamesmead, 'mead,
All of whom we so much heed,
in Carr-Gomm, in Carr-Gomm,
There was Lensbury, Redpoll and dear old Wolvercote,
in the Society of Carr-Gomm.

There was Ealing, Ealing,
Who Stephanie keeps on healing,
in Carr-Gomm, in Carr-Gomm,
There Erika, Erika,
who's come over from America,
in the Society of Carr-Gomm.

There was Walcot Square, square,
Who George keeps from despair,
in Carr-Gomm, in Carr-Gomm,
there was the office, 'fice,
Oh, Robbie your jokes we'll miss,
In the office of the Carr-Gomm.

1993: Re-organisation and centralisation

In 1993, the Carr-Gomm Society underwent a major, nationwide re-organisation dictated by increasing pressure from the Conservative government for tax-funded bodies including charities to streamline in order to ease the administration of grants paid from the public purse. Thus, we were forced to dissolve our 65 autonomous Carr-Gomm town and village committees and centralise all our administration and financing as a national society (the Carr-Gomm Society) at our new central office near London Bridge. Our representatives throughout England, Scotland and Northern Ireland were never able, publicly at least, to say enough how thankful the national committee in London was to everyone, everywhere for all they had done in their own local committees and, through that, for the Society as a whole.

Even though done out of necessity and after much agonising by those in control, the Society's' centralisation action distressed many local volunteers and some disassociated themselves from the national society. Our original system had grown with us; it had absorbed the neighbourhood and community, given people control within their own patch, identified them with their work and given everyone involved as much or as little responsibility as they wanted.

It was hoped that much of this would re-appear in the new organisation, and 12 years down the line it does, slowly, show some signs of reappearing. The national society has now designated three principal districts – North, South and London – each of which is subdivided into groups of counties with their own area offices reporting to national headquarters in London. Hopefully, having a single central office with which to deal will meet the government's requirements while, at the same time, volunteers and neighbours can have a good say in how they choose to run their own houses but with minimal paper work and limited interference from headquarters. Nevertheless, for many of those involved deeply within the work at the time of change in 1993, the transition caused anguish and much unhappiness.

Arguments for and against centralisation are always varied and strong. While an independence of spirit is very important to the success of a Society at local level, a local committee's preference for autonomy has to include independent registration as a charity, VAT and income tax returns, contractual and legal obligations and so on – and this is a tall order for part-time volunteers and neighbours; although as a learning experience it can lead to career enhancement

and the ability to speak with authority on the charity's behalf.

I often feel guilty for imposing the original "federal" system on the Carr-Gomm and other societies but, like Abbeyfield, when Carr-Gomm started in 1964 it was the only way we could cope with the countrywide interest and enquiries; it was easier and more efficient to allow satellite groups to administer themselves rather than have us do it for them from London.

There was a time in 1955 when I decided to stop thinking and theorising and that was when I left the army and started home-helping. Now I seem to be getting back to over-thinking again and so it is, probably, a hint that it is time to end this book.

The dream for our work was that it would help create a world in which love would dispel loneliness; we would try and help draw the warmth and kindness from the hearts and souls of neighbours and thereby overcome loneliness – and that dream remains valid. Today, all the societies have between them around 1,400 houses offering relief from loneliness – whether it be called loneliness, isolation or separation – to more than 11,000 people.

An ideal world would see full occupation, no prejudice and no abuse of power or wealth, the elderly would be valued as much as the young and everyone would have their own self-chosen and happy roof over their heads. But we are very far from such an ideal and the working in the societies with which I am involved was and is evidence of the need to strive continually for such ideals.

When each local group operated under its own legal constitution; links to Carr-Gomm were maintained by serving on general committees, sharing training and so on; the principles, aims and working practices in each group's constitution were exactly the same. With its centralisation, a national constitution was drawn up and is applicable to all local societies. The Abbeyfield Society also found it necessary to centralise and in 2003 formed Abbeyfield UK *(Ch. 24)*.

Allied societies

The local societies who remained autonomous and independent of Carr-Gomm's newly-formed national society in 1993 were the 80 or Houses in East Anglia now called St Matthew Housing *(Ch. 26)*, the Newcastle houses under the Byker Bridge Housing Association and Bath's three houses called the Solo Society; East Grinstead with the Richard Society and Richmond in London became the Solon Society. With them and Abbeyfield UK, Abbeyfield International, Morpeth, Carr-Gomm Scotland and Carr-Gomm, I am linked with ten different societies.

These various societies somehow manage to infuse their efficiency with both enthusiasm and a light touch.

Since 1993 within Carr-Gomm the number of flats had increased to about 300 by the year 2000, and in addition to single people, now couples and single parents were also housed. For the first time, too, residents became active members of the Society's central and local boards and committees. The "Welfare" having evolved to become the Department of Health and Social Security (DHSS) continues to pay state benefits to our residents who qualify, and this income remains vital to the Society's economic viability.

In 1999, in Carr-Gomm's houses three people applied for every vacancy; 30% were self-referred; 24% had mental problems, 8% were ex-offenders, 15% had experienced family breakdown, 22% were female, 3% residents and 5% staff were from ethnic minorities.

In 2000 Susan and I were invited to Edinburgh where Carr-Gomm and Abbeyfield were, wonderfully, forging links. The lovely thing about the Societies is that friends and familiar faces continually re-emerge, sometimes after many years. And meeting to relive memories, make plans or for gossip happens repeatedly – be it in high street tea houses, Boodles, the Travellers Club, the Guards Club, TGI Friday or Macdonalds. So the years move on, memories build, the Millennium has passed and some faces have changed.

ENVOI

So the dream continues, and with it the work. The world is large and there is so much to do. For the Societies mentioned in this book this means, perhaps, that there will be more houses outside the UK than within it. The stories of loneliness and neighbours within our shores which I have told could, after all, have been true for any country in the world.

Our family approaches middle-age and there are grandchildren, while health for Susan and me is much better than for many at our age. Susan has arthritis and I, occasionally, choke but others often have greater problems than these. Sorrow succeeds joy. The sorrow in 2004 of the death of my brother Roddy and Susan's sister Mary.

Having been born before television, penicillin, frozen food, credit cards, split-atoms, electric blankets, computers and walking on the moon were known, we have had to adjust, absorb and take on quite a lot. It has been wonderful and fun. History and the past remain but we are part of the present. What now for the future? What, after all, have I to write about? Certainly nothing more.

One day, maybe, for Susan and me, there will be rest and peace and, perhaps, if either of us is alone, we'll be lonely. At least we'll know where to go to if we are.

INDEX

Carr-Gomm, Richard Culling:
 10 Downing Street, 107
 ADC, 75, 81, 86
 ambition, 59, 75
 anti-semitism, 41
 assistant librarian, 211
 Belsen, 33
 Buttiko clan member, 146
 capture railway, 35
 car crash, 150
 church, 18, 52, 75, 77, 97, 128, 135, 137, 158, 245
 colour blindness, 26
 concentration camp, 33
 desert shoot, 47
 diary, 52, 152
 enlist, 25
 first house, 159
 first real command, 28
 Greenwich, 93, 100, 116, 117, 138
 guardian, 140, 141, 148
 guests on guard, 68–72
 home-help, 78, 97, 153, 186
 hospital, 32, 93, 113, 150, 242
 Imperial Defence College, 52
 lessons for founder, 202
 marriage, 90
 meditations & books, 77, 137, 172
 mini-public life, 135
 museum, 137
 press reaction, 148, 155, 170, 225
 Ruby Wedding, 137
 school, 16, Chap 3
 spying, 61
 start in Bermondsey, 78
 stranger, 207, 249
 tanks, 27–29, 40, 137, Chap 5
 This is Your Life, 91
 tuberculosis, 113
 UK tour, 99, 135
 wounded, 31, 37

Abbeyfield Community Centre (Uganda), 139, 146
Abbeyfield International, 149, 204, 252, 257
Abbeyfield Society, 94, 103, 135, 150, 209, 215, 216, 227, 253, 257, Chaps 21-24
Abdullah, King of Jordan, 46
Achimoto College, Ghana, 140
Adam & Eve, 10
Africa, 51, 53, 81, 94–97, 139, 210, *See also* Uganda, Chaps 11, 14, 18
Agate, John, 120
Allen, Adrienne, 91
Altrincham, Lord, 59
Amin, President Idi, 96, 105, 109–11, 140, 253
Amory, Mark, 6, 56, 108, 109, 142, 148, 164
Andrews, Eamonn, 91
Ankole, 83, 94, 97
Anley, Clare, 245
Anne, the Princess Royal, 193
Anson, Anne, 119, 120, 247
Arnold, Bishop Keith, 207

Australia, 149, 204
autonomy, 43, 189, 191, 207, 256
Avignon, Provence, 251
Bank of England, 66
Barbour, June, 246
Barclay, Joe, 185
Bark, Susan, 231
Barnes, William, 252
Barry, Mrs, 180
Bath, 125, 128, 135, 138, 150, 243, 246, 257
Batheaston, 125, 141, 245
Baynes, Lillian, 136
Bean, Alan, 221
Belfast, 198
Belgium, 204
Bell, Mr, 179
Belsen, 33, 157
Berkshire, Regiment, 25
Bermondsey, 77–82, 89, 101, 116, 185, 190, 211, 214, 216, 229, 247, Chaps 20, 21
& the Kabaka, 106
family connection, 11, 16, 17
Biddlecombe, Richard, 205
Bingley, Lady Juliet, 101, 214
Bisley ranges, 62
Booth, Rev Peter, 187
Bowman, Lois, 247
Boyd of Merton, Lord (Alan Lennox-Boyd), 107, 109, 241
Bradfield College, 105
Brighton, 28, 90, 187–89, 190, 199
Brown, David, 21
Buchanan, Naomi, 246
Buckingham Palace, 27, 66, 72, 113, 117
Buganda, 53, 81, 111, 141, 143, 146, See also Uganda,
Mutesa, Mutebi, Chap 11
Bulteel, Christopher & Jennie, 133, 164, 168
Bunyoro, 83, 94, 95, 97
Burdett, Noel, 206
Buttiko Clan, 146
Buxton, Christopher, 190
Byker Bridge Society, 245, 257
Bywater, Anne, 246
Camps, Professor Sir Francis, 109
Canada, 128, 149, 204
Canvey Island, 189, 190, 199
Carpenter, Betty, 238
Carr, Ellen, 248
Carr, Emily Blanche (grandmother), 12
Carr, Francis Culling (grandfather), 12
Carr-Gomm Society, 100, 101, 135, 253, 257, Chaps 25, 26, 28
shops, 225, 235
Carr-Gomm Society (Scotland), 257
Carr-Gomm, AD (Thea), 10, 23, 75, 81, 98, 117, Chap 2
Carr-Gomm, Adam, 62, 100, 101, 120, 122, 123, 131, 138, 145
Carr-Gomm, Anna, 62, 92, 98, 100, 101, 119, 122, 123, 129, 131, 149, 150
& children, 129, 136, 145
& Piers, 129, 145, 149
Carr-Gomm, Antony (Tony), 13, 25, 81, 114, 116, Chap 2
& Jeannie, 114
Carr-Gomm, David, 62, 100, 101, 115, 120, 122, 123, 128, 132, 145

INDEX

& *Lily, 133*
& *Ros, 92, 133, 144, 150*
Carr-Gomm, Eardley, 13, 81, 114, 136, Chap 2
Carr-Gomm, Elizabeth, 62, 92, 98, 100, 101, 119, 121, 123, 125, 129, 145
 & *children, 129, 145*
 & *Jeffrey, 129, 134*
 & *Robert, 131*
Carr-Gomm, Harriet, 97, 98, 100, 101, 120, 123, 126, 129, 131, 145, 149, 150, 210
Carr-Gomm, Hubert, 16, 236
Carr-Gomm, Lily, 133, *See also* Carr-Gomm, David
Carr-Gomm, Mark Culling, 13, 23, 75, 81, 98, Chap 2
Carr-Gomm, Richard Culling *see separate index, page 260*
Carr-Gomm, Roderick (Roddy), 13, 25, 81, 114, 259, Chap 2
Carr-Gomm, Sarah, 226
Carr-Gomm, Susan, 7, 46, 97–101, 103, 111, 164, 168, 187, 205, 210, 216, 225, 237, 240, 243, 258, 259, Chaps 12, 15-19
Carter, Mr, 179
Caterham, 25
Caumont, battle of, 30
Cazenove, Robert, 243
Charter, 209
Chequers, 67
Childers, Erskine, 19
Childers, Leonard, 11
Childers, Michael, 11
Church, Jeremy, Isabel, 127
Churchill tank, 27, 30, 37, 137
Churchill, Sir Winston, 16, 68, 83, 235, 241

clans, Bugandan, 111, 141, 146, 147
Clayton, Rev Tubby, 171
Coates, Jimmy, 27, 68
Coldstream Guards, 25, 59, 117, 137, 153, 252, Chap 9
Collingham Gardens, 23
Condie, Nell, 232, 248
Coombes, Nanny, 100, 138
Corfu, 97, 116, 124
Courtfield Gardens, 16, 129
Coward, Noel, 70
Crawley, Camilla, 70
Creese-Parsons, Simon, 130
Cresswell, Simon, 247
Cumbria, 136
Cyprus, 46, 49, 53
Darby, Robert, 189, 194, 202
Diana, Princess of Wales, 228
Diggle, Christopher, 219, 247, 251
Diggle, James & Pippa, 243
Edinburgh, 199
Edmunds, Susannah, 217
Eire, 204
Elephant Man, 12
Elephant tank, 28
Eugenia Road, 137, 159, 161, 164, 168, 169, 177
Fairbanks, Douglas, 223
Fiennes, Dean the Hon, Oliver, 228
Fitzpatrick, Finnian, 145
Fleming, Ian, 238
Flensburg, 36
France
 holidays, 17, 55, 134
 Jamais Seul, 251
 wartime, 30
Freddie. *See* Mutesa, HM Kabaka (Freddie)

INDEX

Freemasonry, 23, 223
Germany
 Abbeyfield, 205
 Carr-Gomm Society, 252
 wartime, 32, 33, 35, 36
ghost, family, 12
Gibbs, Canon William, 89, 91, 99
Gibbs, Christopher, 133
Gibbs, Jane, 128, 132, 206
Gibbs, Jenny, 108
Gibbs, Kate, 247
Gibbs, Peter, 90
Gibbs, Susan. *See* Carr-Gomm, Susan
GLC (Greater London Council), 229–34
Glubb, Pasha, 46
Gomm Estates, 13, 17, 78
Gomm Road, 91, 164, 168, 181, 215, 217, 247, 254
Gomm, Field-Marshal Sir William & Lady, 10, 11, 59
Gomm, Jane, 11
Goodwin, Peter, 245
Gough, Archbishop Hugh, 77
Graham Jones, Michael, 247
Graham, Billy & Ruth, 70, 79, 105, 107, 204, 212, 216
Greenwich, 93, 100, 116, 225
Grigg, Sir Edward. *See* Altrincham, Lord
Grixoni, Countess, Kate, 245
Guards Depot, Caterham, 25
Gunnis, Gillie, 191
Hamilton, Niall, 125
Hamilton, Sir Michael & Lavinia, 133
Harrison, Mary, 238, 247
Harrison, Roger, 247
Harwood, Countess (Princess Royal), 67
Haydon, Doll, 111, 248
Heemstra, Baroness van, 161, 204
Heming, grandparents, 10, 14, 15
holidays, 17, 46, 50, 94, 97, 114, 118, 122, 131, 133, 144, 210, 216
Holland, 204
Hollings, Michael, 44
Holness, Bob & Mary, 92, 133
Holness, Rosalind. *See* Carr-Gomm, David & Ros
homelessness, 138
Horace, 125
House of Commons, 21, 66
housekeepers, 160, 163, 177, 181, 183, 192, 217, 218, 231, 238, 239, 248
Hughes, Gloria, 247
Hylton, Lord (Raymond), 99, 121, 194, 202
Inch Kenneth island, 216
Intelligence Services, 61, 139
Israel, 41, 43, 45, 48, 133
Istanbul, 46
Italy, 55, 57, 204
Jamaica, 134, 136
Jamais Seul, 251
Jenkins, Henry, 226
Jersey, 204
Jjunju, 148
Jordan, 46, 49, 53
Kabaka. *See under* Mutesa & Mutebi
Katende, Jehoash. Chap 14
Kime, Emily, 129, 131, 145, *See also* Carr-Gomm, Elizabeth
Kime, Jeffrey, 129, *See also* Carr-Gomm, Elizabeth

Kime, Matilda, 129, 131, 145, *See also* Carr-Gomm, Elizabeth
Kimera, Prince Henry, 143
Kintu, 83
Kiwanuka, Jim & Barbara, 144
Lambeth, Borough of, 228, 244
Langley, Peter John, 126
Lennox-Boyd, Alan. *See* Boyd of Merton, Lord (Alan Lennox-Boyd)
Little, Bob, 126, 149, 243
Luke, St, 7
Lutaya, James, 97
Macclesfield, 185, 190
Macdonald, James, 137, 238, 239, 242
Macdonald, Lady, Mary, 99, 100, 136, 259
MacKay, Neil, 131
Mackenzie, Sir Compton, 203, 212
Mahdi of Sudan, 54
Malta, 52, 53, 55
Margaret, Princess, 86
Marston Bigot, Frome, 137
Mathers, Robbie, 219, 227, 242, 244, 247
Matthew, St. *See* St Matthew Housing Association
Maubec, 130, 134
McColl, Sir Colin, 139
McMullan, Bob, 205
Mells, Somerset, 103, 114, 115, 116, 118–24, 125, 135
Merrick, Joseph. *See* Elephant Man
Milbank, Charles, 129, 251
Milbank, Mark, 37
Miles, Canon Bobby, 171, 187
& *Heather, 136*

Milligan, Rev Barney, 252
Mippy, Miss Jones, 16, 17, 23
Montessori, 131
Morecambe, 199
Morley College, 101
Morocco, 133
Morpeth Mansions, 120, 140, 235, 242
Morpeth Society, 100, 135, 140, 195, 197, 227, 253, 257, Chap 27
Mowden School, 16, 23
Mutebi, HM Kabaka (Ronnie), 86, 105, 108, 110, 111, Chap 18
& *Jjunju, 148*
& *Sylvia, 147, 148*
Mutesa, HM Kabaka (Freddie), 53, 81, 94–97, 140, 141, 142, 253, Chaps 11, 14
& *Damali, 94, 105, 108*
& *Sarah, 86, 105, 108, 140*
New Zealand, 149, 204
Newbery, Peter, 205
Newton, Aubrey, 129, 145, 147, *See also* Carr-Gomm, Anna
Newton, Ollie, 129, 145, 148, *See also* Carr-Gomm, Anna
Newton, Piers, 129, 145, *See also* Carr-Gomm, Anna
Newton, Punch (Miles), 129, 136, 145, 148, *See also* Carr-Gomm, Anna
Newton, Sam, 129, 145, 147, *See also* Carr-Gomm, Anna
Normandy, 30
Norrie, Sir Willoughby, 75
Northern Ireland, 191, 193, 198
Obote, Milton, 94–97, 140, Chap 14
office ditty, 254

INDEX

Olivier, Laurence, 63
Orchard House flat, 106, 116, 141, 214
Osborn Jones, Tim, 219, 247
Owen, Ronnie, 82, 86, 140, 141, 142, Chap 14
  & *the Hon Ardyne, 140, 143*
Oxford, 25, 189, 190, 194, 199
Pactus, Mary, 127, 136, 240
Palestine, 114, Chap 6
Palliser, Sir Michael, 107, 252
Palmer, Edward, 101, 214, 219, 229
Parker, Alice Daisy, 131, *See also* Carr-Gomm, Elizabeth
Parker, Robert, 131, *See also* Carr-Gomm, Elizabeth
patronage, 20, 250
Perry, Rev John & Bridget, 127
Pimpernel Trust, 135, 139
prayer, 44, 77, 80, 161, 170–74, 205, 207, 222, 232
Prince of Wales, HRH Prince Charles, 207
Provence, 129, 134
Quinton, Anthony, 20
Ramsden, Arthur, 153
Ramsden, George, 247
Ramsden, James & Juliet, 133, 238, 241, 247
Ray, Johnny, 72
Richard Society, 257
Robinson, Ian, 219, 242, 244, 247
Ronnie. *See* Mutebi, HM Kabaka (Ronnie)
Rose, Mama, 143, 148
Roxburgh, JF, 20, 21
Rufford Abbey, 28
Russell, Sue, Harry & family, 131

Russia, 11, 136, 240
Sandhurst, 26, 247
Sayer, Doris, 111, 119, 126
Scotland, 191, 208
Scotland Yard, 109
Seaman, Richard, 205
Snowie, Allan, 6, 205
Social Security (DHSS), 227, 258
Solo Society (Bath), 135, 257
Solon Society, 257
Somerset, 103, 114, 116, 118–24, 125
South Africa, 204
Speke Hotel, Kampala, 145
Sri Lanka, 131
Ssese Islands, 97, 145
St George's House, Windsor, 254
St John, Venerable Order, 23, 114, 133, 137, 143, 223
St Matthew Housing Association, 135, 228, 245, 257
Stalin, Joseph, 240
Stanley, the Hon Richard, 219, 254
Stevenson, Robert Louis, 218
Stitt, John & Angela, 101, 137, 214, 247
Stowe School, 211, 250, Chap 3
  old boys, 20, 136
Strickett, Bert, 164, 181
Strutt, Jane, 238, 247
Sudan, 53, 54
Templeton Award, 254
Thamesmead, 229–34
Theophilus, Bishop, 7
This is Your Life, 91
Thomson, John, 219
Timmins, Rev Leslie & Audrey,

90, 170, 212
Toro, 83, 94, 97, 147
Omukama of, 87, 97, 140
Tower of London, 67
Tranmire, Lord (Robin Turton), 173, 194, 241
Tully, Mark, 194, 202
Turnbull, John, 205
Turton, Robin. *See* Tranmire, Lord
Uganda, 41, 53, 81, 94–97, 136, 205, 253, Chaps 11, 14, 18
Abbeyfield Community Centre, 139, 146
Ulundi Road, Greenwich, 93, 116, 117
United States of America, 149, 205

Unwin, Peter, 205
VE Day, 35, 40
Venice, 57
Wales, 191, 199
Walker, Bobby, 215, 230
Walker, Dennis, 219
Walugembe, Prince Richard, 86, 105, 140, 141, 143
Whitteridge, Jane, 111, 217
Wilson, Rev Paul, 219, 247
Windsor Castle, 67, 254
Winn, Godfrey, 8, 70, 212
Wolsey, Gordon, 242
Wynne-Finch, Charles, 52, 55
York, Sarah, Duchess of, 248
Yorkshire, 28, 100
Zimbabwe, 53

© Copyright 2005 Richard Carr-Gomm.
All rights reserved. No part of this publication may be reproduced, stored in a retrieval system, or transmitted, in any form or by any means, electronic, mechanical, photocopying, recording, or otherwise, without the written prior permission of the author.

Note for Librarians: a cataloguing record for this book that includes Dewey Decimal Classification and US Library of Congress numbers is available from the Library and Archives of Canada. The complete cataloguing record can be obtained from their online database at:
www.collectionscanada.ca/amicus/index-e.html
ISBN 1-4120-5490-7

Printed in Victoria, BC, Canada

Printed on paper with minimum 30% recycled fibre.
Trafford's print shop runs on "green energy" from solar, wind and other environmentally-friendly power sources.

TRAFFORD *Offices in Canada, USA, Ireland and UK*

This book was published *on-demand* in cooperation with Trafford Publishing. On-demand publishing is a unique process and service of making a book available for retail sale to the public taking advantage of on-demand manufacturing and Internet marketing. On-demand publishing includes promotions, retail sales, manufacturing, order fulfilment, accounting and collecting royalties on behalf of the author.

10   9   8   7   6   5   4   3   2   1

ISBN 1-41205490-7